HUMAN SERVICE PRACTICE WITH THE ELDERLY

Marion L. Beaver

School of Social Work
University of Pittsburgh

Prentice-Hall, Inc.   Englewood Cliffs, N.J. 07632

Library of Congress Cataloguing in Publication Data

BEAVER, MARION L.
  Human service practice with the elderly.

    Bibliography: p.
    Includes index.
    1. Social work with the aged—United States.
2. Gerontology. 3. Aged—services for—United States.
I. Title. [DNLM: 1. Social work. 2. Geriatrics. 3. Aging. WT 30 B386h]
HV1461.B4 1983   362.6′042   82-24037
ISBN 0-13-447482-1

Editorial/production supervision: Dee Amir Josephson
Cover design: Marvin Warshaw
Manufacturing buyer: John Hall
Cover Photo: Action

Printed in the United States of America

10 9 8 7 6 5 4 3 2 1

ISBN 0-13-447482-1

Prentice-Hall International, Inc., *London*
Prentice-Hall of Australia Pty. Limited, *Sydney*
Editora Prentice-Hall do Brasil, Ltda., *Rio de Janeiro*
Prentice-Hall Canada Inc., *Toronto*
Prentice-Hall of India Private Limited, *New Delhi*
Prentice-Hall of Japan, Inc., *Tokyo*
Prentice-Hall of Southeast Asia Pte. Ltd., *Singapore*
Whitehall Books Limited, *Wellington, New Zealand*

contents

chapter 3   THE BIOPHYSIOLOGICAL ASPECTS OF AGING   55

chapter 4   THE PSYCHOLOGICAL ASPECTS OF AGING   71

chapter 5   THE SOCIAL ASPECTS OF AGING   99

To my father
who died at too young an age

preface

This is an introductory text in gerontology that combines a survey of the field with social work practice. Although there are a number of textbooks in gerontology on the market, few combine theory and practice this way. One function of knowledge for any profession is to develop an effective practice oriented toward specific purposes and goals. The crucial process thus becomes a dialogue between the theoretician and practitioner, between knowledge and action, with each both stimulating and responding to the demands of the other.

Social work with the aging makes use of specialized knowledge and skills about aging and the aged. It is this knowledge base that the author strongly believes should be the starting point for those practitioners who plan to work with older people. Thus, emphasis throughout the text is on gerontological social work, theory, and practice with the elderly.

The first chapter of this book presents an overview of the field of aging. The author defines at the outset the nature and scope of the field. In addition, the reader is provided with an historical perspective of aging to increase his understanding and awareness of the treatment accorded the elderly in the past, and

to point out the changes in the care of older people today. In the second chapter, the reader is provided with demographic data on such characteristics as numbers, racial and ethnic composition, and marital status in order to assess the circumstances of the elderly in American society today. The chapter closes with a general discussion of social work practice with the elderly, including the various roles played by the worker as well as the numerous activities undertaken in the older person's behalf.

Chapter three examines the biological and physiological changes that occur with the passage of time. While the biological aspects of aging are focused on the changes that aging brings to the cells of the body, the physiological aspects emphasize reduction in the performance of organs and organ systems.

Chapter four deals with the psychosocial aspects of aging. Emphasis is placed on sensory and psychomotor processes, perception, mental functioning, creativity, and personality changes with age. Some of the most widely known psychosocial theories of aging are discussed, in order to increase the reader's understanding of the processes of aging. A number of social concepts such as social role, social status, socialization, and age norms are examined for their changing relevance to people as they age in society. Special groups of older people, including minority elderly and elderly women, are singled out for discussion because of the particular problems they present.

The social context of aging, the topic of Chapter five, influences the range and quality of programs and services that are available to the elderly. The ideal service delivery system is one that matches services to need. The pattern of services that exists today is dichotomous. Those services are classified in this text as community versus institutional, public versus private or voluntary, and home care versus institutional care.

Chapter six reviews major federal legislation and government programs to benefit the elderly. The role of professionals and paraprofessionals in the service delivery system is discussed. Problems that exist in the current service delivery system are brought to the reader's attention.

Chapters seven and eight focus on practice with individuals. Chapter seven examines the essential qualities needed by practitioners if they are to work effectively with the elderly. The older person as a client is examined and a number of variables that may have

impacted on his life over time are discussed. The nature of the professional relationship is examined, together with the verbal and non-verbal communications that transpire throughout the social work interview. Case examples are included and discussed in various subsections of the chapter. Chapter eight focuses on such issues as treatment alternatives, the treatment contract, and the importance of time, fees, and absences as they relate to the older client in treatment. Termination is examined in light of its meaning for the older client. The chapter includes case illustrations and practical guidelines and techniques for working with the older adult.

The focus in Chapter nine is on practice with families. The family as a basic unit of growth and experience is discussed. Various types of families, including the nuclear and traditional, ethnic, and aging families, are examined. Aspects of family functioning such as family vulnerability and strength, family roles, family goals and communication patterns are singled out for their importance in understanding and assessing family diagnosis. Chapter ten focuses on practice with groups. The chapter provides a discussion of group processes and methods, together with case illustrations.

The final chapter provides a discussion of community-based services designed to meet the needs of the elderly. Intervention at the community level is also examined. It is within the settings in which community organization takes place that the practitioner is able to influence the ties that bind individuals into small groups, to relate two or more groups, to connect two or more formal organizations, and to relate groups to organizations. The practitioner's purpose may be to improve the relations between individuals, groups, and organizations, or to assist them in collaborating to achieve some tangible goal, or both. Three models of community organization—locality development, the social planning approach, and the social action approach—are described. Examples that relate specifically to each model are included.

This textbook should be of interest to students, educators, and human-service professionals engaged in direct practice with older people. Those students who have little background in gerontology but who are interested in working with older people should find this textbook useful, as will those currently working with older people who wish to upgrade their knowledge and skills and improve the quality of their professional practice. The book should also be helpful to those who anticipate working with the elderly and want to further their understanding of what older people are like and their knowledge of the kinds of skills that are useful in working with them.

The reader will find that the writing style is clear, to the point, and very readable. The topics covered are relevant, up-to-date, and appropriate for an introductory text. Students should appreciate all the implications for practice.

This textbook would not be complete without acknowledging the painstaking and critical efforts of those persons, such as Harry Specht, who read, reviewed, and carefully commented on the original manuscript. Their invaluable comments further refined the structure, and in some instances, the content of the text. Thanks, too, to Prentice-Hall's reviewers Michael Patchner, University of Illinois; Ramon Valle, San Diego State University; and Catharine Zimmerman, Camden County College.

Acknowledgment must also go to those colleagues—Margaret (Betty) E. Hartford and Charlotte J. Dunmore, in particular—who never tired of urging me on to ''write that book.'' Finally, but certainly not last, my thanks to Virginia Rhodes, who typed the bulk of the manuscript, and who, along with Floran Mientkiewicz, Mercedes McBride, and Rosemarie Przybysz typed, edited, and made corrections on the final copy.

This book is formally dedicated to my father. But it is also dedicated to my mother and my aunt Marie, who seem to have found the secret of how to age gracefully.

chapter 1

THE FIELD
OF AGING:
AN OVERVIEW

WHAT IS GERONTOLOGY?

Gerontology is the scientific study of older life and of the special problems of the elderly. By "aging" is meant the progressive changes that take place in a cell, a tissue, an organ system, a total organism, or a group of organisms with the passage of time. All living things change with time in both structure and function; the changes that follow a general trend constitute aging.

Aging is part of the developmental sequence of the entire lifespan. Beginning with conception, this developmental sequence includes prenatal growth and development, birth, infancy, childhood, adolescence, young adulthood, middle age, and senescence. Aging is a normal part of this total process. However, gerontology is concerned primarily with the changes that occur between the attainment of maturity and the death of the individual and with the factors that influence these changes. These factors may range from heredity to climate; they may include social values, customs, and prevailing attitudes (*Gerontology and Geriatrics,* 1969).

The topics of concern to gerontology generally fall into the following categories: (1) social, cultural, and economic problems precipitated by the increasing numbers of older people in the population; (2) psychological aspects of aging, which include intellectual performance and personal adjustment; and (3) biophysiological bases of aging, along with pathological deviations and disease processes (*Gerontology and Geriatrics,* 1969).

The concepts of biologic, social, and psychologic age are useful for describing man as a whole system. The concept "biologic aging" generally considers physical changes in the organism which have been found, in general, to be associated with aging. These changes may be in cell structures, organ systems, or their functioning. "Social age" refers to socially ascribed roles that a person fills— roles that dictate his social behavior. "Psychologic age" refers to age-correlated changes in perceiving, feeling, thinking, and acting in the person as a unique individual. None of these processes occurs independently and each bears some relationship to the other.

Gerontologists agree that aging is multiply determined. Each individual is the sum total of his environment—an environment influenced, of course, by genetic and nongenetic factors as well as by physical and social factors. Although it is commonly agreed that people age at different times and different rates on the various biological, psychological, and social levels (Woodruff and Birren, 1975), this complex of factors generally interacts to determine the aging process.

THE INTERDISCIPLINARY NATURE OF GERONTOLOGY

Gerontology is a complex field of study and practice whose major components are drawn from the physical and behavioral sciences. Members of many disciplines and professions specialize in some area of aging. Among them are social workers, nurses, doctors, biologists, psychologists, public health practitioners, sociologists, architects, economists, political economists, and others studying ways to improve the quality of life for older people.

The body of accumulated knowledge in gerontology is extensive, although there are some who believe we have only begun to scratch the surface in understanding aging (Woodruff & Birren, 1975). Many others believe that there is already a core of knowledge, multidisciplinary in nature, that all people in the field should have about aging and the aged. Many of these same people believe that there is knowledge on aging essential for clusters of related professions such as those concerned with the biomedical sciences, behavioral and social sciences, human services, policy administration, and the environment. Additionally, there are those who believe that there is gerontological knowledge for such professional fields as clinical psychology, nutrition, nursing, and social work (Johnson et al., 1980).

It appears that both inter- and single-disciplinary approaches to gerontology are important. Many educators believe that for the knowledge base in gerontology to be sufficient for training people to work in the field of aging, all areas of life—the biological, psychological, and social—must be studied.

The knowledge base in the field of aging is broad and no one text can pretend to cover it all. This means that some valuable information must necessarily be excluded. However, it is believed that the materials included in the chapters to follow present the basic content and skills essential for those currently working with the elderly and for those preparing for careers in the professional practice of social work.

Two essential subfields of gerontology are social gerontology and geriatrics. Clark Tibbitts, a pioneer in modern scientific gerontology (Kart, 1981), describes social gerontology as "concerned with developmental and group behavior of adults following maturation and with the social phenomena which give rise to and arise out of the presence of older people in the population" (Tibbitts, 1964, p. 139).

Growing old does not occur in a vacuum. Instead, it occurs within a social context. Thus, Tibbitts and others recognize that the social gerontologist must understand how biological and psychological factors influence the ways in which the individual and society adapt to each other.

The essential question to which social gerontology is addressed is, "What happens to human beings socially as they grow old?" Theories such as role theory, activity theory, and disengagement theory have attempted to provide answers to this question. Usually the answers or theoretical explanations given fall within two broad categories: theories that describe and explain how individuals adjust to their own aging; and theories that are concerned with the relationship between a society's social system and its older members (Kart, 1981). Theories that fall into the first category include disengagement theory, activity theory, and role theory. Those that fall into the latter category include the subculture of the aging and age stratification theories.

Geriatrics is that branch of medicine dealing with the diseases and medical treatment or care of older people. More specifically, geriatrics is the medical specialty of gerontology which studies and treats changes and diseases of the aging human system. Geriatricians are medical doctors who have specialized in conditions prevalent among older people.

For several years, practice in geriatric medicine did not carry the same prestige as did practice in other areas such as obstetrics or pediatrics. Prospective physicians have not regarded geriatrics as a rewarding or desirable area in which to work (Kart, 1981). However, as the number of older people in the population continues to grow, and as more funding and physical resources are made available, it is reasonable to assume that more departments of geriatrics will be established in medical schools and hospitals across the country. And since older people require more medical care than people under the age of sixty-five, and since health care expenditures are rapidly soaring, older people need highly trained staff if they are to receive fair value for their money (Butler, 1979).

The processes, problems, and needs of older life are complex.

In fact, most of the vital issues concerning the well-being of the elderly tend to cut across disciplinary lines. Because of this, gerontology continues to insist on the need to integrate a wide variety of the concerns of several disciplines, including the physical and social sciences, the humanities and arts, business and education. It insists also on keeping the whole person firmly fixed at the center of an interdisciplinary emphasis.

Such an approach stresses the importance of contributions among and between disciplines. Even within a specific discipline, a multifaceted perspective may be useful. For example, a careful delineation of the concept of age must take into account biological, psychological, and sociological dimensions.

As we grow older, there appear to be decrements in physiological functioning (Shock, 1961). Although it is not known at this time whether these age-related changes are intrinsic to the aging process per se or whether they are caused by a disease process or by social stress, the aging individual experiences the loss of functional capacity as a general loss of vigor. In addition to this loss of functional capacity, a succession of social losses may occur—loss of job, income, or status; the death of a spouse; the loss of children or beloved friends and neighbors. These social losses can be devastating to the elderly and may serve to depress them. Extreme depression may result in suicide. The suicide rate per elderly white males is higher than that of any other group (Woodruff & Birren, 1975). Butler and Lewis indicate the following:

> Older white men commit suicide at greater rates than black men or women in general (after the different life expectancies of each group are accounted for). We surmise that the explanation lies in the severe loss of status (ageism) that affects white men, who as a group had held the greatest power and influence in society. Black men and most women have long been accustomed to a lesser status (through racism and sexism) and ironically do not have to suffer such a drastic fall in old age. In fact, there are some indications that black people enjoy a rise in status as they age (1982, p. 80).

It is quite possible that some of the suicides could have been prevented, particularly those related to depression. Depressive reactions are widespread among the elderly and they are treatable. Conscious efforts are required to make outreach services available to those elderly individuals who have become isolated and withdrawn.

Old age must offer the older person something to live for (Butler & Lewis, 1977).

What does the loss of status and prestige and the subsequent rise in depression, isolation and suicide among the elderly mean for the helping professional? It suggests that multiple skills and intervention strategies are essential on a variety of levels to meet effectively the specific needs and problems of older people. Practitioners are needed to provide the elderly with health care, social services, and other human services. Architects and planners are needed to intervene on a neighborhood level. Qualified administrators and managers of housing projects are needed to develop appropriate programs and services for the elderly. Maximizing health care in old age is a major concern for health care providers. Education is a basic strategy to provide the aged with information about health care and nutrition.

Researchers are needed to strengthen the knowledge base of gerontology, and the effectiveness of those who work in the field. Observing and understanding phenomena is a critical feature of scientific inquiry. Gerontologists gather data systematically through such methods as questionnaires or interviews, sometimes using mechanical devices such as videotapes, tape recorders, and so on. They also act as observers. Frequently, a variety of techniques is employed in a research study in order to assess more accurately the validity or truthfulness of the observations.

Before researchers can observe behavior, they must design their study. The type of research design that is used will depend upon the type of question(s) being asked. For instance, if we were to investigate the effects of a new exercise program on the level of well-being of seventy-year-old retired men, we would use an experimental design. The study would consist of an experimental group that would be exposed to the program, and a control group that would not. A Pretest-Posttest control group design would be used. The Pretest-Posttest control group design is an experimental design in which subjects are assigned to experimental and control groups by random methods and are given a pretest on the dependent variable Y. "The treatment is introduced only to the experimental subjects for a specified time, after which the two groups are measured on the dependent variable" (Ary et al., 1979, p. 249). Thus it would be possible to determine how much of the shift in level of well-being could be attributed to the new exercise program. In a design such as this, the experimenter is able to exert a considerable amount of control over a variety of experimental variables and conditions.

The survey design is the most common method of data collection in social research. In survey research, the researcher asks a selected set of individuals a specific set of questions. Survey studies seek to obtain quantitative descriptions among specified variables. Quantitative descriptions are obtained through the use of various measuring devices to describe relationships among variables (Tripodi et al., 1969). Thus, statistical concepts such as correlation, proportions, and so forth are employed.

Researchers might compare two or more samples at one point in time. For example, marital satisfaction may be assessed in a comparison of three distinct groups, such as couples in their forties, fifties, and sixties married for the first time. Or the researcher might explore the relations among a series of variables, systematically collecting information on a variety of variables that are defined sufficiently so that they can be measured. For instance, information could be collected on income, racial or cultural background, family status, work history, health status, and so on in community-based women seventy-five years of age and over, and living alone. The investigator would then determine whether there are any significant correlations among these variables. Developing an adequate survey instrument (either a questionnaire or an interview schedule) is a long process that requires knowledge and skill.

Any time a researcher is interested in actual behavior, observational methods are to be preferred. For example, the researcher might be interested in observing behavior among older people in a nursing home, on a hospital ward, or at a political rally. Observational methods can be used by social work practitioner/researchers and others to learn more about the lives of those being studied, from their own point of view (Ramos, 1981). The data collected on the people being studied are descriptive. Early in the process the researcher must make some decisions. Who should be studied? On what aspects of, say, older people's lives should the investigator focus? Why should these people be studied, and of what benefit will the resulting data be?

Because the data collected through observational methods are descriptive, the report is usually written in the form of a case study or ethnography. In writing a case study, the observer presents a detailed description of the individual, or group of individuals studied. Also included is an analysis of the importance of the description. Observational methods enable researchers to gain new insights into the groups they are studying.

In order to function in, understand, and make decisions about the world in which they live, researchers have always sought to explain and predict that world. The research process is "widely believed to be the most accurate source of prediction and explanation" (Crandall, 1980, p. 80). The research process is a systematic, exhaustive, objective, scholarly, and empirical method of investigating a variety of questions in a variety of areas. In gerontology, the goal of research is to learn more about the biological, psychological, and social processes of aging—not for the purpose of extending or lengthening the life span, but to improve the quality of life for older people (*Gerontology and Geriatrics,* 1969).

If the quality of life is to improve for older people, it is essential that those practicing in the field of aging keep abreast of the current developments, research innovations, and empirical findings in this changing field. Research studies on aging should seek to develop and extend knowledge about the aging process and the conditions of the aged—knowledge that is useful in the development of better practices and in the formulation of more effective policies that relate to older people.

The material in the chapters to follow will continue to emphasize the strong interdisciplinary thrust that dominates gerontology. It will draw on major research findings that will be examined in terms of their implications for practice. The major focus of the text will be on social work practice with the elderly. This is currently the weakest area in the social work literature. One major reason that this area is lacking in substance is because the social work profession has been relatively slow to make a substantial commitment to aging as a field of study. Strides are now being made by the profession to remedy this deficiency. There is a substantive body of knowledge about aging, and multiple skills and methods that must be mastered by those social workers who plan to work with the elderly.

From this substantive body of information, that knowledge of aging needed for direct practice with the elderly has been selected with care. In addition, skills and interventive techniques useful for the beginning student practicing with the elderly have been identified. These are discussed in relation to their appropriateness for working with individuals, families, groups, or communities.

SOCIAL WORK CONCERNS

Social work has as its primary concern the interaction of people with their social environment. The social environment may include the family, agencies and organizations, the judicial system, the school system, and the health and welfare system. Helping people to deal effectively with these systems—many of which are large and complex—as well as linking various systems with one another in behalf of the client, requires knowledge and expertise. When working with older clients, the worker may discover that some are intimidated about applying for services such as food stamps, Medicaid, or rent rebates. Their reluctance to apply for the service may be related to the belief that their application will be rejected, that they will not be understood, or that their worthiness will be questioned. The worker may have to take the initiative to establish the older client's eligibility for the service, or enable him to effectively deal with the system himself. An essential part of the social worker's function is to get the various service delivery systems—for example, food stamps, Medicaid, rent rebates—to work in the best interest of the client.

Services to older people may be provided on an individual, group (family and small-group), or community basis. To work successfully with older people, it is important to understand their social status as it is now in relation to the changes that have occurred over time. In addition, it is important to understand the aging process itself, as well as the strengths and weaknesses of the elderly in coping with their status and problems (Harbert & Ginsberg, 1979).

The nature of aging is shaped by its social context—the whole social environment in which aging occurs. The social environment encompasses the family or friends and peers at one level, and the society or culture at another level. The position of the aged in a society will depend upon a number of factors including the structure of the society, the political climate, attitudes toward aging, services to older people, family structure, and so on (Ward, 1979).

We are living in a society characterized by rapid social, political, economic, and technological change. Yet relatively little is known about how these factors of change are affecting the elderly in terms of their socioeconomic circumstances, levels of need, patterns of family living and community relations. Change, however induced, cannot take place without people being hurt (Titmuss, 1968). In consequence, new and different social needs are continually arising. For instance, there are many problems posed by the "graying" of America's suburbs. The lack of jobs and of affordable housing has forced a significant number of young adults to vacate the suburbs in a number of states, leaving behind a predominantly older population. Many of these people are now living on fixed incomes and are unable to keep up with the high cost of living, as they once were. In addition, the housing industry is depressed; housing to meet the diversified and changing needs of elderly individuals is not available. Another set of problems is related to the differential growth of age groups within the older population itself. It is the "old old" (those seventy-five years of age and over) who are the fastest growing group in our society and who generate the most intensive demand for health care services, particularly long-term care services (Soldo, 1980). Another issue relates to the dwindling federal dollar spent on social services for the elderly. In 1980, 0.9 of every dollar was spent on such programs. A year later, the shortage of funds for such programs was reduced even more.

AGING IN AN HISTORICAL PERSPECTIVE

An examination of some historical antecedents helps one to better understand both the prevailing attitudes as well as the treatment accorded the aged in that particular society. Evidence from the past points to shifts and changes in the care and treatment of older persons. Although serious methodological limitations are inherent in a comparative reporting of such data, nevertheless a picture emerges that provides some understanding of cultural variations.

The ancient Hebrews, known historically for their experiences with hostile and forbidding environments and for their attempts to find a stable and accepting homeland, demonstrated a great deal of respect for the elderly patriarch. Abraham, for example, is the archetype of a patriarch, a man vested with complete power over his family. This power could be tempered only by love and by the religiously enjoined respect of those legally under his sway (Bensman & Rosenberg, 1976). Other biblical patriarchs included Isaac, Jacob, and Jacob's twelve sons. Such men were accorded considerable prestige by the members of their families.

Long life was viewed by the ancient Hebrews more as a blessing than as a burden. One has only to read the book of Genesis for examples of unsurpassed and prosperous longevity. Adam lived to be

930 years old, Seth died at the age of 912, Noah lived to be 950 years, and Methuselah died at the ripe old age of 969 (Koller, 1968).

Wisdom and old age were inextricably linked together. Younger men were less experienced and inclined to make hasty and ill-conceived decisions. According to rabbinic teaching, even if senility deprived old men of their hard-earned wisdom they were still to be respected.

The aged and the aging were also highly respected in conservative outlying districts of ancient Greece (Koller, 1968). But in cities like Athens attitudes toward the elderly were generally negative and condescending. The Greeks were interested in the present and made every effort to live life to the fullest. They dreaded and feared old age, perhaps because even men of power would inevitably lose not only their health and attractive physical appearance, but their status and influence as well.

Aristotle perceived youth in a positive light. He noted:

> They have high aspirations; for they have never yet been humiliated by the experience of life, but are unacquainted with the limiting force of circumstances. . . . If the young commit a fault, it is always on the side of excess and exaggeration. . . . They regard themselves as omniscient and are positive in their assertions; this is, in fact, the reason for their carrying everything too far. (Conger, 1971, p. 1119)

Old age was viewed by Aristotle in a more negative vein. For instance, in describing those who have grown old, Aristotle stated that the elderly err

> . . . in everything more on the side of defect than they ought. And they always "suppose" but never "know" certainly; and questioning everything, they always subjoin a "perhaps" or a "possibly." And they talk of everything in this undecisive tone, asserting nothing decisively. . . . Moreover they are apt to be suspicious from distrust, and they are distrustful from their experience. (Aristotle, Bk. II, Ch. XIII)

The Greeks endowed their gods with such youthful qualities as beauty, strength, vast amounts of energy, and lust for life. Such gods were ageless, and apparently were the epitome of what life ought to be.

The ancient Romans' view of aging was quite similar to that of the Greeks. Nowhere were their views better portrayed than in the comedies of such writers as Plautus, which played before appreciative audiences. Old men were generally portrayed as vicious, miserly, lecherous, thoughtless, and tyrannical.

However, not all elderly men were perceived in this light. Some had the good fortune of being assigned as moral guardians to young boys from wealthy families. These trusted elderly servants were held in high regard as they accompanied the young boys to school, stayed with them during school hours, and brought them safely home (Koller, 1968). Nevertheless, the majority of ancient Roman authors consistently portrayed the elderly in a negative and highly uncomplimentary way.

The scientific mode of thought of the sixteenth and seventeenth centuries ushered in new ways of thinking; it stressed observation, experimentation, and verification. One of its chief proponents was Francis Bacon. Bacon wrote that "the end of our foundation is knowledge of causes, and secret motions of things; and the enlargening of the bounds of human empire, to the effecting of all things possible" (quoted in Gruman, 1966, p. 80). The implications that Bacon's statement has for gerontology is that "by undertaking a systematic study of the processes of aging, one might discover the causes of aging" (Birren & Clayton, 1975, p. 6).

Despite the new mode of thought, however, the basic ambivalence about aging prevailed. Bacon himself reflects this ambivalence in his discussion of the qualities essential to youth and old age:

> Men of age object too much, consult too long, adventure too little, repent too soon, and seldom drive business home to the full period, but content themselves with a mediocrity of success.... [yet] age doth profit rather in the powers of understanding, than in virtues of the will and affections. (Quoted in Hendricks and Hendricks, 1977, p. 40)

Shakespeare sounded this negative theme in such plays as *As You Like It* and *King Lear.* The title character of *King Lear,* written in the early seventeenth century, is an impetuous old man who by his own folly brings down upon his head punishment that chastens and transforms him. His daughter, Cordelia, is the instrument of Fate in the re-education of a man who has reached old age without achieving the wisdom and the humility that maturity should bring.

Old age was clearly viewed by Shakespeare as a time of

misfortune and decline. This theme is vividly portrayed in his eleventh Sonnet:

> When forty winters shall besiege thy brow
> And dig deep trenches in thy beauty's field
> Thy youth's proud livery, so gazed on now,
> Will be a tattered weed, of small worth held.

A number of books were written on and advances made in physiology, anatomy, pathology, and chemistry during the seventeenth and eighteenth centuries (Kart, 1981), despite the fact that pre-enlightenment thinking still largely prevailed. Cotton Mather (1665-1728) was one of the first Americans to write about aging. Mather wrote about aging from a theological perspective; he conceived of illness as punishment for original sin and maintained that only through temperance could longevity be achieved (Kart, 1981). Another American, William Barton, also addressed the issue of aging and longevity. In his *Observations on the Progress of Population and the Probabilities of the Duration of Human Life, in the United States of America* (1791), he attempted to show that people of America lived longer and were healthier than people in Europe (Kart, 1981).

Benjamin Rush (1746-1813), a famous physician, teacher, soldier, statesman, writer, and reformer, was one of the first Americans to describe the changes in body and mind that accompany old age. He refuted the idea that old age was a disease. The breadth of his interests was matched only by the intensity of his feelings. Rush approached every issue "as if the fate of the world hung in balance" (Brenner, 1970, pp. 31-32). The scientific mode of thought was in the air and the writers and scientists of the day were convinced that the principles of life would be discovered by observation and experimentation rather than by theory (Kart, 1981).

In the early twentieth century, American scientists such as Minot (*The Problems of Age, Growth and Death,* 1908), and Pearl (*Biology of Death,* 1922), and the Russian biologist Metchnikoff (*The Prolongation of Life,* 1908), were among those interested in explaining the phenomenon of aging (Birren & Clayton, 1975). However, some of the hypotheses of these early scientists were weak or incomplete. For example, Metchnikoff believed that the longevity of yogurt-eaters from Middle Europe was attributable to the fact that yogurt cleansed the gastrointestinal tract of bacteria; these, he thought, caused an increasing toxicity of the organism with age (Birren & Clayton, 1975). This reasoning on the part of Metchnikoff was faulty because, as Birren and Clayton point out, "If a rat's gastrointestinal flora are destroyed, the rat will suffer from vitamin deficiency because the flora synthesize the vitamins needed for normal functioning" (1972, pp. 19-20).

Other scientists in Europe were also interested in aging. For instance, Charcot, the French physician, was concerned with the clinical aspects of old age. Charcot was of the belief that the management of diseases of aging and the aged should be based on an established clinical regimen (Kart, 1981).

A Belgian mathematician, Quetelet, is considered by some to be the first gerontologist. Quetelet was one of the first scientists to apply the concept of measures of central tendency in his investigations into aging and birth and death rates in the early 1800s (Schwartz & Peterson, 1979).

In 1922, G. Stanley Hall, a psychologist and president of Clark University, wrote a book entitled *Senescence, the Last Half of Life*. Hall's concern with his own retirement led him to write this book. Until the publication of Hall's book, psychologists regarded old age as the inverse, or regression, of development (Birren & Clayton, 1975). However, Hall stated that:

> As a psychologist, I am convinced that the psychic states of old people have great significance. Senescence, like adolescence, has its own feelings, thoughts, and wills, as well as its own physiology, and their regimen is important as well as that of the body. Individual differences here are probably greater than in youth. (1922, p. 100)

Hall was of the belief that senescence required that one "construct a new self just as we do at adolescence, a self that both adds to and subtracts much from the old personality of our prime" (p. 411). On the basis of questionnaire data and his own observations, Hall found that "people did not necessarily show an increase in religious interest as they grew older" (Birren & Clayton, 1975, p. 20); nor were the elderly more fearful of death than were the young.

By 1930, the problems commonly associated with growing old "were being described frequently as a social problem and the aged as a problem group" (Maddox & Wiley, 1976, p. 4). Prompted by the growing numbers of older people in the population, their increasing life expectancy, and their inability to maintain themselves economically, many viewed with alarm the social implications these factors would have for the rest of the population. According to Maddox and Wiley, "human suffering among aged persons in the form of incapacity, isolation, and poverty were considered to be prevalent enough to warrant social concern and social action" (1976, p. 5). This view was reflected in the passage of the Social Security Act of 1935 (Ward, 1979).

During the post-World War II era, gerontological research began to accelerate. The Gerontological Society of America was founded in 1945. The society publishes, on a monthly basis, two well-known journals in the field of aging: *The Journal of Gerontology* and *The Gerontologist*. The American Geriatric Society was founded in 1950. Research and interest in aging continued to grow, and "the literature generated between 1950 and 1960 equalled the production of the literature in the entire preceding 115 years" (Birren & Clayton, 1975, p. 24). Since gerontology is a product of the twentieth century, it is a field of study that should continue to grow.

AGING AND THE AGED IN AMERICA, 1607-1789

The United States in its early years was an expanding country with a vast frontier and a predominantly agricultural economy. The unrestricted opportunities firmly established the American tradition of the "rugged individualist" who through hard work, initiative, and thrift could be expected to accumulate sufficient resources to meet any future threats to his economic security. This expectation was reinforced by the fact that there was little unemployment, and by the role of family groups in assuming responsibility for their members who were in need (*Gerontology and Geriatrics*, 1969).

Colonial life was rigorous and all hands were needed to keep the system going. The well-being, the very existence, of the colonies depended upon the maximum contribution of each of the colonists (Axinn & Levin, 1975). So extreme were the early deprivations that sheer survival was dependent on mutual aid. Most people did not live to reach old age; death was a constant companion. Thus, numerically and proportionately, the numbers of people living to reach old age in colonial America was small. Public awareness of the problems that are today commonly associated with old age had not surfaced.

The colonists were basically a religious group and brought from England a compassionate concern for "impotent" people—young, aged, infirm, and handicapped (Pumphrey & Pumphrey, 1961, Introduction). Whenever the individual or a family member was unable to provide economic aid to an "impotent" person, the colonists would join together and provide assistance through voluntary mutual aid. However, mutual aid was only to be extended in times of urgency and distress. The colonists held firmly to the belief that, to the extent possible, every individual had a primary obligation to provide for and care for himself and his family.

The economic virtues of thrift, industry, and sobriety were accorded a prominent place by the early settlers (Feldman & Scherz, 1967). Poverty and dependency came to be regarded as a sign of spiritual disgrace, of inner evil. Wealth became a mark of virtue. Very limited assistance was given to the poor. In fact, charity—that is, economic assistance—was limited to local residents who were not poor at the time they were accepted into the immediate community but who fell on "hard times" (Dentler, 1972, p. 115).

The incorporation of the English Poor Laws into the legislative framework of American colonial governments differentiated the deserving poor from the undeserving poor. Those defined as "deserving" were colonists who conformed to current religious and political beliefs and moral codes and who exhibited a "keenness to work" (Dentler, 1972). The Puritan ethic placed a great deal of emphasis on hard work. Through hard work the individual could maximize his independence as well as his family's wealth and well-being. Although poverty could not be equated with unworthiness, it could suggest a moral flaw in the individual's character. Given this kind of social attitude, little attention was paid to environmental factors such as disease, pollution, filth, housing shortages, and discrimination that differentially affected the lives of individuals (Feldman & Scherz, 1967).

The kind of care that the elderly received depended mostly on their socioeconomic level. While emphasis throughout the colonies was on individual and family responsibility, the elderly poor were still in a precarious position of dependency. Those elderly who were better off financially could expect to receive optimal care throughout their lives. Even a favored old slave who had worked for an aristocratic family for most of his life could expect to receive a ceremonious burial when he died.

In colonial times, local villages and towns assumed responsibility for selected categories of individuals who were in need through no fault of their own. Even though the colonists were supportive of those who were defined as "unemployables," they diligently sought to find effective methods to deter the able-bodied poor from seeking relief.

In the seventeenth century, the almshouse system[1] of relief was adopted as the most economical method of providing for the poor (Coll, 1969). Among those who were cared for in the almshouse were the old, the mentally ill, widows, and orphans. Eventually almshouse care was challenged as the most efficient method of caring for the destitute. The almshouses were badly constructed, poorly ventilated, and poorly heated. The rooms were crowded with all manner of inmates. Care was anything but humane. The care of the elderly, of worthy adults who had suffered temporary reverses, of the insane, and of children was found to be especially outrageous (Axinn & Levin, 1975). Even though the aged and infirm aroused sympathy from most people, there were still those that claimed that the indigent aged should have saved for old age or misfortune (Coll, 1969).

THE GROWTH OF INDUSTRIAL SOCIETY

Until 1870, more than half the nation's adult workers were farmers. In the years that followed, however, industry developed rapidly, creating a highly specialized and urbanized economy. This rapid growth and expansion continued until World War I. Cities grew as factories attracted people away from rural areas. New career opportunities in the cities opened up, especially for the young, who tended to be the most mobile. The cities held promise of exciting changes and a new way of life. Once there, many young adults married and established permanent residence, thus breaking up the extended family. Many of those who were left behind were aging or aged family members who had become attached to their communities and had no

---

[1] Almshouses were poorhouses or workhouses for people too poor to support themselves. The first almshouse was established in Rensselaerswyck, New York in 1657.

desire to leave. Unfortunately, many of these people were either too old or too sick to work, or were severely limited in their ability to manage life on the farm without help from younger family members. They soon found themselves in economic distress. Poverty, due to industrial rather than individual causes, became a way of life for these older members of society. Thus, the shift from a predominantly agricultural to a highly mechanized industrialized society created new risks to the family's financial security and lessened the ability of families to take care of their own members. In a period when productivity was high, the nonproductive were perceived by some to be responsible for their own social misfortune.

This orientation reflects the kind of societal attitudes that hold the individual responsible for his own welfare. Because societal attitudes have for years associated work with independence and self-reliance, failure to work and failure to provide are regarded as marks of personal inadequacy. A popular point of view among many people in American society is the belief that unlimited opportunities are available to the individual if he wants to work.

Social and Environmental Problems

With industrialism and urban growth, numerous social and environmental problems were intensified. Industrial development aggravated such social problems as alcoholism, crime, delinquency, prostitution, drug addiction, and severe unemployment. It brought to light such environmental problems as pollution, overcrowding, and excessive noise. Nevertheless, this period was one in which science, invention, and health technology progressed rapidly. Health technology succeeded in prolonging life. As life was prolonged, death was less effective in creating openings in the labor force. The new technology created new occupations, but the young became the primary recipients. The aged remained in the more traditional occupations such as agriculture, railroad and factory work, and mining—some of which, in time, became obsolete. Displacement from occupations such as these meant a permanent job-loss for older workers; they would not be retrained. Employers believed that older workers were too difficult to train for new jobs; they did not catch on fast enough, and the short time they had left to work after being retrained made training economically unsound.

Many older workers who were forced to relinquish their jobs

had no meaningful activities to substitute for them. This made adjustment to retirement all the more difficult. In addition, older workers who were forced to retire had no savings or other source(s) of income to fall back on once they became unemployed.

To help meet the hazards of industrial life, unemployed workers with limited means of support frequently sought economic aid from community organizations. Prior to the nineteenth century, state governments assumed little direct responsibility in social welfare[2] activities, and assistance to those in need remained a local responsibility.

The participation of state governments in social welfare came about largely through the activities of Dorothea Dix, a staunch advocate of the humane care for the treatment of the insane. In 1841, she became acutely aware of the inappropriateness of local care for the mentally ill and launched a crusade to get the states to take full responsibility (Pumphrey & Pumphrey, 1961). As a result of Miss Dix's efforts, the Massachusetts legislators agreed to appropriate funds to enlarge the existing asylum in Worcester to accommodate the insane being held there. In addition, new institutions for the mentally ill, such as the Trenton asylum in New Jersey, were created and existing ones enlarged.

In spite of this progress at the state level in the area of mental health, however, Miss Dix believed that adequate care of the mentally ill could best be financed at the federal level (Pumphrey, 1965). She proposed that the federal government appropriate 10 million acres of public lands for the establishment of hospitals for the insane and 2.5 million acres for institutions for the education of the deaf.

In 1854, Congress passed a bill incorporating Miss Dix's proposals, but President Franklin Pierce vetoed the bill on the grounds that "charitable activities were reserved by the Constitution to the states" (Pumphrey, 1965, p. 262). The Pierce veto was significant: it became the "controlling doctrine in American social welfare for two generations because federal assistance for state welfare programs was not available until the 1930's" (Pumphrey, 1965, p. 33).

Thus, during the early twentieth century, state governments emerged as the major instruments of social welfare (Dentler, 1972).

---

[2] Social welfare is here referred to as "society's organized efforts to help those persons recognized as unable to care for themselves or meet their social obligations" (Pumphrey, 1965, p. 19).

Statewide measures were adopted to provide aid through cash allowances to certain categories of the poor. Mothers' pension laws, for example, were adopted in a number of states before World War I. Arizona was the first state to enact old-age pension legislation; but its act, passed in 1914, was declared unconstitutional. Nine years later similar laws were enacted by Montana, Nevada, and Pennsylvania. By January, 1935—on the eve of the adoption of the Social Security Act—twenty-eight states had old-age pension laws but all had serious limitations. In every case, the applicant had to prove that he was in need and that he had no close relatives upon whom he could call for aid. The age limit was usually high—seventy years in thirteen states, sixty-eight in North Dakota. Far more serious, however, were the residence requirements. Arizona, for example, required that a person live thirty-five years in the state before receiving a pension (Dentler, 1972). Finally, only a limited number of older people who were eligible to receive old-age pensions actually received them. Of approximately 7,500,000 persons in the United States who were sixty-five on January 1, 1935, only 231,000—or about 3 percent—were actually receiving old-age pensions (Dentler, 1972).

Workmen's compensation was the first social insurance program to be introduced in the United States. A federal law covering civilian employees of the federal government engaged in hazardous jobs was adopted in 1908, and the first state workmen's compensation law to be held constitutional was enacted in 1911. By 1929, workmen's compensation laws were in effect in all but four states.

EMERGING PERSPECTIVES IN SOCIAL WELFARE

The period from the turn of the century to the Depression of the 1930s saw the development of new power supplies, greater mechanization in industry and agriculture, and enormous advances in scientific management (Axinn & Levin, 1975). The Gross National Product climbed as a result of technological progress and relatively steady employment levels.

Between 1900 and 1930 the population of the United States increased by 46.8 million to reach 123 million. During those same years, the total number of persons living in urban areas increased by

38 million to a total of 69 million. Forty percent of the population lived in urban areas in 1900; this rose to 51 percent in 1920 and 56 percent in 1930 (Axinn & Levin, 1975). In 1900 the United States was a "youthful" country, demographically speaking, with only 4 percent of the population sixty-five years of age and over.

With industralization had come a collection of problems including city slums, factory reform, unassimilated immigrants, and class animosity (Leuchtenburg, 1958). And always there was poverty. On the surface the economy appeared sound, but a disproportionate accumulation of the wealth was in the hands of a few people. A report by the Commission on Industrial Relations indicated that 50 to 66 percent of working-class families were poor and that a third lived in abject poverty (Axinn & Levin, 1975). Many elderly Americans were included in this latter group.

The years from 1890 to 1914 marked the Progressive Era. Characteristic of the Progressive Era was its emphasis on reform. Around 1880, various segments of the population had become aware that the Protestant ethic which emphasized individualism and acting in one's own best interest, and the prevalent laissez-faire[3] economical view, together justified unfair business practices such as cut-throat competition, formation of monopolies, deplorable safety and working conditions, and exploitation of the working class through low pay, long hours, and child labor (Zastrow, 1982). The evils of unlimited competition and abuses by those with economic power placed the bulk of the population (many of whom were barely above the subsistence level) in a disadvantaged position.

A new kind of social thinking stressed that by manipulating the environment, and by social and economic controls, all men could benefit (Ward, 1979). This new thinking, in direct opposition to Social Darwinism[4] and laissez-faire economical views, "called upon the federal government to take on new and different functions; to

---

[3] Laissez-faire economical theory asserted that the owners of business and industry should fix the rules of competition, the conditions of labor, and so on, as they pleased, without governmental regulation or control.

[4] Social Darwinism was based on Charles Darwin's theory of evolution. Darwin theorized that higher forms of life evolved from lower forms by the process of survival of the fittest. Herbert Spencer extended this theory: struggle, destruction, and survival of the fit were essential to progress in human society as well.

establish legislation to regulate business practices, and to provide
social welfare programs'' (Zastrow, 1982, p. 18). The result of this
new thinking was that more attention was focused on the social needs
of the poor. In addition, the federal government began to place
limited funds into such programs as housing, health, and slum
clearance.

The last years of the nineteenth century also witnessed the
development of a new impulse in Christianity, particularly in Protestantism. Whereas traditional Protestantism placed emphasis on
individual believers and their obligation to serve God, the new idea
stressed dedicating oneself to the service of one's fellow human beings. Protestant clergy and lay people in both England and the
United States became aware of the social problems developing in
their respective countries and began to turn their attention to social
reform—to saving society. This new concern for the preservation of
society came to be known as the Social Gospel (Handel, 1982). From
1870 to 1900, the Social Gospel movement challenged the dominant
values and beliefs of the doctrine of laissez-faire (Zastrow, 1982).
Social Gospel advocates judged that laissez-faire was incompatible
with Christian principles.

As communication and literacy improved, more people
became acutely aware of the facts of poverty and depression. Recur-
rent business depressions began to dispel the myth that all was well
with the economic and social system and that poverty should be attributed to individual fault. Whatever the causes, the results of this
change in attitude can be illustrated by the extent to which social insurance measures were adopted prior to 1914.

Though most of the states had adopted workmen's compensation laws just before World War I, that was fully a quarter of a century after they had been introduced in Europe (Diamond, 1972). One
reason that the development of a system of social security in the
United States lagged behind that in other industrial nations is that
this country placed unbounded confidence in individual effort as a
means of achieving economic security. This was despite the fact that
60 percent of American families had incomes below $2,000 in 1929
(Axinn & Levin, 1975). Most of the population, including the elderly,
had no reserves to fall back on when the Great Depression set in.

The Depression of the 1930s brought home very poignantly

the fact that anyone could be poor and unemployed as a result of the malfunctioning of society. Not until the Depression was it recognized that federal action was required to cope with the economic risks of unemployment, old age, death, and disability. In 1935, President Franklin D. Roosevelt proposed to the Congress legislation embodying the recommendations of a specially created Committee on Economic Security. As a result, the Social Security Act was enacted on August 14, 1935. It was a milestone in American political and social history.

The role of the federal government in the provision of social services during the Depression came at a time when 25 percent of the labor force (13 million persons) were unemployed and many more could only find part-time employment (Axinn & Levin, 1975). Those who had followed the rules of economic virtue—hard work, thrift, and so on—went down, along with those who had gambled on the stock market (Stein, 1971).

Population Sixty-five and Over Increases

In 1900 only 3 million people in a total population of 76 million were 65 years of age and over. By 1940, the group had nearly tripled in size to 9.0 million (Current Population Reports, 1976).

Aging first came into national focus in 1950 when President Truman directed the Federal Security Agency to hold the First National Conference on Aging to assess the problems emerging as a result of the extraordinary increase in the number of elderly persons in the population. Particular attention was focused on the problems of poverty, unemployment, and rising health costs among the elderly. The problems persisted, however, and in some respects became more severe with time.

By 1958, the magnitude and complexity of these problems reached a point that prompted the Congress to enact legislation requesting President Eisenhower to call the first White House Conference on Aging in January, 1961. This conference, like the National Conference on Aging in 1950, was highly publicized and heightened public awareness of the problems associated with older life. The year 1965 saw the passage of the Older Americans Act which created for the first time a central point for the aged within the federal government—the Administration on Aging. Medicare, or Title XVIII of the Social Security Act, was passed in 1965; it provided a national system of health insurance for the elderly. Medicaid, or Title XIX of the Social Security Act, was also passed in 1965 and became effective July 1, 1966.

In spite of these strides, many older people were increasingly disadvantaged. Inflation continued at a steady rate and even though money incomes were increased through raised Social Security benefits, many people were relatively poorer. In addition, employment opportunities for retirees did not materialize to enable them to earn additional income; property taxes climbed to such levels that many older home owners were forced to sell their homes and move into cheap, rented quarters (*White House Conference on Aging,* 1971). The production of housing designed to meet the diversified and changing needs of aging persons lagged. Health services remained fragmented and uncoordinated and were not prepared to accommodate the needs of the rapidly rising numbers of older people.

Long-term care was narrowly referred to by providers of health care as a secondary, custodial function of the health care system. The clients of long-term care were persons of any age with chronic or continuing conditions living in nursing homes and rehabilitation facilities. The overwhelming proportion of people residing in such facilities were chronically ill or disabled elderly. (Today long-term care is broader in focus and takes into consideration a range of care sources and settings—including non-institutional settings.)

Congress continued to maintain a strong interest in older people. Soon after his inauguration, President Nixon appointed a special task force to study the problems of older Americans. In November, 1971, the Second White House Conference on Aging was held. The conference planners hoped that this conference would move in the direction of a national policy on aging and that all levels of government would be involved in finding effective ways of meeting the needs of the elderly. There is some question whether this conference or the previous one generated worthwhile information or policies. Nevertheless, the 1971 White House Conference on Aging generated recommendations in many areas including income, employment, health care, housing, nutrition, education, and transportation.

The Federal Government's Role
in Meeting Needs of the Elderly

The most universal problem of the aged is insufficient income. People with insufficient income can save very little even when they are educated toward wise consumer behavior. Lack of savings among the elderly results in severely limited capital for food, medical care, transportation, and so on. Poverty and the problems of the elderly impoverished present a distressing picture to the larger society. In the face of this, society has devised service interventions designed to change an unacceptable to a more acceptable way of life for older individuals.

The Social Security system has undergone several revisions since it was first developed. As originally formulated, Social Security payments were not intended to take the place of an individual's monthly salary. Rather, they were meant to supplement the family's savings. Social Security was intended to prevent poverty by providing adequate levels of subsistence for those who had previously worked, but were now too old to work, or were disabled, or dependent. (Strictly speaking, wage-related benefits do the most for those who have earned the most and thus paid in the most.)

World War II brought full employment and rising incomes to millions of Americans. For oppressed minorities, "particularly blacks and women, the period offered increased opportunity for economic, educational, and social equality" (Axinn & Levin, 1975, p. 226). Unprecedented economic growth in America continued at a steady rate during the 1950s. Millions of families had extra money to spend on comforts and luxuries. The majority of middle- and upper-class citizens assumed that poverty no longer existed in America.

In the midst of this great prosperity there arose a renewed awareness that America's growing affluence was unevenly distributed. John Kenneth Galbraith, a widely read economist, asserted that there "was a problem of poverty in the midst of so much prosperity" (Friedlander & Apte, 1980, p. 312). But few people paid attention to Galbraith's assertion. Concern with the meagre quality of life for many in affluent America was stressed in Michael Harrington's *The Other America: Poverty in the United States*.[5] This book,

---

[5] Harrington, M. *The Other America: Poverty in the United States*. New York: Macmillan, 1962.

along with Galbraith's *The Affluent Society,*[6] "expressed and in turn gave impetus to a new mood of social discontent and a rising tide of pressure for social action" (Piore, 1977, p. 527).

During the years from 1946 to 1964, "the issue of poverty was treated in federal politics as if there were no solution other than continued growth in the economy on the one hand and occasional minor reforms of public welfare assistance on the other" (Dentler, 1972, p. 118). In the early 1960s, Presidents Kennedy and Johnson reexamined poverty and found one-fourth of the nation ill-fed, ill-clothed, and ill-housed. "President Kennedy strongly encouraged the development of a legislative package to combat poverty. About a month before his assassination in 1963, the Council of Economic Advisors prepared a document entitled Program for a Concerted Assault on Poverty" (Friedlander & Apte, 1980, p. 315). The Economic Opportunity Act was passed on August 20, 1964. The declaration of purpose of the new law established public policy in relation to the elimination of poverty:

> The United States can achieve its full economic and social potential as a nation only if every individual has the opportunity to contribute to the full extent of his capabilities and to participate in the workings of our society. It is therefore the policy of the United States to eliminate the paradox of poverty in the midst of plenty in this Nation by opening to everyone the opportunity for education and training, the opportunity to work and the opportunity to live in decency and dignity. (U.S. 88th Congress, 2nd session, Public Law No. 88-452, Sec. 2).

The War on Poverty thus declared was the first federal attack on the problem in thirty years to go beyond the concept of social insurance for the aged and the disabled. This overdue, under-funded attack on a major social problem was called off because of the Vietnam conflict (Dentler, 1972).

The great positive development to come out of the War on Poverty was a national awareness of the scope of poverty and the social fact that there are available solutions for its treatment and elimination. This awareness has stimulated, among other things, a continuing tradition of improved social security benefits for the aged (Dentler, 1972).

---

[6] Galbraith, J. K. *The Affluent Society.* Boston: Houghton Mifflin, 1958.

In November, 1980, Ronald Reagan, a conservative Republican, was elected fortieth President of the United States. On assuming the Presidency, he made it clear that there existed a huge federal budget deficit and measures would have to be taken to eliminate it. The central themes of the Reagan administration and Congress were federal budget reductions and tax policy changes. President Reagan proposed a vast restructuring of the thirty social services, mental health, and health programs that made up the non-cash social welfare system in the United States. Many of the federal programs employing social workers suffered cuts up to 20 percent.

What emerged in the early months of the Reagan presidency was not just a struggle over the elimination of a federal budget deficit. Rather, it was a struggle over the philosophy of government, the limits of its involvement in domestic programs, and its distribution of national resources. It must be borne in mind that the impact of government policy in social matters has been profound, particularly during the latter part of the twentieth century, and millions of Americans have looked to the government for a solution to social problems. For many, social policy has meant social welfare programs for the poor, the elderly, and the handicapped, among others.

In the 1980s, the cost of living will no doubt continue to rise, the condition of older Americans threatens to grow worse, and the number of older people in the population will increase. Clearly a realistic national policy regarding the older population is sorely needed.

The Third White House Conference on Aging was held in December, 1981. A total of 2,260 delegates, representing all of the fifty states, were in attendance. The Conference opened amid charges and countercharges that the Reagan administration had tried to control delegate input on committees dealing with such controversial issues as income and health. Apparently, these key committees were "stacked" with delegates considered "favorable" to the administration. Leaked documents alleged to be from conference staff files showed, for example, that the Economic Well-Being Committee, which had official jurisdiction over Social Security, had no less than one hundred and five "favorable" members and twelve "not favorable." Another committee considered crucial by both advocates of the cause of the aged and by the administration, the Health Care and Services Committee charged with Medicare and Medicaid issues, had ninety-four members listed as favorable to the administration and thirty-two not favorable (*Older American Reports,* 1981).

Despite charges of stacked committees, the administration was unable to block passage of a liberal slate of some six hundred resolutions calling for expansion of many programs Reagan wanted curtailed or even eliminated. Report recommendations that emerged from the Conference called for public endorsement of no benefit cuts in Social Security, restoration of the Social Security minimum benefit, and expansion of health benefits under Medicare and Medicaid to include home health visits, drugs, dental and eye care (*Older American Reports,* 1981).

These are only a few of the recommendations made by the Conference. However, in light of the growing numbers of older people, the vulnerable position in which many of them find themselves, and the difficult times in which we live, society must redouble its efforts if older people are to be helped to make effective life transitions, and improve the quality of their lives.

SUMMARY

Gerontology is the scientific study of older life and of the special problems of the elderly. The field of aging is broad and encompasses the biophysiological, psychological, and social aspects of old age. Although people age on each of these three levels, aging is influenced by both heredity and environment.

Social gerontology and geriatrics are two sub-fields of gerontology. Social gerontology is concerned with practical issues and problems confronting the elderly; geriatrics is the branch of medicine that deals with the diseases and medical care of older people.

Aging is accompanied by a number of losses, some of which are inherent to the aging process, others of which are disease-related. There are also a number of social losses—for example, the death of spouse, the loss of job, income, or status—that people experience as they grow old. These losses can be devastating to older people experiencing them.

Research in aging is essential if gerontologists and others are to find effective methods of improving the quality of life. Experimental, survey, and observational research methods are used by researchers to gain knowledge about aging.

When viewed within an historical perspective, cultural variations in the perception of old age emerge. The ancient Hebrews, for example, valued wisdom and old age. However, in cities like Athens, Greek attitudes toward the elderly were negative and condescending. Aristotle viewed aging in a negative light, as did William Shakespeare.

The scientific mode of thought was ushered in during the sixteenth and seventeenth centuries. Although some of the old ways of thinking prevailed for a while, significant throughout the scientific era was an emphasis on the causes of aging. During that period, well-known Americans such as Benjamin Rush and others wrote about and were interested in aging.

Life in colonial America was rigorous and maximum contribution was required from each of the colonists. Few people lived to reach old age. Whenever a colonist identified as an "impotent" person required economic aid, assistance was given through voluntary mutual aid. The almshouse system of relief became a popular method of providing for the poor during the seventeenth century.

As the nation grew and industry expanded new career opportunities became available to the young. Those who were either too old or too sick to work were disadvantaged and often found themselves in economic distress. Society viewed these people as responsible for their own misfortune.

Dorothea Dix, well-known nineteenth-century humanitarian, tried to rescue the insane from jails and almshouses. She was an advocate of humane care for the treatment of the insane and was eventually instrumental in getting the states to assume responsibility for their care rather than relying on local units of government.

As America entered the twentieth century, technological advances increased rapidly. However, a number of social problems including city slums, unassimilated immigrants, and poverty followed. Some states passed workmen's compensation laws or Mothers' Pension programs in an effort to deal with poverty. Statewide approaches to poverty were not sufficient to meet the economic needs of so many people when the Great Depression of the 1930s arrived. Most people, including the elderly, had minimal resources to fall back on. To solve the problems—especially those of unemployment and old age—a permanent system of social security was needed. Thus, the Social Security Act was signed into law on August 14, 1935, and the fundamental federal law in the field of social welfare in the United States was created.

chapter 2

THE ELDERLY POPULATION

THE DEMOGRAPHY OF AGING

Demography is defined as the "science of vital statistics, as of births, deaths, marriages, etc. of populations" (*Webster's New World Dictionary,* 1970). One way to make this rather abstract subject more meaningful is to raise questions that relate specifically to a description and analysis of the elderly population. For instance, how many older Americans are there? How are they distributed over the United States? What are their living arrangements? What is their marital status? To what extent is the population sixty-five years of age and over increasing? How many older people live in poverty? Answers to questions such as these are important at several different levels of government and for several different reasons.

At the national level, information about the number of people over the age of sixty-five and their characteristics, as well as recent trends affecting them, are basic to the formulation of policies relating to social security, education, taxation, health and medical insurance. At the state level, population facts and principles are of primary importance in connection with plans and policies relative to old-age benefits, hospitalization, and the planning, development, and implementation of innovative programs for the elderly. At the local level, knowledge of basic facts about people sixty-five years of age and over is essential for the intelligent shaping of public policies (Smith & Zopf, 1976). Questions such as those related to the location of health care facilities, the planning or improvement of transportation systems for the elderly, and the location of housing to extend the span of independent living must all be studied in close relationship to population facts and trends.

In addition, information such as this is useful to students of gerontology because it helps them to understand better the nature and position of older persons in contemporary society (Cutler & Harootyan, 1975), and the extent to which their numbers have increased and continue to increase in the general population. The latter notion is of vital importance when one considers the press of humanity upon our current supply of available resources.

The discussion in this chapter on the demographic aspects of aging focuses primarily on age variations in numbers, characteristics, and vital processes, that is, births and deaths, of those persons in the population sixty-five years of age and over. However, the reader should be aware that any discussion of the demographic aspects of aging as it relates to the individual's physical condition (for example, life, health) and social and economic characteristics (for example, labor force participation, income, living arrangements) is of special concern to the public as the individual advances in age. Such individual changes are collectively reflected in the data on the demographic characteristics of the population (Siegel et al., 1976).

Grouping data into age categories such as sixty-five to sixty-nine years, seventy to seventy-four, seventy-five to seventy-nine, and so on, frequently conceals the fact that the elderly are not a homogeneous group. People age at different rates and changes begin to occur in people at different chronological ages (Loether, 1975). Some persons manifest changes such as decreased muscular strength, stooped posture, loss of elasticity of the skin, and decrements, especially in vision and hearing, at a much earlier age than others. Grouped data do not describe individual differences such as these. This means that in summarizing grouped data some important information is almost always lost. Nevertheless, grouped data are frequently employed to reveal or emphasize a group pattern. This approach tends to make for a smoother description of the data.

Although the information presented in this chapter comes from official government sources (*Facts About Older Americans,* 1978; *Current Population Reports,* 1976) the figures for the older ages are no doubt subject to a substantial degree of error. The figures are affected not only by the failure to count everyone or to register all births, deaths, and migratory movements, but also by the misreporting of age and other characteristics. Persons from the various minority groups were particularly concerned about the failure of the 1970 census to count what they believe to be a significant number of their members. Failure to provide as accurate a count as possible of minority persons (or any group in the population) could affect their representation in the Congress, in state legislatures, in county, city, and town councils.

A number of systems—such as schools, the federal government, businesses, states, cities, and citizen groups—use the census figures to plan their work and to measure the problems and progress of the United States. Another very significant use of these figures is for the distribution of funds by legislative bodies to communities. It is for these reasons that an all-out effort was made by the Bureau of the

Census to count as accurately as possible the total number of people in the nation as of April 1, 1980. The 1980 census apparently revealed a truer picture of the number of elderly minority persons, for example, in the total population, largely because of the concerted effort to find such persons.

In spite of these obvious limitations in the reported data on the older population, it is believed that the general magnitudes, relations, and patterns are reflected satisfactorily by the reported figures (Siegel et al., 1976). The reader is advised, however, to exercise caution in interpreting these data.

Number

Demographically, aging is defined essentially in terms of chronological age, on the assumption that for large populations the aging process, functional age, and physiological age follow chronological age closely (Siegel et al., 1976). It must be pointed out that the older population is not a homogeneous group and that its characteristics tend to vary sharply within the band sixty-five years of age and over. However, for convenience and simplicity, the single broad group sixty-five and over is often selected for detailed consideration.

It still seems to be the case that the attainment of age sixty-five marks the point of retirement for many workers. Sixty-five is the age of qualification for Social Security benefits and Medicare coverage. It figures in several important pieces of legislation affecting the older population, including Federal and State tax laws (*Current Population Reports,* 1976).

The older population of the United States is large and continues to grow rapidly. In 1977, there were 23.5 million men and women over the age of sixty-five. This meant that one in every nine persons in the United States was sixty-five years of age and over. Between 1900 and 1977, the percentage of the U.S. population aged sixty-five and over more than doubled (4.1 percent in 1900, 10.9 percent in 1977), while the number increased over seven-fold from 3.1 million to 23 million (*Facts about Older Americans,* 1978). (See Figure 2-1.)

The population sixty-five and over is expected to show substantial percentage increases during the 1980s. The general rise in the number of births in the nineteenth century and in the first decades of

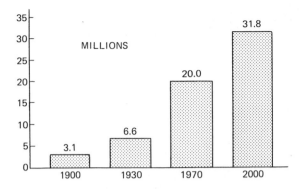

The Older Population in the Twentieth Century

Year	Number (000's)	Percent of Total	Men (000's)	Women (000's)	Ratio Women/Men
1900	3,080	4.1	1,555	1,525	98/100
1930	6,634	5.4	3,325	3,309	100/100
1970	19,972	9.8	8,367	11,605	139/100
1977	23,494	10.9	9,569	13,925	146/100
2000	31,822	12.2 – 12.9	12,717	19,105	150/100

FIGURE 2-1   Growth of the Older Population in the Twentieth Century. Source: *Facts About Older Americans,* 1978, U.S Government Printing Office, DHEW Pub. No. (OHDS) 79-20006.

this century largely accounts for past and prospective rapid increases in the number of elderly persons until about 1990 (*Current Population Reports,* 1976).

During 1976, about 1.8 million persons reached the age of sixty-five and 1.2 million persons sixty-five and over died. This resulted in a net increase of 537,000 older Americans (1,470 per day). The population sixty-five and over increased rapidly during the 1960-70 period (20 percent), much more rapidly than the population as a whole (13 percent). (See Table 2-1 and Figure 2-2).

Yet the growth rate of this age group during the 1960s was well below its growth rate during the 1950s (35 percent), and the preceding decades (23.7 percent in 1920; 36.0 percent in 1930; 34.7 percent in 1940, and 37.3 percent in 1950). The population sixty-five and over is expected to show substantial increases for years to come, although the increases will be much smaller than before 1960 (*Current Population Reports,* 1976).

The rapid drop in the number of births during the 1920s to the

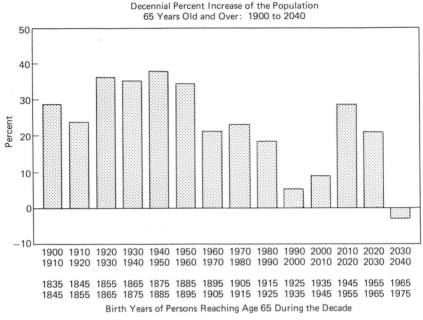

Decennial Percent Increase of the Population
65 Years Old and Over: 1900 to 2040

1900	1910	1920	1930	1940	1950	1960	1970	1980	1990	2000	2010	2020	2030
1910	1920	1930	1940	1950	1960	1970	1980	1990	2000	2010	2020	2030	2040

1835	1845	1855	1865	1875	1885	1895	1905	1915	1925	1935	1945	1955	1965
1845	1855	1865	1875	1885	1895	1905	1915	1925	1935	1945	1955	1965	1975

Birth Years of Persons Reaching Age 65 During the Decade

FIGURE 2-2 Demographic Aspects of Aging and the Older Population in the United States.   Source: *Current Population Reports,* 1976, U.S. Dept. of Commerce Bureau of the Census, Special Studies Series P-23, No. 59, May 1976.

1940s is expected to result in a decrease in the size of the population sixty-five and over from about 1990 to 2010. However, the births of the post-war "baby boom," 1945-1959, will ultimately have their impact on the size of the aged population. Early in the next century (2010 to 2020) the number of persons sixty-five and over will leap forward (by 9.6 million, or 29 percent) as those cohorts[1] attain age sixty-five. Two other demographic factors that eventually affect a population's composition are mortality and immigration. Mortality reduces the initial cohort of births, and net migration typically increases it (Kart, 1981).

At present death rates, the older population is expected to increase 35 percent to 32 million by 2000. If the present low birth rate persists, these 32 million will be 12.2 percent of the total population of about 260 million.

The age structure of the U.S. population is depicted by the

[1] A birth cohort is all of the individuals who are born within the same period of time, usually five years.

TABLE 2-1 Decennial Percent Increase of Population by Broad Age Groups: 1950 to 2010

(A MINUS SIGN (–) DENOTES A DECREASE.
PERIODS EXTEND FROM JULY 1 OF INITIAL YEAR
TO JUNE 30 OF TERMINAL YEAR)

Age and projection series	1950 to 1960	1960 to 1970	1970 to 1980	1980 to 1990	1990 to 2000	2000 to 2010
All ages .... II.	18.7	13.4	8.7	10.0	7.1	6.2
Range ...... { III.			7.6	6.9	4.0	2.1
I.			10.2	14.2	11.4	12.2
Under 15 years ..... II.	36.8	3.2	-11.6	13.4	0.8	-0.4
Range ...... { III.			-15.7	-0.1	-3.8	-8.3
I.			-6.5	30.2	7.6	10.2
15 to 24 years ..... II.	9.9	48.5	13.7	-16.2	11.8	5.7
Range ...... { III.				-16.6	-4.0	0.5
I.				-15.8	31.2	13.6
25 to 44 years ..... II.	3.2	2.7	27.7	25.5	-2.3	-3.5
Range ...... { III.					-2.5	-10.6
I.					2.1	5.5
45 to 54 years	17.9	13.3	-2.9	11.4	41.8	13.1
55 to 64 years	16.6	19.4	12.8	-2.7	12.0	41.7
65 to 74 years	30.1	13.0	23.4	13.8	-2.6	13.3
75 to 84 years	41.2	31.7	14.2	26.6	15.6	-2.4
85 years and over	59.3	52.3	44.6	20.1	29.4	19.4

Source: Current Population Reports, 1976, U.S. Dept. of Commerce Bureau of the Census, Special Studies Series P-25, Nos. 311, 519, and 601.

37

Bureau of the Census according to birth cohorts. Population reports published by the Bureau of the Census reveal that there are greater numbers of people in the United States under the age of sixty-five than there are over that age. However, these reports also indicate that the proportion of persons age sixty-five and over has more than doubled in the last eighty years (See Table 2–2).

Race and Ethnic Composition

The proportion of the population sixty-five years old and over varies by race and ethnic origin. A much smaller proportion of the black than the white population is sixty-five and over (8 percent as

TABLE 2-2   Percent of Population Sixty-five and Over and Median Age of Total U.S. Population, 1900–1980, and Projections Under Varying Fertility Assumptions, 1990–2040.

YEAR	% OF TOTAL POPULATION AGED 65 AND OVER	MEDIAN AGE OF TOTAL POPULATION
	Estimates	
1900	4.1	22.9
1910	4.3	24.1
1920	4.7	25.3
1930	5.5	26.5
1940	6.9	29.0
1950	8.2	30.2
1960	9.3	29.5
1970	9.9	28.1
1980	11.2	30.2
	Projections[a]	
1990	12.1 (11.7 – 12.6)	32.8 (31.4 – 33.7)
2000	12.2 (11.3 – 12.9)	35.5 (32.5 – 37.3)
2010	12.7 (11.1 – 13.9)	36.6 (31.1 – 40.2)
2020	15.5 (12.7 – 17.8)	37.0 (31.4 – 41.7)
2030	18.3 (14.0 – 22.1)	38.0 (31.2 – 43.2)
2040	17.8 (12.5 – 22.8)	37.8 (30.7 – 43.9)

[a] Base data of projections are for July 1, 1976. Main projection assumes replacement-level fertility (2.1 children per woman). Range in parentheses is that implied by above-replacement-level fertility (2.7 children per woman) and below-replacement-level fertility (1.7 children per woman).

Sources: U.S. Bureau of the Census. *Historical Statistics of the United States, Colonial Times to 1970;* and *Current Population Reports,* Series P–25, No. 704, ''Projections of the Population of the United States: 1977–2050.''

against 11 percent in 1977). This difference is the result of higher fertility rates and lower life expectancies of minority group members. It also reflects the large immigration of whites prior to World War I (*Current Population Reports,* 1976).

Older blacks and other nonwhite elderly have frequently been perceived as people in triple jeopardy in that they are old, poor, and members of a minority group. These groups—elderly blacks, Asian-Americans, Native Americans, and those of Hispanic descent—have been and continue to be disadvantaged on several counts. Their relative deprivation is a continuation of earlier patterns of discrimination in employment, housing, and education. Thus, low life-time earnings, irregular employment, and fewer years in jobs covered by Social Security, all mean lower-than-average benefits in retirement (Hess & Markson, 1980). This situation, in turn, has implications for health status, diet, and nutrition.

The population of Hispanic origin currently has a very low proportion of persons sixty-five and over (4 percent in 1977), and a marked distinction in sex ratio at these ages (87 males per 100 females in 1975), in comparison with the white population as a whole and even the black population. The relevant explanatory factors may be similar to those applicable in the comparison of the black and white populations.

Sex Composition

Women make up a substantial proportion of the older adult population, whereas at some younger ages there is an excess of males, and at others a small excess of females. In 1890 there were one hundred and two men aged sixty-five and older for every hundred women in the same age group. Only forty years ago just as many males as females were reported at age sixty-five and over, but there has been a steady decline in the population of men and an increasing excess of women since that time (*Current Population Reports,* 1976). By 1977, the number of men had decreased to one hundred for every one hundred forty-six women. By the year 2000, it is estimated that the number will shrink even further, reaching sixty-five males per every hundred females. As a consequence, services for the aged in the years ahead will be dominated increasingly by the problems of those in advanced old age and by the problems of single women.

Geographical Distribution

Elderly persons tend to be most numerous in the largest states (*Current Population Reports,* 1976). In 1977, less than half (45 percent) of the elderly lived in seven states. California and New York had over 2 million; Florida, Illinois, Ohio, Pennsylvania, and Texas had over 1 million each.

The highest growth in percentage from 1970 to 1977 has been in seven states. The sixty-five and over group has grown by more than 30 percent in the following seven states: Nevada (64 percent), Arizona (55 percent), Florida (47 percent), Hawaii (44 percent), New Mexico (39 percent), Alaska (37 percent), and South Carolina (30 percent). Most of these states have warm climates and a low level of industrialization, which many of the elderly find very appealing (Butler & Lewis, 1977).

The sixty-five-and-over group was 12 percent or more of the total population in eleven states in 1975—Florida (17.1 percent), Arkansas (13.3 percent), Iowa (13.0 percent), Missouri (12.9 percent), Nebraska (12.8 percent), South Dakota (12.7 percent), Kansas and Rhode Island (12.6 percent), Oklahoma (12.4 percent), Pennsylvania (12.1 percent), and Maine (12.0 percent) (*Facts About Older Americans,* 1978).

There were eleven states in which over one-fifth of persons sixty-five years of age and over were below the poverty level in 1975—Mississippi (37.0 percent), Georgia (31.9 percent), Alabama (31.6 percent), Louisiana (29.3 percent), Arkansas (29.1 percent), South Carolina (26.8 percent), Tennessee (26.0 percent), North Carolina (24.7 percent), Kentucky (22.6 percent), Texas (22.5 percent), and Oklahoma (22.1 percent) (*Facts About Older Americans,* 1978). Elderly people, both black and white, live most frequently in central parts of cities and in rural locations (Butler & Lewis, 1977).

Life-Expectancy

The proportional growth of older people in our population is impressive. More and more people are living to reach their seventies and eighties, and even beyond. A child born in 1976 can expect to live seventy-three years, about twenty-six years longer than a child born in 1900. The major part of the increase in life-expectancy has occurred because of reduced death rates for children and young adults (*Facts About Older Americans,* 1978). Until the start of the twentieth century, childhood diseases caused the death of many people before they reached adulthood, much less old age. But this is no longer true. Children today rarely die of such childhood diseases as diphtheria, whooping cough, or scarlet fever (Jones, 1977). Progress in public health and medicine has reduced the rates of illness and mortality among the young (Kart, 1981).

At age sixty-five, life-expectancy is fourteen years for men and eighteen years for women. Assuming that the 1976 death rates do not change in the future, 82 percent of female children born today will live to the age of sixty-five as compared with only 68 percent of male children born at the same time. (*Facts About Older Americans,* 1978).

The mortality rate of males in the United States is well above that of females throughout the age scale. More than 1.2 million older people died in 1976, sixty-seven per 1,000 men, forty-six per 1,000 women. The death rate for the under sixty-five group was three per 1,000. The leading causes of death among older persons were heart disease (44 percent), cancer (18 percent), and stroke (13 percent). All of the above are chronic conditions.

THE SOCIAL AND ECONOMIC CHARACTERISTICS OF THE ELDERLY

In this section we consider the leading social and economic characteristics of the older population. These characteristics are described under the following headings: (1) marital status; (2) living arrangements; (3) educational attainment; (4) extent of poverty; (5) income level; and (6) labor force participation.

Marital Status

There are striking differences in the marital status of elderly men and women. In 1977, most older men (77 percent) were married and lived with their wives; few lived alone. Most older women (52 percent) were widows. There were five times as many widows as widowers, a substantial proportion of them living alone.

A number of factors explain the high proportion of widows to widowers. The principal factor is the much higher mortality rate of married men as compared with their wives—a joint effect of the higher mortality rate of men than women and the fact that husbands

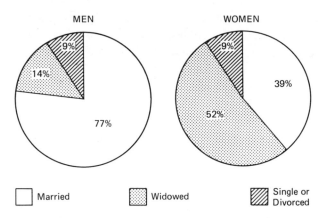

MEN   WOMEN

9%   14%   77%   9%   52%   39%

☐ Married   ▨ Widowed   ▨ Single or Divorced

FIGURE 2-3   Distribution of Older Persons by Marital Status: 1977. Source: *Facts About Older Americans,* 1978, U.S. Government Printing Office, DHEW Pub. No. (OHDS) 79-20006.

are typically older than their wives by a few years (*Current Population Reports,* 1976). A second factor is the higher remarriage rates of widowers, who frequently take wives from among women under sixty-five. In 1977, about one-third (35 percent) of older married men had wives under sixty-five years of age. Older men seem to have greater marital options than do older women. It is socially acceptable for a man to marry a woman in either his own age group or in a younger or older age group (Butler & Lewis, 1977). However, older women are frequently frowned upon if they marry a man who is considerably younger than they. (See Figure 2-3.)

Living Arrangements

Only a small proportion of the elderly live in institutions. About 4 percent of the elderly population, approximately one million people, lived in institutions of all kinds—homes for the aged, nursing homes, mental institutions, foster homes, and so on—in 1977. This means that 96 percent of the aged live in the community, either by themselves or more often with a spouse, family, or friends.

Most older people live in a family setting. Among the noninstitutional population, the numbers of older men and older women living in a family setting were about the same (7.6 million men and 7.5 million women), but since there are many more older women than men (146 to 100), the proportion of older men in family settings was 83 percent, and of women, 58 percent (*Facts About Older Americans*, 1978). (See Figure 2-4.)

Approximately one-third of older Americans (7.0 million; 1.6 million men and 5.5 million women) lived alone in 1977 or with non-relatives (42 percent of all older women, but only 17 percent of all older men). Men, because of their shorter life-span, usually live with a spouse and/or family. The proportion of older people living in family settings decreases rapidly with advancing age.

Educational Attainment

Most older people cannot compete with the young in educational attainment as measured in terms of the percent of high school graduates and the median years of school completed. Older persons had completed an average of 9.5 years of school in 1977. About 37 percent had finished high school, and 8 percent had four or more years of college (*Facts About Older Americans*, 1978).

The level of educational attainment of the elderly population has, however, been increasing rapidly. This trend toward a higher level of education for the entire adult population is expected to continue in the future as younger persons with more education move into older age groups.

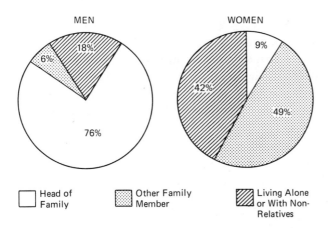

FIGURE 2-4   Living Arrangements (Noninstitutional Population). Source: *Facts About Older Americans*, 1978, U.S. Government Printing Office, DHEW Pub. No. (OHDS) 79-20006.

It is reasonable to expect that, in the future, better educated cohorts of the elderly will be better informed and in better health, they will no doubt be more actively involved in community and civic affairs and more vocal about government involvement in major areas of their lives than were earlier cohorts.

Extent of Poverty

Large numbers of the population do not become poor until they grow old. It should be noted, however, that the proportion of the elderly population below the poverty level has been falling sharply in the last decade and a half. For instance, in 1974 only 16 percent of the elderly were poor, as compared with 35 percent in 1959; for those living in families the proportion fell from 27 percent in 1959 to 8.5 percent in 1974. On the other hand, 36 percent of elderly blacks were still below the poverty level in 1974. (*Current Population Reports,* 1976).

In 1976, about 15 percent (3.3 million persons) of the population sixty-five years of age and over were below the poverty level. Among elderly whites, one of every eight (13 percent) was poor, but about one-third (35 percent) of elderly blacks and one-fourth (28 percent) of elderly Hispanic persons were poor. The disadvantage is particularly great when the family is headed by a female. The sex and race of the family head is an important factor in the poverty status of families. Over a third of black female family heads sixty-five and over have incomes below the poverty level. The proportion below the poverty level was much higher for elderly persons living alone or with nonrelatives (30 percent) than for those living in families (8 percent). Persons sixty-five years of age and over who reside outside the nation's metropolitan areas were more likely to be poor than were elderly metropolitan residents (20 percent as against 12 percent). (*Facts About Older Americans,* 1978).

Of the 8.1 million families with a family head sixty-five years of age and over, 726,000, or 9 percent, were below the poverty level. The major portion (82 percent) of the income received by poor families was derived from public sources such as Social Security, Supplemental Security Income, and public assistance. For non-poor families with a head sixty-five years of age and over, only one-third (34 percent) of the income was from such sources. About 37 percent was received in the form of wages, salaries, and self-employment income.

About two-thirds or 2.1 million of the elderly poor were persons living alone or with non-relatives. As with elderly families, nearly all (93 percent) of the income received by the elderly poor was from public sources. Of the 4.2 million elderly families which received more than half of their income from public sources, only 15 percent were poor. However, about 39 percent of the 5 million elderly individuals who received over half of their income from these sources were below the poverty level.

Income of Older Persons[2]

Although elderly people represent a little over 12 percent of the total population, they constitute one-fifth of the nation's poor. One of every nine couples with a husband sixty-five years of age and over received incomes of less than $4,000 in 1976. At the other end of the income scale, one of every five elderly couples had incomes of $15,000 or more. The median income for these couples was $8,070.

The income of elderly persons living alone or with non-relatives was skewed toward the lower end of the income distribution. Nearly two of every five elderly individuals received incomes under $3,000, while only one of five received more than $6,000. The median income for these individuals was $3,495. (See Figure 2-5.)

Labor Force Participation[3]

The proportion of elderly males in the labor force has been dropping rapidly over the past quarter-century. Thus, the male labor force participation rate decreased from two in three older men in 1900 to one in five in 1977. One the other hand, the female rate rose slightly from one in twelve in 1900 to one in ten during the 1950s, but dropped again to one in twelve in the 1970s.

About 2.9 million or 13 percent of older people were in the labor force—either working or actively seeking work—in 1977. This means that 20 percent of the older men (1.8 million) and about 8 percent of the older women (1.1 million) are in the labor force. Together they make up 3 percent of the United States labor force. About one-

[2] Most of the information in this section is derived from *Facts About Older Americans,* 1978.

[3] A large portion of the information in this section is derived from *Facts About Older Americans,* 1978.

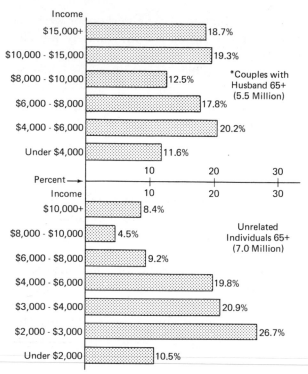

* For couples, data are restricted to 2 person families in order
  to exclude income received by other family members in
  larger families.

FIGURE 2–5   Percent Distribution by Income: 1976. Source: *Facts About
Older Americans,* 1978, U.S. Government Printing Office,
DHEW Pub. No. (OHDS) 79–20006.

sixth of the older men who work are in agricultural jobs, and over
one-third are self-employed.

The proportion of black men who participate in the labor force
is similar to that of whites. However, black men earn less, do
physically more demanding work, and are in poorer health than
white males. Moreover, black males die on an average of seven and a
half years sooner than white males (Butler & Lewis, 1977).

The proportion of black women who work has been historically higher than that of white women. This may be due to the fact that
they need to supplement their husbands' earnings to make ends
meet, or because there is a greater need to support themselves (Butler
& Lewis, 1977). The type of work that many older black Americans

performed in the past was either domestic or service-related work. For years these jobs were not covered under the Social Security Act. Although this situation has now been rectified, many older blacks refuse to retire because of their fear of receiving few benefits, or none at all.

HEALTH STATUS AND HEALTH CARE UTILIZATION[4]

It is well known that older people not only get sick more frequently, but also visit the doctor more often than their younger counterparts. In 1976, about 39 percent of older persons were limited in their major activity (working or keeping house) due to illness, as compared to only 7 percent of younger persons.

The elderly person with severe functional limitations frequently suffers from physical and social isolation (Bierman & Hazzard, 1973). In 1972, about 18 percent of those sixty-five and over had an interference with their mobility due to chronic conditions—6 percent had some trouble getting around alone, 7 percent needed a mechanical aid to get around, and 5 percent were homebound.

The severe chronic health problems that many of the elderly experience frequently require more doctor visits, and more and longer hospital stays. In 1976, older people had about a one in six chance of being hospitalized during a year, whereas for persons under sixty-five the likelihood was one in ten. Among those hospitalized during the year, the proportion with more than one stay was greater for older persons than for younger persons (26 percent *vs.* 15 percent) and the average length of stay was about five days longer (11.6 *vs.* 6.9 days).

On the average, older people had more physician visits than did persons under sixty-five (6.9 *vs.* 4.7 visits) in 1976, and a higher proportion had visited a doctor within the last six months (70 percent *vs.* 68 percent).

The Costs of Health Care

Health care for the elderly is expensive. In 1976, the nation spent $120 billion for personal health care. About $36 billion or 29

[4] Most of the information in this section was taken from *Facts About Older Americans,* 1978.

percent of this amount was spent for older persons. The per capita health care cost for an older person was $1,521, nearly three times as much as the $547 spent for younger adults. Benefits from government programs, including Medicare ($15.0 billion) and Medicaid ($5.6 billion), accounted for about two-thirds of the health expenditures of older persons as compared with three-tenths of those of adults under sixty-five.

The average health bill per individual for the total population in 1975 was $475; the average health bill for those sixty-five and over was $1,360 (Harris, 1978). The cost of health care continues to be a major problem for older adults. With rising inflation and the high costs of such basic necessities as housing, food, clothing, and medical care, little or nothing is left for leisure, education, travel, or anything else that might enhance the life satisfaction of the elderly (Schwartz & Peterson, 1979).

As people advance in age they are more likely to have chronic conditions and to require more frequent treatment and longer hospital or home care. The cost of the health care received is expensive, and instead of improving, the older person may get progressively worse. Consider the case of Mr. Greenberg:

> William Greenberg is experiencing advanced forms of senility. Almost 30 years ago, in 1954, he developed diabetes. This was controlled with strict dieting and weight loss. At age 85 he had a severe heart attack and survived as a result of recent advances in drug therapy. He stopped working, changed his diet, began to take newly discovered drugs to lower the fatty substances in his blood, and by age 90 his coronary arteries were again functioning normally. But he began to lose his memory, fall frequently (a hip fracture was repaired after one such event), and lose his personal cleanliness so that he began to need constant care. Now at age 104 he is bedridden, recognizes no one, but has a healthy appetite and normally functioning heart, lungs, and kidneys. His care costs $80,000 annually. Who should pay the bills? (Chalmers & Stern, 1981, p. 19).

For those elderly with limited income resources, the chances of receiving adequate health care when they become ill is minimal. On the other hand, the health care available to the rich is often superior to that available to the poor.

Prevention of deterioration has not been a major interventive medical strategy in this country; rather, cure has been emphasized.

The preventive approach would stress how health can best be maintained in the older individual. For instance, preventive health care would place emphasis on health education. Health education would enable individuals to become knowledgeable about "how their body functions and teach them how to look for pathological signs" (Crandall, 1980, p. 167). Cure, on the other hand, is "an attempt to eliminate the symptoms of an illness or disease or an attempt to strengthen the remaining abilities of the individual" (Crandall, 1980, p. 168). Chalmers and Stern put the case for prevention succinctly:

> Most doctors agree that a greater emphasis on preventive medicine would
> be an important first step toward decreasing the need for expensive
> treatment. Americans need to focus more on better nutrition and
> exercise, as well as on the elimination of alcohol, tobacco, and
> carcinogens from their diet and environment. In addition, more of our
> health care dollars should be spent to learn how to treat the chronically ill
> more efficiently, and more basic research should be conducted on the
> processes of aging, especially in the brain. If we can postpone
> deterioration of the brain and joints, we can enable older people to keep
> working longer. Prolonging their productivity will diminish the financial
> burden on the working young—assuming that an expanding economy
> can keep both young and old at work. (Chalmers & Stern, 1981, p. 17).

SOCIAL WORK PRACTICE AND THE ELDERLY

Social work, like other helping professions, emerged in response to human needs. Social work has its own philosophy, purpose, methods, and procedures. Its basic aim is the optimal social functioning of human beings. To achieve this aim social workers must be well grounded in knowledge about human behavior and the social situation as well as in sound practice methods that are sufficiently grounded in research. However, there are few studies in the literature concerning social work practice with the elderly, despite the fact that social workers frequently find themselves working directly with a variety of older people, and also provide services to individuals, families, couples and groups on behalf of the elderly.

Social workers' professional methods inevitably reflect their beliefs about the nature of human beings, as do the methods of other helping professions. For instance, when people believed that mental illness was a consequence of being possessed by the devil, "the methods devised to cure such conditions were unbelievably cruel, designed to drive the devil out" (Combs et al., 1971). Similarly, if we believe that older people are senile, overly talkative, intolerant, cantankerous, and shallow, then we will deal with them accordingly. To create effective and efficient helping relationships, we need the very best and most accurate understandings about people we can possibly acquire.

Social work practice is concerned with the interactions between individuals and their social environment. Its essential focus is on helping people use their social environment to meet their needs (Gilbert et al., 1980). People are complex beings. Their social environments are also complex. The social environment includes the family, friends, neighbors, peers, schools, the workplace, the church, and a variety of other organizations and institutions. A major concern of social work is to enchance older people's problem-solving and coping capacities, to link them with appropriate resources and opportunities in the community, and to promote more effective relationships between older people and societal resource systems.

Older people may be experiencing distress in their lives as a result of physical, social, and emotional problems. The social worker is in an advantageous position to help them to utilize their own problem-solving capacities and coping abilities to deal more effectively with the situation. For instance, the social worker can encourage an older woman to discuss her ambivalent feelings about her husband's retirement. An airing of feelings may help her to organize her thinking, see the situation in a different light, and make plans along with her husband to cope with it better. The social worker can also share information with the older couple about resources in the community that the retired husband can utilize during the day to fill his time in a more meaningful way. The social worker can be instrumental in linking the older retiree to appropriate community resources.

The social work profession has long been concerned about making practice more effective. This is an essential aim since social workers apply relevant knowledge, methods, skills, and techniques in their work with a variety of clients and client groups. Goals are always specified, as the worker and client move toward an agreed-upon end. This process is always planned and it is carried out in an orderly and systematic fashion.

The worker's activities will be many and varied. He may conduct formal and informal interviews with the older client, with the family as a unit as well as with individual members of the family, with the older couple, or with staff at various agencies providing services to the older client. In addition, the worker may apply a variety of techniques and skills such as psychological support, development of insight, direct suggestion and advice. Hollis (1977), however, indicates that both suggestion and advice should be given tentatively and with the implication that the client is free to reject what is offered, but might like to try it out. Other useful techniques include information-giving, interpretation, and clarification.

The worker assumes a variety of roles in carrying out his several activities. For instance, the worker may be the locator of a resource. This is frequently an essential role when working with older clients who have limited knowledge of what resources exist. The worker may also function in the role of enabler. In this role the social worker helps the client develop the means, opportunity and capacity to utilize the resource to the best of his ability. The worker may become a mediator on the client's behalf. In this role, the worker acts as a conciliator to reconcile differences between the client and an unresponsive resource. The worker may also act as an advocate for both the older client and his family. In this role, the worker may speak up on behalf of the client, write letters on his behalf, streamline access to services, negotiate on his behalf and assist the older person to speak up for himself to demand the kind of programs and services to which he is entitled as a social benefit (Lowy, 1979).

As the social worker carries out his tasks, any one role may assume priority over another. For instance, the client might wish to be helped to be more assertive himself and develop his own capacity to deal with his situation. In this instance, the worker would perform in an educative-teaching role. At other times, no matter how hard the client tries, his efforts to deal effectively with the system are thwarted at every turn, and so the worker may have to assume the responsibility of mediator. There should always be judicious and careful interplay between each of the various roles.

Individual Counseling

Working with older people on an individual basis may mean interviewing older clients at home, in general or psychiatric hospitals, public welfare departments, senior centers, or wherever necessary. The elderly face a variety of problems for which counseling can be useful (Pressey & Pressey, 1972). Older couples frequently undergo serious disturbances in the marital relationship when a spouse, generally the husband, retires. Some older retirees have difficulty adjusting to the role change that retirement brings; widowhood may create personal difficulties and family upset. Therapeutic sessions with some older people may take longer than with younger persons.

A range of services such as homemaker, nutritional programs, transportation, economic aid, and housing may be needed because of the multiplicity of problems the older client presents. Inadequate income may affect diet, nutrition, and health care; some older people may need an advocate to act on their behalf when some of their basic rights have been violated. For instance, elderly persons in nursing homes are frequently treated in an inhumane manner by nursing home staff. They are also evicted at times without advanced notice or due process (Harbert & Ginsberg, 1979).

Group Counseling

The group has been used as an effective method in working with the elderly. Group work has been offered to older people in institutional settings, senior centers, hospitals, churches, and settlement houses. A group is frequently used for meeting some of the needs of its participants. Such needs include loss of social contact, lack of self-esteem, loneliness, and isolation. Social workers may help older persons overcome a variety of social and emotional problems through group services.

Groups may be used for recreational, occupational, and educational purposes as well as for counseling and therapy. Group services to community dwellers are accessible to those who are relatively intact mentally, physically, and functionally. Increasingly, day care programs are utilizing the group work approach for the mildly impaired elderly.

An understanding of the influence and contribution of the older person as a member of the family constellation is also important to the practice of social work. The family to which the older person belongs "is far more than a collection of individuals occupying a specific physical and psychological space together" (Goldenberg & Goldenberg, 1980, p. 3). Rather, a family is a natural social system, with properties all its own. The family is, in every sense, the product of evolution. For instance, the family has evolved a "set of rules, roles, a power structure, forms of communication and ways of negotiation and problem solving that allow various tasks to be performed effectively" (Goldenberg & Goldenberg, 1980, p. 3).

The family can be viewed as a "functioning unit in which the adults and children interact with one another and consequently affect one another" (Kimmel, 1974, pp. 194–195). The older person has a history within the family, influences the family system as a whole, and affects how each family member perceives the family. Thus, in order to understand the older person as a family member, the social worker must examine his or her relationships with all other members of the family.

Programs and Services

In the past, programs and services for older people in the community tended to be spotty and experimental (Mathiasen, 1965). The overall picture is still one of fragmentation, and, in many instances, of duplication and lack of coordination. For example, health care and health-related services are provided by a number of different programs in the same community. Older persons in need of help must struggle through a maze of independent applications for Medicaid, Title XX, and Title III programs. Often this means several trips to several different state and local social service departments scattered all over town (Soldo, 1980), and there is no single source of evaluation and access to this confusing array.

The major influence on programs for older adults has been the Older Americans Act (OAA), initially passed by Congress in 1965 (Gelfand & Olsen, 1980). The Act has been amended seven times. Impetus was given to community planning for older people by the Act of 1965, which authorized money grants to the states to help them establish and strengthen agencies on aging and develop services and opportunities for the elderly (Brody, 1977). The result has been a variety of access services (transportation, outreach, information and referral), ''in-home services'' (homemakers, home health aides, visiting, and telephone reassurance efforts), and legal services. Other services include nutrition programs (at congregate meal sites and meals-on-wheels), community service employment, and senior centers.

SUMMARY

Since the turn of the twentieth century, the number of older people in the population has grown considerably. In 1900 there were only 3 million people sixty-five years of age and over. By 1980 there were 25 million people over the age of sixty-five. Changes in fertility, mortality, and migration have all contributed to this growth. Minorities constitute a smaller proportion than whites of the population aged sixty-five. Minority elderly are perceived to be in triple jeopardy because they are old, poor, and members of a minority group. Elderly women make up a substantial proportion of the older population.

Social work, like other helping professions, emerged in response to human needs. Professions, like social work, require special knowledge and skill. What social workers believe to be important inevitably determines the professional methods they use in dealing with people. Social work is concerned with the interactions between individuals and their social environment. The social environment includes complex social systems such as the health and welfare system. When older people have difficulty dealing with the system, the social worker may have to intervene on their behalf. A growing concern is how to enable people to maintain optimal levels of health as they grow older. Social workers frequently find themselves performing in a variety of roles as they work with older people on an individual basis, as members of families and other small groups, and as residents of a community.

The service delivery system that currently exists to meet the needs of the elderly is characterized by duplication, fragmentation, and lack of coordination. These features help to explain why it is so difficult for the older person to negotiate the system.

chapter 3

THE BIO-PHYSIOLOGICAL ASPECTS OF AGING

The previous chapter brought into clearer focus the characteristics of the aged and the problems they experience as they grow old. There seems to be little disagreement among gerontologists that as individuals age there is a decline of biological and physical capacity. Physical decline is closely associated with one's attitude about oneself. If the changes experienced by the individual interfere with his ability to negotiate his environment, they are bound to affect his well-being, delimit his competence, and reduce his social interaction.

> Mr. C., a sixty-nine-year-old retired salesman, has always prided himself on his agility and ability to maintain a rather youthful appearance despite his age. Nevertheless, recently he has become more aware of some obvious physical changes to his body including slackness of skin, brown spots and increasing wrinkles.
>
> Since his wife's death five years ago, Mr. C. has dated a variety of women ranging in age from forty-five to fifty-seven. A recent date with one of the younger women found her alarmed when she noticed the wrinkles and brown spots on his hands and wondered just how old he really was. Having learned this, she refused to go out with him again.
>
> This was a blow to Mr. C's ego and he found himself dating less and less and spending more time around the house.

This is not an uncommon incident, although some other person might have handled the situation differently. For years, Mr. C. experienced his body as ''good,'' as acceptable and pleasurable. His image of himself was closely related to his body concept. To discover that a younger woman viewed the physical changes in his body as marks of aging was stressful to him. He could no longer hide the fact that he was growing old. His age and altered appearance had caught up with him. The negative stereotypes of aging always include biological decline; our body no longer responds quickly to our wishes and our changed appearance announces that we are no longer young (Huyck, 1974).

Many people have difficulty accepting the readily visible physical changes that accompany the aging process. The famous French beauty Ninon de l'Enclos is supposedly the ideal of all lovely ladies who dread the marks of age. Mme. de l'Enclos was called "the woman who never grew old" and was said to be beautiful and still attracting young lovers almost up to the time of her death at the age of ninety-one, in 1705. Contemporary accounts relate that she faithfully did exercises to avoid wrinkles in her neck and that she owed her youthful skin to a beauty mask made of fresh milk, lemon juice, and brandy.

BIOLOGICAL ASPECTS OF AGING

Aging is a biological process that occurs in all organisms; the length of life is one index of the rate of aging. Aging proceeds at a gradual rate, and represents a progressive loss of vigor and of resistance (Bierman & Hazzard, 1973). Genetic and other prenatal influences set the stage for the aging sequence, and postnatal environmental factors— including demographic, economic, psychological and social factors— act to modify this sequence (Wilson, 1974).

There is a view that asserts that "biological deteriorations create a susceptibility to disease, and susceptibility to particular diseases leads to mortality" (Kart, 1981, p. 45). Normally as people age there are declines in some physical capabilities. Changes in physical appearance and declines in physical ability are what most people notice first. These changes are customarily placed in the category of biological aging.

Controversy still prevails around the issue of whether old age is or is not an illness. Many people, at some point in their lives, are afflicted with some form of illness or disease which shortens their lifespan. "Changes that occur as a result of disease processes may be categorized as relating to pathological aging" (Kart, 1981, p. 45).

Eventually everyone must face progressive loss of vigor and ability to resist disease. For this process biologists use the term senescence. Senescence refers to the degenerative changes that occur after adulthood has been reached and which will ultimately contribute to the death of the person.

What causes senescence (normal biological aging) is still unknown. Some biologists believe that there is evidence to prove that the final death of an individual is caused by an increasing death of nondividing cells.

The cell has been referred to as the basic unit of life. During youth, newly formed cells in the body outnumber dying cells. This constitutes the growth period. During adulthood, the number of dying cells is balanced by the number of new cells. During aging, new cells are outnumbered by dying cells. So aging, biologically speaking, can be thought of as a constant loss of cells.

Generally, when cells get worn out they divide and form new cells. These new cells begin to perform whatever biochemical functions and processes they should. Old cells that have gone through many cell divisions do not perform their biochemical operations as well as young cells. There is only a limited number of cell divisions available.

The physical symptoms of senescence—that is, those important bodily changes that occur as one ages can be identified. With age, the skin tends to become wrinkled and rough, and pigment plaques are not unusual. The skin is more vulnerable; it is easily broken and heals slowly. There is a stiffening of the joints, particularly at the hip and knee. With age, there is a reduction in height; typically, a stooped posture is seen in older individuals. Muscular strength and coordination decline. The sensations of touch and pain are reduced. Visual acuity declines with age; cataracts, another vision difficulty, are found increasingly. Taste and smell become less sensitive as the person ages. Reflexes are less marked and reaction time is slowed. Short-term memory is reduced, although long-term memory appears to be retained.

It is well known that there are marked individual differences in the onset and rate of physical change with age. All individuals do not age at the same rate. However, physiological capacities decrease linearly and death rates rise exponentially with increasing chronological age (Jarvik & Cohen, 1974).

Various theoretical explanations have been advanced to account for the physical changes that accompany advancing age. None of these theories is wholly adequate but each contributes to our understanding of aging. Some theories stress hereditary factors, pointing to genetic differences in resistance to disease and longevity of individual cells. Other theories emphasize the accumulation of waste materials in the body cells, which eventually clog the cells and cause them to die from lack of nutrients; researchers are trying to find ways to cleanse the body cells and thus retard or even reverse physical aging (Huyck, 1974). Four well-known theories of biological aging are outlined below.

Theories of Biological Aging

The Exhaustion Hypothesis.   The exhaustion hypothesis assumes that aging is due to the depletion of some essential material in the cell. There is little biochemical evidence to support this theory.

The Collagen Theory.   Collagen is a substance found in connective tissue (Atchley, 1977). Large amounts of collagen are found in the skin, bones, and tendons. Collagen is an important component of the walls of blood vessels and contributes to their strength as well as to the strength of scars. Collagen stiffens with age, and, as a result, tissues containing collagen lose elasticity.

> With increasing age, the collagen in the connective tissue becomes more rigid. Some individuals have speculated that this rigidity may make the transmission of nutrients and the expulsion of waste products more difficult and thus have an impact on the various organs. (Crandall, 1980, p. 132)

The increased stiffness is caused by change over time in the cross linkages between the strands of the collagen molecules (Atchley, 1977). The actual amount of collagen in tissues may decrease with age, or there may be proliferation of collagen due to some stimulus, such as death of parenchynal cells, inflammation, or physical injury (Sinex, 1975).

The Autoimmune Theory.   Atchley (1977) gives a clear description of the autoimmune theory:

> The autoimmune theory holds that as age increases, mutations cause some of the cells of the body to produce proteins that are not recognizable as part of "self" and are responded to as if they were foreign substances. When foreign substances appear in the body, the body produces antibodies that attempt to neutralize the effect of the foreign substance. This response to invasion is called an immune reaction. When antibodies respond to mutations within the body, their response is called an immune reaction. (p. 35)

Crandall explains: "In the autoimmune response the body is essentially destroying itself. Studies have shown that life expectancy is increased if the autoimmune responses are slowed down" (1980, p. 133).

   The Genetic Mutation Theory.   It has long been known that nucleic acids are localized within the chromosomes in the nucleus and that, when the cell divides, these chromosomes normally replicate or reproduce themselves. Occasionally, for reasons not yet clearly understood, there is a change in the number of chromosomes, or chromosomal breakage, in which there is loss of or rearrangement of gene fragments resulting in gene mutation. A mutation is any change in a chromosome or a gene occurring spontaneously, and is, obviously, inheritable.
   "The genetic mutation theory relates to the fact that the functioning of cells in our bodies is controlled by the genetic material, DNA" (Atchley, 1977, p. 35). DNA molecules make up the genes that are within the chromosomes that are within the nuclei of all cells. These molecules regulate the cells through intermediate RNA molecules (Bell & Rose, 1975). The aging process may be related to errors in the reading out of the genetic code. Thus, if there occurs a progressive accumulation of faulty copying in clonally dividing somatic cells (such as mutation or cross linkages in RNA and DNA), some of the progressive functional deterioration seen in the aging organism might be explained (Bierman & Hazzard, 1973).
   None of these theories is adequate for explaining how and why the body ages. Whatever the ultimate cause of aging, humans do not die of old age; they die of diseases. By sorting out and systematically studying those factors that contribute to the normal processes of aging from those that do not, gerontologists are beginning to develop a more realistic picture of biological and physiological aging.

PHYSIOLOGICAL ASPECTS OF AGING

Since the probability of death increases with age, it is assumed that changes take place within the individual with the passage of time. The general pattern of change is a gradual reduction in the performance of organ systems; this reduction begins in the early thirties and continues throughout life. There is no evidence that aging begins precipitously at any given chronological age. There are wide individual differences in aging among different people, so that some individuals of seventy or even seventy-five may possess the performance capacities of the average fifty- to-fifty-five-year-old.

Age, however, reduces the ability of the individual to deal with physiological stresses. Even abilities that show no age change in the resting state show significant differences in the degree of displacement and rate of recovery following a stimulus. For example, when the blood sugar level is raised experimentally it requires more time to return to normal in an elderly person than in a young person, even though fasting blood sugar levels are the same in young and old. Experimental evidence indicates that aging is accompanied by loss of reserve capacities in many organ systems (*Gerontology and Geriatrics,* 1969, p. 365).

Although aging and disease are often mistakenly regarded as synonymous, no disease is limited solely to the later years of life. Certain disorders, however, are common; they include arteriosclerosis (hardening of the arteries), hypertension (high blood pressure), diabetes, arthritis, and cancer. Of these, the disorders involving the circulation and therefore the heart are by far the most important. Heart disease and stroke, along with cancer, are the leading causes of death in elderly people. Their causation is largely from within the body. ''They arise as a result of the summation of many superimposed insults and in no two instances are the causative factors necessarily identical'' (*Gerontology and Geriatrics,* 1969, p. 365).

Aging in Organs and Organ Systems

The examination of aging at the level of organs and organ systems shows that many processes begin to decline long before death. In multicellular organisms, aging occurs at various levels of organization: organs and organ systems, tissues, cells, subcellular particles, and molecules. Such physiologic aging is apparent in man after the age of thirty.

Not only do individuals age at different rates, but organs and sub-systems within the individual age differently (Keller & Hughston, 1981). For instance, there are differential declines in the cardiovascular system, the respiratory system, the sexual system, the auditory system, the visual system, and reserve capacity, skin, balance, response patterns, mentation, and so forth. Some functions, notably cardiovascular work performance and sexual function in males, clearly reach their peak at the end of the adolescent growth period (Bierman & Hazzard, 1973).

The Brain

As the individual ages, a number of changes take place in the nervous system. The changes referred to result from complex events, including cell death, oxygen deprivation, and chemical changes in the cells themselves. Brain cells do no reproduce. Thus, when cells are lost from disease, toxins, trauma, or other causes the decrease in number over time can result in a decrease in efficiency of the brain's functioning.

The brain is probably one of the most critical organs in the human body. It is the central part of the nervous system, the center of thought, and the organ that receives sensory impulses and transmits motor impulses (*Webster's New World Dictionary*, 1970, p. 171). Since it is the center of thought, it enables the individual to organize and cope with his world.

The weight of the brain varies with age. By age seventy-five, brain weight diminishes to about 92 percent of what it was at age thirty. In a study of atrophic changes and neuronal death of old men Bondareff (1977) found that

> the brains of old men that come to autopsy typically demonstrate a decrement in brain weight and a decrease in brain volume resulting in a shrunken gross appearance. Although in most cases it has not been possible to know with certainty whether the apparent atrophic change has resulted from . . . , a degenerative disease of the aged, . . . or so-called normal aging, atrophic changes of some sort typically are taken as sine qua non of the aging process. (p. 162)

Sexual Behavior

Studies report a decline in sexual activity with age (Masters & Johnson, 1966, 1970). There is, however, considerable controversy over why this reduction occurs (Kalish, 1975). Men are often worried about loss of potency. Sexual potency is not only pleasurable in itself, but a symbol of masculinity and worth as a person. Loss of sexual attractiveness may threaten the female's security in the marital relationship and for this reason she may welcome a diminishing of sexual interest on the part of her mate (Smith & Bierman, 1973).

In spite of a general decrease in sexual activity with age, active participation has been found in men and women in their seventies and eighties. Those who are married have a decidedly higher incidence of sexual activity than those not presently married (Kalish, 1975).

In the past, the failure of society to recognize the sexual needs of older people was serious, but not critical. Today, when 25 million people have reached or passed the age of sixty-five, society can hardly afford to perpetuate the myths about sexlessness in these years. The research of Masters and Johnson and others on the sexual behavior of older persons has clearly established that, under the proper physical and emotional conditions, the capacity to enjoy sex is not lost in the later years but simply slows down gradually, along with other physical capacities (Huyck, 1974).

Loss of Reproductive Capacity: Menopause

For women, the main physiological event of the adult years is probably the menopause, the gradual cessation of the menstrual periods. (The term climacteric refers more generally to the variety of changes which occur during this time.) Women generally complete the menopause between the ages of forty-eight and fifty-two.

There are still a number of myths surrounding this event that have helped to perpetuate a negative image. For instance, much of the psychiatric literature describes menopause as a traumatic experience for a woman because she can no longer bear children (Huyck, 1975). Apparently the woman perceives herself as no longer desirable—and certainly not as sexy—if she knows she can no longer have children.

It turns out that little stock can be put in this statement. Systematic research on women in various stages of the menopause was conducted by Neugarten and her associates (1968) at the University of Chicago. These researchers found that, while about half of all the women they interviewed agreed that the menopause is an unpleasant experience, those who are past it are much more likely to associate it with positive changes rather than negative changes once it is over (Troll, 1975). Other events in their lives produced emotional stress, but seldom the lack of reproductive ability (Huyck, 1974).

It is believed that a similar kind of phenomenon takes place among men. In the medical journals of a number of European countries, it is called "climacterium virile" (Huyck, 1974). The same phenomenon in this country has been referred to as the male menopause or the male climacteric syndrome. The male climacteric syndrome is defined as

> A cluster of physiologic, constitutional and psychological symptoms occurring in some men aged approximately 45 to 60, associated with hormonal changes and often loosely resembling the female climacteric syndrome. The symptoms include: nervousness, decrease or loss of sexual potential, depression, decreased memory and concentration, decreased or absent libido, fatigue, sleep disturbances, irritability, loss of interest and self-confidence, indecisiveness, numbness and tingling, fear of impending danger, excitability, less often headaches, vertigo, tachycardia, constipation, crying, hot flashes, chilly sensations, itching, sweating, cold hands and feet (Huyck, 1974, pp. 38–39).

Hormonal therapy has been found to be very effective in the relief of the general symptoms among men, but does little to relieve the psychological symptoms.

Some research related to the male menopause has been done with psychologically disturbed patients. The history of these patients showed a compulsive drive for achievement and success. They were ambitious, active, aggressive, hard workers, and good family providers. Close psychological examination of these patients revealed that the glandular disturbance of the menopause had mobilized and brought to the surface old longings and anxieties that were only partly overcome, or incompletely sublimated, during the previous years of apparent emotional equilibrium (Huyck, 1974). The obvious suggestion is that perhaps the male climacteric is associated in some way with personality factors (as is the case with ulcers) or with socioeconomic factors (as with gout).

Although the production of male hormones (testosterone) diminishes gradually from age forty on, given good health and an amenable partner a man should be able to function sexually well into old age.

LONGEVITY

Genetic Influences on Longevity

There are certain unknown features of the biologic process of aging that appear to be inherited. Short life-spans seem to be inherited, in that a predisposition to a fatal condition like cancer or heart disease may be genetically determined. The reverse also seems to be true: longevity seems to be inherited. Sex also appears to affect longevity, with the advantage to the female (Bierman & Hazzard, 1973).

In Western culture, women outlive men by eight years or more. One possible explanation for this might relate to the pressures men experience in the competitive working world (although women are beginning to enter the world of work in greater numbers, and to re-enter it at older ages, and will begin to experience these same pressures). However, this explanation loses its credibility when we realize that the female outlives the male in many animal and insect species.

Long-lived Parents Make for Long-lived Offspring. Biologists say, "If you want to live long, choose long-lived parents." A study by Alexander Graham Bell (1918), found a positive relationship between age at death of parents and age at death of offspring. A study by Kallman and Jarvik (1959) also indicated a positive relationship between longevity in parent and offspring. The maternal influences were found to be greater than the paternal ones.

However, genetic factors must be viewed in relation to physical and social determinants. For instance, Botwinick (1981) points out that

> favorable cultural traits may run in a family. The children of the wealthy not only have more money, but they also tend to be healthier than children of the poor. A higher economic status results in better nutrition, better housing, and better sanitation, all of which makes for a longer life. (p. 4)

Environmental Influences on Longevity

A number of factors in the physical environment may influence the aging process. Such things as air pollution, cigarette smoking, lack of exercise, inadequate diet, and even insufficient income can influence how long a person will live. A proper diet, exercise, a little or no smoking are believed to be essential in warding off heart attacks. Studies indicate that smoking, chronic health problems, and a higher death rate go hand in hand. For instance, Retherford (1975) estimates that one-half of the sex differential in mortality after age thirty-seven is derived from males' higher consumption of tobacco.

In terms of food, scientists believe that we should restrict our intake of sugar, salt, saturated fats, carbohydrates, and alcohol. It appears that the lower the intake of these substances, the longer the life.

Radiation may also have an effect on the aging process. It is not unreasonable to expect that the greater the exposure to radiation, the greater the likelihood of a shortened life-span. Radiation is believed to destroy chromosomes, and it is believed that chromosome loss accelerates the aging process. Other scientists, however, hypothesize a kind of spontaneous recovery process within the cell so that the effects of radiation decrease with time (Botwinick, 1973).

Cigarette smoking is known to be related to morbidity and mortality from lung and oral cancer, pulmonary diseases, and cardiovascular disease. However, cessation or appreciable reduction of cigarette smoking has been shown to decrease excess disease and death (Bierman & Hazzard, 1973).

The psychological and emotional stress commonly associated with work and home has been increasingly identified as a major predisposing factor in cardiovascular dysfunction (Weg, 1975). Additional convincing evidence "clearly demonstrates not only the psychological and emotional trauma but also the noxious physical consequences of environmental stress" (Schwartz & Peterson, 1979, p. 194).

The consequences of drug addiction (narcotics) and drug dependence (tranquilizers and stimulants) on abusers of various ages have been written about. Habits of abuse that impose risks on the physical, social, and psychological well-being of the individual can continue on into old age. Drug addiction and drug dependence serve to increase and exacerbate whatever current chronic health problems the older person may have.

The health problems related to chronic excessive intake of alcohol are multifaceted and constitute a major concern particularly among middle-aged adults (Bierman & Hazzard, 1973). However, studies have shown that there is an actual decrease in alcohol consumption and dependence with the approach of old age.

Each of these environmental influences is believed to generate a specific impact on the aging process. However, the impact that each has will vary greatly in intensity and effect upon the older person. Most people want to maintain an optimal state of physical and emotional well-being. How well the individual, particularly the older person, is able to do this will depend on social, motivational, cultural, and physical factors.

CHRONIC CONDITIONS AMONG THE ELDERLY

Chronic conditions such as heart disease, stroke and cancer are more prevalent among older persons than younger ones. These illnesses are debilitating and may seriously affect an older person's mobility. Further, chronic disease seriously affects the welfare of the community because of its relationship to other social and economic problems, because it affects large numbers of people including the elderly, because it causes long and costly debility, and because it is the leading cause of death (Upham, 1949).

Chronic illness has increased over the past several years (Schwartz & Peterson, 1979). This increase, however, derives mostly from the fact that more people are living longer and consequently the total amount of chronic illness is greater. What has happened in recent decades is that longer life-spans have led to larger numbers of chronically ill, dependent people, maintained by expensive technology.

Chronic illness frequently necessitates many changes in diet, housing, social activities, and style of life. The older person with a chronic illness has to observe regimes of rest and activity, is more vulnerable to emotional strain, and carries an increasing load of stress and anxiety (Upham, 1949). Chronic illness is wearing, especially for the older person, and requires constant medical attention.

If the elderly person receives suitable medical care and the specific supports he needs to carry out the doctor's recommendations, the progress of his illness may be retarded and its recurrences limited. So, in order to maintain some semblance of independence, supportive efforts (understanding the nature of the illness and the need for medication, having transportation in order to get to the doctor, and so on) are definitely needed.

Anyone who works with an older person must take into consideration his physical condition. A careful assessment must be made of any expectation of independence as well as of those social, emotional, physical, and financial supports that are available to him. Knowledge of which physiological declines are the most crucial and what preventive measures can be used enables the older individual to weave a reasonable self-prescription for independence (Keller & Hughston, 1981).

Preventive Measures

What kind of preventive measures can be taken to maintain for as long as possible the quality of life conducive to maximal levels of functioning? A few of the more obvious ones are discussed below.

1. Exercise.   Making exercise an integral part of everyday living has been recommended for years. Appropriate and regular exercise and physical training are known to improve functional level, regardless of age. Neurophysiologic studies have demonstrated that retention of capacities may depend on their continued use and exercise (Bierman & Hazzard, 1973). Fischer et al. (1965) reported better physical performance and functional capacities in a sample of physically active older men than in a comparable sample of sedentary older men. Another study (Barry et al. 1966) has shown significant improvement in physical working capacity and cardiac function as a result of conditioning in older people. However, the investigators' sample size was only of eight older people.

Many people (both young and old) resist exercise regimes of any kind because they are time-consuming and require a certain amount of effort. Caution is in order when an older person decides to undertake an exercise program. A doctor should be consulted by the older person before beginning a vigorous exercise program. It is believed that the exercise engaged in should "help to maintain normal posture, correct joint alignment, prevent contractures, preserve strength for ambulation, stimulate circulation and metabolism, and provide emotional satisfaction'' (Bierman & Hazzard, 1973, p. 179).

While some older people may engage in a program of calisthenics, others may engage in such purposeful exercise as walking, playing tennis or golf, working in the garden, or bicycle riding. Whatever the form of exercise, it should be undertaken on a regular basis and it should be appropriate to the person's interests.

2. Diet.   To maintain an optimal level of health into old age is a much sought-after goal. Unfortunately, however, many people are plagued with health problems as they grow older. Poor diet and nutrition are believed to be major contributors to poor health. Diets lacking in minerals, proteins, and vitamins have a telling effect on the physiological functioning of the body. For instance, the morbidity related to gallstones, hepatic dysfunction, and osteoarthritis that is frequently consequent to obesity could be moderated by diet control and loss of weight (Weg, 1975).

When dietary patterns among the elderly are examined, it is necessary to take into consideration the complex of social, motivational, financial, cultural, and physical factors, as well as habit patterns, knowledge base, and the like (Schwartz & Peterson, 1979). The older person's dietary habits will most likely be affected if there is a breakdown in one or some combination of these elements. Nutritionists and dietary experts believe that where nutritional deficiencies are found among older persons these deficiencies appear to be more closely linked to level of income, general health, feelings of well-being, and life-style habits than to old age itself (Schwartz & Peterson, 1979).

3. Stress.   Psychological and emotional stress has been increasingly identified as a major predisposing factor in cardiovascular dysfunction; specifically, these disturbances include atherosclerosis, coronary heart disease and hypertension (Weg, 1975).

Americans typically live at a fast pace. This characteristic is vividly demonstrated on jobs that require a great deal of travel, an endless flow of creative ideas, and the rapid development of bigger and better products. Younger people may have the endurance to withstand various degrees of stress that older people cannot. As people grow older, the ability to maintain competence under such pressure diminishes and certain physical disabilities become the norm. Schwartz & Peterson (1979) point out that those "physical factors within a normal range not affecting the behavior of young persons may affect the behavior of older persons when physical function reaches an abnormal level (in intensity and duration)" (p. 195).

SUMMARY

Aging is accompanied by biological and physical decline. Gerontologists refer to this as senescence. Research findings have not revealed what causes senescence. However, some of the physical symptoms have been identified. Some age-related biological changes that manifest themselves in obvious physical alterations include graying hair, wrinkled and rough skin, stooped posture, and pigment plaques. As people age, there are also changes in the various organs and organ systems of the body.

A number of theoretical explanations abound as to why people grow old. Such theories include the collagen, autoimmune, and genetic mutation explanations. None of these theories is adequate for explaining how and why the body ages. Some biogerontologists believe that aging can be thought of as a constant loss of cells, and that there is enough evidence to indicate that the final death of an individual is caused by an increasing death of nondividing cells of major organs.

Sexual activity declines with age. However, men and women should be able to function sexually well into old age, given good general health.

A variety of factors influence the aging process. These include genetic as well as environmental factors. Genetic factors, however, must be viewed in relation to physical and social determinants. A number of factors in the physical environment may also influence how long a person will live. Factors such as air pollution, inadequate diet, cigarette smoking, lack of exercise and insufficient income have all been identified as environmental influences. An adequate diet and appropriate and regular exercise are preventive measures that are known to maintain the quality of life conducive to maximal levels of functioning.

chapter 4

THE
PSYCHOLOGICAL
ASPECTS
OF AGING

This chapter and the next are concerned with the psychological and the social aspects of aging. Although treated in two separate chapters, the intent is not to convey the impression that these two major aspects of aging are separate and discrete from each other, or from the biological aspect, already discussed. They are not. A change in one area may well affect changes in each of the others.

For instance, suppose a person retires. It is possible for his income to drop more than 50 percent. In order to save money, he cuts back on the amount and quality of food that he buys. He then eats a poorer diet that results in decreased vigor and activity and this makes him increasingly susceptible to disease. He becomes ill. More money must be spent for drugs, which means he has less money for food. He may become psychologically depressed about his status in life (Ernst & Shore, 1976). Thus, social changes may affect biological changes, which, in turn, produce a psychological effect. The interweaving of these factors and the difficulties of sorting them out have complicated the tasks of gerontologists (Brody, 1977).

This chapter examines the psychological processes that interact to produce age-related changes.

CHANGES ON THE PSYCHOLOGICAL LEVEL

The psychology of aging is a wide realm that encompasses the sensory and psychomotor processes, perception, mental ability, drives, motives, and emotions (Atchley, 1977). A number of changes are known to take place on the psychological level as the individual ages. For instance, aging is usually accompanied by gradual impairment of a number of sensory functions. Quantitative measurements of auditory acuity have demonstrated that hearing loss with increasing age is greater in males than in females and is more severe for high-pitched tones than for low tones. Similarly, visual acuity diminishes with increasing age, but is more closely related to the development of diseases of the eye than to age itself.

Perhaps the most noticeable feature of aging is the gradual slowing of psychomotor responses. However, when the elderly individual is given ample time to respond to a stimulus he is able to discriminate almost as well as a young person. Experimental evidence indicates that older people can continue to learn throughout their lives, although their rate of acquisition of a new skill may be somewhat slower than that of young adults and is greatly influenced by the degree of motivation. Often the personality changes with age.

Several of these age-related changes are described separately and examined for their effect on the social functioning of the older individual.

Personality Changes with Age

Personality refers to the complex psychological processes occurring in a human being as he functions in his daily life, motivated and directed by a host of internal and external forces. To put it differently, personality is the organization in the individual of those processes that intervene between environmental conditions and behavioral response. The processes referred to include perception, cognition, memory, learning, and the activation of emotional reactions—as they are organized and regulated in the individual (LeVine, 1973). It is these intervening processes that cause individuals to respond differently to such things as birth, death, aging, pain, stress, and to various pressures and opportunities in the social environment.

Each individual possesses a unique set of attributes that sets him apart from every other individual. These attributes also help to make the individual recognizably similar in different situations and at different times over the years (Kimmel, 1974). Since these qualities help to make the personality relatively stable, it is possible to predict how an individual will behave in different situations.

The individual's personality is shaped by his environment and his response to a variety of situations. It reflects his unique adaptation to his past experiences. An individual's inner core is seen as fairly consistent once it is formed and it is this unique set of personality characteristics that are sufficiently stable across different situations—such as school, work, family, and old age—to make an identifiable personality that is generally consistent.

But people also change. As the individual takes on new social roles and encounters new experiences, moving through the various life-stages, his usual ways of responding may change. In addition, external situations continue to have an effect on each individual as he shifts and changes in various ways.

There are a number of significant events or situations that occur in the individual's life that are likely to have some effect on his personality. Such events include: becoming a spouse, becoming a parent, going through retirement or a second marriage, being widowed. Nevertheless, studies of personality continuity—particularly those that have measured self-description of personality—have found considerable continuity (Kimmel, 1974). In addition, cognitive styles—for example, self-defined typologies of ourselves and of the world—have been found to be stable across situations and over time (Mischel, 1969).

Thus, the human personality is both relatively stable and continuous as well as reflectively flexible and changeable. That is, it can change while at the same time remaining fairly consistent (Kimmel, 1974). Whitbourne and Weinstock (1979) point out that

> beneath the many changes that occur within and around each adult, there is a common theme: the individual has his own unique way of relating to people and events, which is determined by the particular characteristics that form the self. (p. 2)

The gerontological literature presently points to a decrease in emphasis on the individual's external world and an increasing importance of internal processes. With new cohorts of elderly, however, this characteristic may change. As a variety of social roles becomes available to older people when they retire, and as more people are encouraged to remain in the labor force once they reach their sixty-fifth birthday, both the internal and external aspects of the personality may come to be of equal significance.

Nevertheless, advanced old age may bring on increased internalization, that is, more concern with one's own emotions, physical functions, and inner-world orientation (Kimmel, 1974). It is these older individuals whom a number of people tend to label as rigid, senile, set in their ways, and intolerant. But it is difficult to state whether these persons were always somewhat inhibited; whether their behavior is a reflection of society's negative view of older people that would have us believe "out of sight, out of mind"; whether health problems interfere with outgoingness; whether high crime rates in the neighborhood, limited incomes, and reluctance to make new friends after loved ones have died lead the elderly to isolate themselves—or all of the above. Still, it is important for the worker to detect any signs of introversion, assess how exaggerated or real it is, and evaluate its impact on the older person's intra- and interpersonality.

No one is exactly the same from childhood on. We continue to grow and develop our personalities throughout life. Some changes may be subtle, others more obvious.

Life-Cycle Perspectives

One perspective by which social gerontologists view the aged and the aging process is the life-cycle, life-span developmental process (Neugarten et al., 1964; Lowenthal, 1974). This perspective views life as a continuous ongoing process—each stage evolving in an orderly way out of earlier stages of life.

The well-known psychoanalyst, Erik Erikson, postulated a step-by-step process of growth. He theorized that each stage arrives at its appointed time and that preparations for each specified stage-related task are laid in earlier stages (Erikson, 1963). The student should be familiar with Erikson's theory of ego development, one of the few examples of a developmental theory of personality that specifically encompasses adulthood as well as childhood and adolescence.

Erikson formulated eight stages of ego development from infancy to old age, each stage presenting a task or a crisis for the expanding ego. Erikson's model is psychosocial rather than psychosexual. He proposed that four stages occur during childhood.

The first stage is marked by the conflict of trust versus mistrust. How does the growth of trust come about? It results from the infant's experiences with people and objects, as well as from his developing cognitive and motor skills. Through his contacts with the mother, the young infant either establishes a basic feeling that the world is a place in which his needs will be taken care of as they arise, or he comes to feel that the world is a threatening place not to be counted upon.

Stage two deals with the conflict between the sense of autonomy and feelings of doubt. At this time (about one to three years of age) children are exploring their world. Parents should encourage exploration and not impose too many punishments, so that children may leave this state without possessing self-doubt.

In the third stage, the four- to five-year-old has the task of building initiative rather than guilt. Again, how others (adults) react to the child's activities and explorations will influence whether a sense of pride and initiative is felt or guilt results.

The fourth stage occurs between the ages of six and eleven. The school-age child is confronted with the task of industry versus inferiority. Those who are encouraged to be interested in and explore things will leave this stage enjoying productivity and being industrious. If the child is met with little encouragement and success, he will most likely feel inferior.

Stage five occurs during adolescence and is a time of confronting what one is about. "Who and what am I?"—this is the dominant preoccupation of the pubescent youth. The task to be accomplished is ego identity. Although a number of issues are salient during this stage, the focus is on being able to resolve one's own conflicts mentally. Failure to establish an ego identity results in what Erikson calls "ego diffusion."

After ego identity is established, the young person once again turns his interests outside himself. Only after having defined his sense of self is an individual ready to establish intimacy with another. Intimacy means a sharing of self without fear of losing one's identify. Failure at this stage results in inability to establish truly mutual relationships, in work, in friendship, in marriage (Whipple, 1966).

The seventh stage occurs once individuals reach middle age. "Generativity" is the concept Erikson uses to express the desire of two mature people, who have found a satisfying mutuality in their relationship, to combine their personalities and energies in the production and care of offspring (Whipple, 1966). Erikson (1963) points out that

> generativity is primarily the concern in establishing and guiding the next generation, although there are individuals who, through misfortune or because of special and genuine gifts in other directions, do not apply this drive to their own offspring. (p. 267).

Those who do not become parents may achieve generativity through creative and unselfish behavior. The biological status of parenthood does not necessarily constitute genuine generativity (Whipple, 1966).

During the middle years, Erikson feels, the individual develops an increased empathy for others, not only in family life, but in his work, in his community, and in the world at large (Whipple, 1966). The failure of generativity results in stagnation. Adults who are self-absorbed cannot look beyond their own needs. They relate to others only in terms of how others can serve them. This type of existence may be satisfactory until the process of aging and its attendant consequences set in (Goldberg & Deutsch, 1977).

In the eighth stage, the issue of integrity versus despair must be resolved. The sense of integrity arises from the individual's ability to look back on his life with satisfaction (Elkind, 1977). Erikson (1963) best expresses the meaning of ego integrity when he states,

> only in him who in some way has taken care of things and people and has adapted himself to triumphs and disappointments adherent to being, the originator of others or the generator of products and ideas—only in him may gradually ripen the fruits of these seven stages. (p. 268)

Thus, the crucial task during this stage is to evaluate one's life and accomplishments as a meaningful "adventure in history." According to Whipple (1966):

> The individual who has, with reasonable success, met life head on, lived through exaltation and despair, been the originator of ideas and children, destroyed as well as created can finally accept himself as a member of the human race and feel a sense of oneness with other human beings even those in different cultures and distant times. (p. 361)

The negative resolution of this stage is a sense of despair—an existential sense of total meaninglessness, a feeling that one's entire life was wasted or should have been different (Kimmel, 1974). This despair in turn, produces a disgust with the world and the self (Rogers, 1979).

OTHER AGE-RELATED PSYCHOLOGICAL CHANGES

Intelligence

Intelligence is the capacity of an individual to behave effectively and efficiently. It refers to the behavior which a person can normally deliver when called upon to do so. This means that intelligence is not static nor is it a fixed quantity. Instead, it is open to change and development (Combs et al., 1971).

Intelligence is commonly measured by intelligence tests, whose results are summarized in a statistic known as the intelligence quotient (IQ). Historically, the results of intelligence tests indicate declines with advancing age. Consequently, we often think that age causes a reduction in a person's ability to learn. "While it is recognized that learning ability does change in some people as they age, many authors feel that the change is more the result of other changes than a result of age alone" (Ernst & Shore, 1976, p. 22).

The study of intellectual functioning in old age is attendant with difficulties. For instance, how valid and reliable are the intelligence tests for an older population? How is intelligence to be defined and measured? What types of sampling techniques should be used? What research methodology should be utilized?

Most aging research on intelligence is either cross-sectional or longitudinal in methodology. Cross-sectional methods use two or more samples of persons representing different age groups who are studied at one point in time. The groups are measured for a selected variable, or series of variables, which the investigator wishes to study. Longitudinal studies follow an individual or group of individuals over a relatively long period with repeated measures taken on selected variables at subsequent points in time.

Longitudinal research yields data on adult intelligence (up to about age fifty) that suggest that performance increases less rapidly during adolescence, until it reaches a plateau between the ages of twenty-five to thirty. Performance then declines slightly with age for subjects of average intelligence, but is maintained or increases slightly for initially more able subjects at least to age fifty (Botwinick, 1967). However, cross-sectional measures of IQ have typically shown a decline for older cohorts beginning at mid-life (Schwartz & Peterson, 1979).

Much of the decline is accounted for by declines on those subtests of the standard IQ test that measure performance aspects of intelligence. A close look at the subtests that measure verbal abilities reveals little or no change with age. The performance tests are scored on the basis of the amount of time required to perform the task; a rapid performance is given a higher score than a slower one (Kimmel, 1974). When the aged are given all the time they need on tests that are heavily dependent upon school skills, their performance is only slightly poorer than that of young adults.

Thus, the general decline in intellectual functioning is largely a result of declines in the performance aspects of the standard intelligence tests, which may result from slower performances. In other words, the slowing down of reaction time and other central nervous system functions with age may account for much of the decline in intellectual performance noted among elderly subjects (Kimmel, 1974).

Memory

Memory refers to the retention of specific events which have occurred at a given time in a given place (Craik, 1977). Whenever memory is discussed, almost inevitably the memory system is referred to as short-term and long-term, or as primary and secondary. Short-term memory refers to recall after a relatively brief delay. Age differences in short-term memory have been investigated by Craik (1968), Raymond (1971) and others. Craik and Raymond compared the recency effect (that is, recall after a brief period—from one hour to several days) of young subjects to that of old subjects (Walsh, 1975). They concluded that short-term memory was unimpaired with aging.

Long-term memory refers to the recall of events that occurred in the past and have neither been frequently rehearsed nor thought of (Crandall, 1980). Studies indicate that older adults have difficulty in retrieving information stored in long-term memory (Walsh, 1975). There seems to be some uncertainty about the way in which older people retrieve such information. The suggestion has been made that older persons fail to elaborate minimal retrieval cues in order to make them more effective. While the younger person can actively reconstruct aspects of the initial situation, the older person either does not or cannot engage in these reconstructive activities (Craik, 1977).

More well-controlled experimental studies are needed in this area. Social work practitioners are bound to fall behind the most current ideas in memory research because much that exists is both voluminous and confusing.

Learning

Although memory and learning are different aspects of the same underlying mechanism, it is conceptually useful to differentiate between them. Learning may be defined as the acquisition of general rules and knowledge of the world, while memory refers to the retention of specific events that occurred at a given time in a given place (Craik, 1977). We learned early in life that Columbus discovered America, that the shortest distance between two points is a straight line, that $10 + 10 = 20$. The time and place of learning are not important for our utilization of these pieces of knowledge (Craik, 1977). But recalling a specific incident requires our remembering a definite time and place.

In spite of evidence to the contrary some people believe that older people are resistant to learning anything new. Researchers continue to stress that there are factors other than true age decline that may contribute to the discrepancies between young and old found in a number of learning experiments. Apparently there is a group of variables, identified as performance or noncognitive factors, that account for a decline of learning ability in old age (Goldberg & Deutsch, 1977).

As people grow older, a number of changes take place within the body. Some of the changes are attributable to a slowing down of the organs and organ systems of the body. Almost inevitably there is a slowing down or impairment of the central nervous system—which results in slower reactions on the part of the person. This physical slowing down has implications when it comes to performing on various tests, especially if the tests are timed.

Older people need a longer time in which to respond. It takes them a longer time to get the answers out, and they seem to benefit from a longer response period. They usually pace themselves well and use the extra time to advantage. Whatever the reasons older people require more time to give an answer, it is incumbent upon social workers to be patient with older clients. They should not be anxious to hurry clients to answer what seems to many of the young a simple question requiring only a straightforward answer.

In terms of motivation, some people are very relaxed when they take an examination; others are more anxious. If the person is highly anxious when he takes a test, this may be detrimental to his performance, because anxiety interferes with his thinking processes. Research findings indicate that the elderly are more physiologically aroused than younger groups during and after learning tasks. In addition, older people tend to be overly cautious when taking a test and make errors of omission (for example, failure to respond to a cue word) rather than errors of commission. However, when the elderly are given more time to respond, the number of omission errors decreases (Goldberg & Deutsch, 1977).

Tasks must have some meaning for older people if they are to perform well on examinations. Frequently, verbal learning tasks have little or no essential interest to older adults. Denney and Wright (1976) suggest that one explanation for the relatively poorer performance of the older person is that he is not very interested in what he has been asked to do.

There is no doubt a host of other variables that influence the older person's performance on learning tasks. Nevertheless, age still appears to be a factor in learning. Even in those instances in which older people are given enough time to finish a meaningful task, they still do not perform as well as younger age groups.

If older people are given certain tasks to perform, clear instructions should accompany the tasks. There are some educational classes on television that address the needs of the older learner. Workers should be aware of a variety of resources, including the influential role television plays in the life of the older person.

Problem–Solving Ability

The literature on problem-solving in old age is relatively scanty. Atchley (1977) defines problem-solving as "the development of decisions out of the processes of reason, logic, and thinking" (p. 56). A number of cross-sectional research studies have shown decline with age in both verbal and nonverbal situations. Older people show poorer performance on a number of tasks including completing analogies, constructing sentences from odd words, logical reasoning, tasks of analysis and synthesis, and tasks of inventiveness. Many psychologists have attributed the decline in performance of the elderly to rigidity and loss of abstractive ability (Dibner, 1975). A major task among psychologists is "to explain how it comes about that people cease to be able to do complex things which they once did well" (Rabbitt, 1977, p. 606). That is, old people have been shown to be less able than the young on some tasks. It has been proposed that

the reasons the older person has difficulty in problem-solving are due to their difficulty in organizing complex material, in making fine discriminations among stimuli, and in withholding responses even though he may think they are wrong. (Dibner, 1975, p. 78)

For instance, in problem-solving tasks in the laboratory, the aged take more time and hesitate when pressed. And even when given more time, the older person shows some decrement in problem-solving.

Although older people are less able to integrate or organize information than the young, they know their limitations. They are very well aware when the demands of a task exceed their capacities, and can adapt reasonably well to any decrements in performance.

Psychomotor Performance

Notable among studies related to psychomotor performance are those that investigate changes in reaction time with age. Reaction time (that is, the period elapsing between the appearance of a signal and the beginning of a responding movement) slows with age. The slowing down of the psychomotor system is characteristic of any individual who survives beyond middle age (Birren, 1965). Apparently this change in reaction time is a normal aging phenomenon; it occurs uniformly, without regard to disease (Woodruff, 1975). Probably the most important change in motor performance that comes with age is lack of speed (Welford, 1977).

It is difficult to determine why changes in reaction time occur with age. An essential question is whether the changes are due to some basic deterioration in the sensorimotor mechanisms, or whether they result from changes in the strategy of performance—such as increased caution (Welford, 1977). In terms of capacity, existing evidence suggests that cardiovascular impairments are associated with the slowing of several types of performance, both motor and intellectual, and that the likelihood of these impairments increases with age (Botwinick & Storandt, 1974).

Botwinick & Thompson (1968) undertook an interesting study in which they compared the reaction times of a group of subjects sixty-eight to eighty-six to those of young athletes aged eighteen to twenty-seven, and non-athletes of the same age. They found that while the reaction times of the older subjects were significantly slower than those of the young athletes, they were not significantly slower than those of young men of the same age who were not athletes. This finding is useful because it suggests that part of the slowness shown by older people is attributable to lack of physical fitness, which might be associated with poorer blood supply to the brain (Welford, 1977). The point has already been made that exercise can increase physical capacities in older people.

Older people have found ways to compensate for their lack of speed. For instance, in facing complex tasks, older people may use such compensatory techniques as working more slowly, more carefully, or dividing the tasks into small units to be handled sequentially (Dibner, 1975).

Changes in Sensory Processes

Vision.   It is through the five basic senses of vision, hearing, taste, touch, and smell that individuals receive information from the environment that is essential to their survival. After the age of forty-five, however, visual difficulties tend to increase, and become particularly marked as time goes on. For instance, the most common causes of blindness are those which predominantly affect the elderly. Number one on the list is cataract formation. According to Hendricks and Hendricks (1981), when this occurs

> the lens becomes thicker, shows evidence of yellowing, and eventually becomes opaque. As a consequence, less light filters into the eye, compounding the visual difficulties caused by the gradual loss of the lens's ability to alter its shape, a trait essential for accurate focus on near as well as distant objects. (p. 153)

As the eyes' power of accommodation decreases, eyeglasses are required. Removal of the opaque lens may restore some vision, but the addition of a contact lens usually is required to achieve satisfactory visual acuity. Research findings indicate that most elderly persons need reading glasses for close work.

A second frequently found cause of blindness, particularly among older persons, is glaucoma, characterized by increased pressure within, and hardening of, the eyeball. As in the case of cataracts, glaucoma usually progresses rather slowly, with vague visual disturbances and gradual impairment of vision. Halos around lights, headaches and the need for frequent changes of eyeglasses (particularly by those people over forty) are symptoms that should be investigated by an ophthalmologist. There are different forms of glaucoma and each type requires different management. Since continued high pressure of the aqueous humor, a nutrient fluid that circulates in the anterior chamber of the eye, may cause destruction of the optic nerve fibers, in order to avoid blindness it is important to obtain ongoing treatment beginning early in the disease.

Blindness caused by diabetes is increasing in the United States, especially among the elderly. Disorders of the eye directly related to diabetes include: (1) optic atrophy, in which the optic nerve fibers die; (2) cataracts, which occur earlier and with greater frequency among diabetics; and (3) diabetic retinopathy, in which the retina can be damaged by blood vessel hemorrhages and other causes.

Farsightedness is a common visual condition that occurs with advancing age. In this condition, the light rays are not bent sharply enough to focus on the retina, with the result that the eye cannot focus properly on nearby objects. This condition can be corrected through the use of eyeglasses.

At least 16 percent of the institutionalized elderly exhibit some degree of visual difficulty (Ernst & Shore, 1976). Some of the behaviors which nursing home patients with problems of vision may exhibit are coordination difficulties (that is, walking, manipulating objects, finding food on a plate), positioning objects (that is, placing objects directly in the line of vision), squinting the eyes, and an inability to copy. Ernst and Shore (1976) observe that "often, because of visual problems, a person cannot look at an object and draw it accurately. His impaired visual capacity prevents him from drawing the object as he sees it" (p. 37).

In terms of practical applications, it is reasonable to assume that early detection and intervention can be useful in staving off any serious incidences of these diseases. Routine tests by the general practitioner can help identify both glaucoma and diabetic retinopathy (Fozard & Thomas, 1973). There are many ways to compensate for poor vision, such as putting large lettering on doors, hallways, and medicines; using bright colors on faucet tops; and placing large numbers on telephones. In addition, a number of articles exist that contain medical advice on visual problems of the elderly and the most effective rehabilitation strategies. However, there are at present no guidelines for helping professionals such as social workers to explain to the elderly the advantages and disadvantages of such things as spectacles and low vision aids (Bell, 1968).

Hearing.   Clinical manifestations of deterioration are increasingly evident in the human auditory system with age. The existing data show that the major functional changes in hearing are associated with disturbances in the inner ear and related neural pathways. Mechanical processes are altered and deficiencies occur in the metabolic and neuronal processes that are essential for normal hearing (Corso, 1977).

There is no question that, with advancing years, the functional changes in hearing significantly interfere with the communication process. This is bound to affect how the older person feels about himself as well as his ability to communicate adequately with others. Consequently, the aging individual is inclined to restrict the degree and scope of his social interaction. Social workers who find themselves working with partially or totally deaf older persons should learn to speak to them slowly and distinctly so that they will more easily grasp what is being said. In addition, workers should become sensitive to the social and psychological difficulties hearing loss presents. However, older people can be taught how to compensate for hearing loss. A good hearing aid is one way, although some older people resist wearing one. In that case, care must be taken to educate the elderly persons to the advantages of wearing such a device, as well as to allow them to express their feelings and anxieties about having to place such a foreign object in their ears. Use of headphones for listening to records, radio, and television is another way to compensate for hearing loss (Crandall, 1980). Headphones enable the aged to hear programs without being disturbed by outside noises, and without disturbing others.

Taste and Smell.   Both taste and smell are obvious features of the environment that determine many of the older person's reactions. Both are essential for judging the adequacy of food (Engen, 1977). Although a number of investigators have observed that taste sensitivity decreases with age, this conclusion must be viewed cautiously.

Some experiments have not been able to verify it. More knowledge is needed in this area before generalizations which may be of practical value in diagnosing sensory deficits or influencing diets can be made (Engen, 1977).

Nevertheless, a number of behaviors can be observed that are indicative of changes in taste. One such indicator is loss of, or increased, appetite. Ernst and Shore (1976) observe that "the person who is experiencing taste changes may quit eating because nothing tastes good anymore, or may eat excessive amounts in order to achieve some taste sensation" (p. 76). In this situation, weight gain or weight loss may be attributable to changes in taste sensation. Again, the older individual may constantly complain about the foods not tasting right. This could be another indication of changed taste. A person whose tongue is excessively white may be experiencing some difficulty in tasting the food. The taste buds may be covered from lack of regular dental hygiene (Ernst & Shore, 1976). Although changes in taste do occur in some persons, no significant changes are likely to occur before the person has reached the age of seventy.

The interpretation of smell is closely related to the sense of taste. The smell of food is just as important in stimulating appetite and the flow of digestive juices as is the sense of taste. As with the sense of taste, no firm conclusions can be drawn about smell. If odor sensitivity changes, it appears to do so early in life and, perhaps, more under the influence of maturation or learning than aging (Engen, 1977).

There are certain behaviors that may be related to olfactory changes. These include not reacting. Most people will react in some way to various odors, especially those that are unpleasant. If an especially unpleasant odor is present and "the person fails to react, he may have experienced a decline in the ability to smell" (Ernst & Shore, 1976, p. 83). People who constantly experience nasal congestion may have difficulty distinguishing odors. Some people make comments that may be related to their inability to smell. For instance, Ernst and Shore (1976) point out that "the person may actually tell you that he cannot smell a particular object such as a bouquet of flowers or he may comment that he simply cannot detect a particular odor" (p. 84). An obvious concern for those older people who have lost the ability to smell is that in case of a fire their lives may be in grave danger.

Touch.   The touch receptors are small rounded bodies called tactile corpuscles. They are found mostly in the dermis and are especially close together in the tips of the fingers and the toes. The receptors for pain are the most widely distributed sensory end organs. The tip of the tongue also contains many touch receptors and so is very sensitive; the back of the neck is relatively insensitive.

Loss in touch sensitivity has been reported to occur in 25 percent of an aged population (Kenshalo, 1977). Those working with elderly persons who have lost their tactile sensation can increase their communication with them through touch therapy. "Touching another person is a way of communicating with him. If the person has lost tactile sensation, touch and stimulation may help him overcome some of the losses" (Ernst & Shore, 1976, p. 63). Communicating through touch can be initiated with the hope that some means may be devised to enable family and significant others to interact with those older people who have difficulty verbalizing (Ernst & Shore, 1976).

Creativity

Creativity is a difficult concept to define or measure. What is creativity? How can it be measured? Is there a specific age or average age at which an individual can reach the highest level of creativity? The creative individual is one who originates or produces some product or work of art that is imaginative, artistic, and demonstrates intellectual inventiveness. Historical evidence supports the view that age in itself is no deterrent to creativity; many examples of major achievements in the arts and sciences by people of advanced age have been reported.

Lehman approached the issue of problem-solving from a very different perspective. He studied the creativity of notable engineers and technologists (1966). Peak creative potential, according to his findings, appeared to occur in the years thirty-five to forty; the years forty to fifty were comparable to the years twenty to thirty, but the decline accelerated thereafter. Lehman (1953) cited a number of reasons why men made their greatest contribution before the age of forty. These included the better education of younger people, physical decline, motivational changes (including resting on one's laurels), and increase in family and administrative responsibilities after mid-life (Dibner, 1975).

These findings do not mean that older people cannot be creative. They can be. Naturally, some activities require more skills than others, but there is no reason why older people should not be encouraged to participate in creative activities as long as they are motivated and physically able to do so. There is no reason why older people should not take up for the first time such activities as painting, photography, or metal-working.

To date, the evidence on whether individuals become more or less creative with advancing age is contradictory. It should be pointed out that major impairment of either memory or learning will have consequences for the ability to think or create. However, it appears likely that where there is *slight* loss of memory or difficulty in learning new materials, the creative older person will develop ways to counteract this difficulty. As a result, his daily functioning will be impaired only slightly—if at all.

MENTAL DISORDERS OF OLD AGE

Old age predisposes people toward psychiatric illness for two reasons. First, the biological and psychological effects of aging increase the older person's vulnerability to physical and mental illness. Second, social isolation and emotional stresses often become both more common and less easily dealt with as people grow old. There is a sharp rise in mental illness with advancing age. Older persons with mental disorders are also likely to have various forms of physical illness.

The mental disorders of old age are of two kinds: organic disorders which have a physical cause and functional disorders for which no physical cause has been found and for which the origins appear to be emotional (Butler & Lewis, 1977). Chronic brain syndrome (an organic disorder) and functional disorders account for more than 93 percent of the mental disorders of those older persons residing in mental hospitals (Brody, 1977). There is a paucity of data regarding the environmental and biological influences of maladaptation, the etiology of various disorders, and life-cycle development in the social structure as these affect the mental health of the elderly (Jarvik & Cohen, 1974).

Organic Brain Syndromes (OBS)

Organic brain syndromes are mental conditions caused by or associated with impairment of brain tissue function (Butler & Lewis, 1977). The characteristic features of such disorders are (1) disturbance and impairment of memory; (2) impairment of intellectual function or comprehension; (3) impairment of judgment; (4) impairment of orientation; and (5) shallow or labile affect. This constellation of symptoms characterizes organic brain disorder, especially in full-blown and advanced states (Butler & Lewis, 1977). In the population sixty-five years of age and older, approximately half of all persons with significant mental impairments have organic brain syndromes due to brain cell death or brain cell malfunction (Redick et al., 1973).

In some elderly persons with OBS, the brain impairments may represent the only disturbance observed, with basic personality and behavior remaining unchanged (Butler & Lewis, 1977). Cases such as this "are uncomplicated in the sense that the person attempts to make suitable adjustments to disorders and has insight into what has happened to his intellectual abilities" (p. 77), especially in the early stages of OBS. Older people who exhibit this form of OBS can function fairly well with little assistance from others. However, when OBS is accompanied by emotional symptoms, the situation becomes more complex. This is because the changes that are observed in the person may result in an initial diagnosis of some form of personality change or neurotic disorder, depending on which behavioral changes predominate. A group of rather ill-defined emotional or behavioral changes may be first to appear—for example, depression, loss of interest, fatigue, listlessness, or agitation (Pfeiffer, 1977). Other signs may include irritability, social withdrawal, emotional outbursts, irregular work attendance, and a change in behavioral standards (that is, inability to remain oriented to one's environment, difficulty assimilating new information, and so on). At times, these changes are present months or even years before anyone in the patient's surroundings notices any clear-cut memory deficit, confusion, or disorientation (Pfeiffer, 1977).

As the deficit increases, the individual may become forgetful, confused, bewildered, and perplexed. He may be prone to wander and get lost and inclined to neglect personal hygiene. In the more severe forms, these characteristics are exacerbated. The individual may then exhibit, for example, loss of recognition of near relatives, helplessness in feeding and walking, incontinence, delusions, hallucinations, and abnormal mood states such as agitation, depression and fatuous euphoria (Merskey, 1980). The patient may proceed to a stage in which he no longer responds to his own name (Pfeiffer, 1977).

With even greater severity of brain deficit the patient will lapse into a coma, if the onset is rapid. Or he will become bedridden, with loss of sphincter control, and will become subject to decubitus ulcers and local or systemic infections, if the progress of brain impairment is slow (Pfeiffer, 1977).

Clinicians who regularly deal with people with OBS need a short, portable, reliable, and valid instrument to determine the presence and degree of intellectual impairment. Such an instrument is available in the form of a ten-question mental status questionnaire, standardized on a population of some 1,000 elderly persons and validated on a clinical population of mentally impaired elderly (Pfeiffer, 1975).

Reversible Organic Brain Syndromes–or "Acute" Brain Syndromes. The concept of "acuteness" carries with it the notion of rapid onset, dramatic symptoms, and short duration—none of which is reliably present in the brain syndromes of older people. The concept "reversible" is a much more exact definition, since reversibility of the brain pathology remains the one consistent characteristic (Butler & Lewis, 1977).

Reversible organic brain syndromes are essentially due to temporary malfunctioning of a significant proportion of cortical cells, in general due to metabolic malfunction or drug intoxication (Engel & Romano, 1959). Based on clinical studies, it is estimated that from 10 to 20 percent of older persons with organic brain syndromes have a reversible form of the disorder (Pfeiffer, 1977).

The person with reversible brain syndrome may exhibit such symptoms as anxiety, mild confusion, stupor, hallucinations, and delusions of persecution. The person may also be disoriented, mistaking one person for another. Other intellectual functions may also be impaired.

In terms of the course of illness, reversible brain syndrome follows a pattern of extremes. According to Butler and Lewis (1977), both a high immediate death rate and a high discharge rate from the hospital are typical of reversible brain syndrome. Although mortality rates are substantial (an estimated 40 percent die, either from exhaustion or from accompanying physical illness), the person who survives the crisis has a good chance of returning to the community. (pp. 81–82).

The basic strategy of treatment in the reversible brain syndromes is the "elimination of the offending metabolic deficiency or the elimination of the offending drug" (Pfeiffer, 1977, p. 663), that is, tranquilizers, bromides, barbiturates, and so on.

Chronic Brain Syndrome (CBS)–Irreversible. The basic characteristic of chronic brain syndrome is its irreversibility. Once brain damage has occurred, there is no full return to normal physical condition. Brain cells have no capacity for regeneration. However, even though damage is permanent and irreparable, many of the emotional and physical symptoms can be treated, resulting in support and actual improvement of functioning (Butler & Lewis, 1977). There are three types of irreversible chronic brain syndrome: (1) senile dementia, (2) the presenile dementias, and (3) arteriosclerotic brain disease.

Senile dementia is characterized by gradually developing generalized intellectual and cognitive impairment. It is associated with diffuse brain cell loss of unknown etiology. The disorder occurs more frequently in women than in men, probably because of their longer life-span, with the age of onset from sixty to ninety years, the average being seventy-five.[1] Early features of senile dementia are errors in judgment, decline in personal care and habits, impairment of capacity for abstract thought, apathy, and lack of interest. As the deterioration increases, mental symptoms proliferate and the traditional five signs of organic dysfunction become more evident (Butler & Lewis, 1977). The five characteristic signs of organic dysfunction are: (1) disturbance and impairment of memory; (2) impairment of intellectual function or comprehension; (3) impairment of judgment; (4) impairment of orientation; and (5) shallow affect. These symptoms vary with the "extent of brain impairment, the rapidity of onset, the personality resources of the individual and the quality of the surrounding environment" (Pfeiffer, 1977, p. 660). Senile

[1] For a more comprehensive description of organic brain disorders, see, for instance, Butler, R. N. & Lewis, M. I. *Aging and Mental Health.* Saint Louis: Mosby, 1977, chapter 5.

dementia is one of the main causes of death in old age. Average survival after the onset of symptoms is five years.

The presenile dementias are a group of cortical brain diseases that look clinically like the senile dementia seen in older people but occur earlier, in the forty and fifty year age groups (Butler & Lewis, 1977). Alzheimer's and Pick's diseases are the two common forms. Alzheimer's disease is associated with characteristic neuropathological changes, especially plaques and neurofibrillary tangles and granulo-vacuolar degeneration, which are most pronounced in the temporal lobes (Merskey, 1980). Survival from the date of onset ranges from months to over ten years. Pick's disease has a somewhat different, more localized distribution of brain lesions (Mansvelt, 1954), but the clinical manifestations of the two disorders can hardly be distinguished (Pfeiffer, 1972).

The other major type of organic brain syndrome is arteriosclerotic brain disease. Here the organic brain syndrome is due to localized death of brain tissue related to occlusive arterial or arteriolar disease, with subsequent infarction of brain tissue. Arteriosclerotic brain disease may be marked by episodes of deterioration with partial recovery, by major or minor strokes, by the occasional presence of physical signs of vascular lesions and by the occurrence of emotional lability (that is, sudden and unjustified variations from one mood extreme, such as elation, to another, such as depression). This disorder has a somewhat better prognosis than Alzheimer's disease but the distinction between the two often cannot be made with any reasonable degree of certainty (Merskey, 1980).

Functional Disorders[2]

Bereavement, the loss of one's occupation, and social isolation are probably, in addition to severe physical illness, the worst stresses that people are called upon to face during their lives. All of these stresses occur most commonly in later life when the individual is biologically failing and is least able to cope with them. It, therefore, often happens that older people have to contend from a position of

[2] For a fuller description of functional disorders in old age, see for instance, Pfeiffer, E. Psychopathology in Social Psychology. In J. E. Birren & K. W. Schaie (Eds.), *Handbook of the Psychology of Aging.* New York: Van Nostrand Reinhold, 1977, chapter 27.

weakness with difficulties which would be a strain to anyone (Merskey, 1980).

Affective disturbances, particularly depressions, are the most common functional psychiatric disorders in the later years (Pfeiffer, 1977). Depression in this age group can vary greatly in duration and in degree. Many elderly persons experience fleeting episodes of sadness, loss of energy, and short-lived lack of interest, frequently in response to some adverse situation or loss.

The Characteristics of Depression.   Depressions of significant degree and duration have both psychological and physical manifestations (Pfeiffer, 1977). The psychological characteristics of depression include abject and painful sadness, generalized withdrawal of interest and inhibition of activity, and a pervasive pessimism, manifesting itself as diminished self-esteem and a gloomy evaluation of one's future and present situation. In addition, depressed patients often experience difficulty in making decisions, even minor ones, and their thought processes and speech are significantly slowed down, as are their physical movements (Pfeiffer, 1977). Often a considerable amount of tension and anxiety is associated with depressive affect.

The physical symptoms of depression are also prominent. In many elderly patients they may be the first sign of a depressive condition. In fact, many older persons prefer to mention their physical rather than their psychological symptoms. The prominent physical signs of depression include loss of appetite, significant weight loss, fatigue early in the morning, sleeplessness, wakening in the very early hours, and constipation or, more rarely, diarrhea. Obviously, this group of symptoms could be associated with significant physical illnesses. Thus, a thorough medical examination and a psychosocial diagnosis are both in order (Pfeiffer, 1977).

The most characteristic feature of all depressive disorders is that they are episodic in nature. Generally, they occur in persons who have previously gotten along reasonably well, without severe degrees of pathology, other than perhaps a previous episode of depression (Pfeiffer, 1977).

Suicide in Old Age.   Suicidal ideas often accompany severe depressive illness. They may take the form of relatively passive wishes for death, or they may be the starting point for an active plan to commit suicide. They must be taken very seriously when they occur in older persons. It is estimated that as many as 80 percent of the aged who are predisposed to suicide are depressed (Benson & Brodie, 1975). A smaller fraction of those who commit suicide is made up of persons who have used alcohol to excess and a still smaller fraction of persons with organic brain syndrome. A small percentage of those committing suicide suffer from an untreatable terminal illness (Pfeiffer, 1977).

When an older person attempts suicide, he almost always intends to die. Older people use all the usual methods of killing themselves: drugs, guns, hanging, and jumping off high places (Butler & Lewis, 1977). Rescue from a suicide attempt in old age is often accidental or due to poor planning of the attempt. Persons attempting suicide in old age should be hospitalized (Pfeiffer, 1977).

Paranoid Reactions.   Following depressive reactions, paranoid reactions are probably the most common functional psychiatric disturbances in old age. Paranoia is the attribution to other people of motivations which do not in fact exist (Fish, 1959; Post, 1966). Paranoid patients are suspicious of persons and events around them and they often construct faulty—that is, unrealistic—explanations of events which happen to them. Paranoid states are usually of short duration but are sometimes chronic, as in classic paranoia. They tend to occur under adverse conditions—imprisonment, deafness, isolation, disfigurement, infections, drunkenness, involution, or blindness (Butler & Lewis, 1977).

Paranoid depressions are common in older persons who are experiencing various kinds of sensory deficits, particularly hearing losses, and also in persons with decreased intellectual capacity (Retterstol, 1966). Typically, such an elderly person might misplace her glasses or wallet, or some other valued or needed possession, and then accuse those around her of theft. Or, a woman might notice that she has been receiving less and less mail. Rather than coming up with the explanation that she was simply writing fewer letters and was involved in fewer business transactions, she instead comes to the conclusion that the postman is stealing the mail from her (Pfeiffer, 1977).

Paranoid reactions in old age are quite responsive to appropriate treatment and intervention. There must be an understanding of the etiology. Such understanding dictates the correction of sensory or cognitive deficits; the provision of a relatively stable, friendly, familiar environment; and so on.

Hypochondriasis. After depressive and paranoid reactions, hypochondriasis is probably the most frequent functional psychiatric disorder in the later years (Pfeiffer, 1977). Hypochondriasis is more common in older women than men, and it seems to increase in frequency with advancing age (Earley & von Mering, 1969).

Hypochondriasis is an overconcern with one's physical and emotional health, accompanied by various bodily complaints for which there is no physical basis (Butler & Lewis, 1977). Even so, an older person complaining of physical symptoms should have a thorough physical examination. The diagnosis of hypochondriasis cannot be made on the basis of a psychiatric examination alone nor can it be made solely on the basis of a negative physical examination. It must be made, instead, on the basis of essentially negative physical findings and specific psychological observations (Pfeiffer, 1976).

When a hypochondriacal patient seeks help, he presents himself as someone physically disabled and not as someone emotionally distrubed. Efforts at restructuring the symptomatology of the hypochondriacal patient from physical symptoms to psychological symptoms are consequently doomed to failure (Pfeiffer, 1977). However, medical help, while not curing the problem, may be valuable if it can lead the patient to examine the real reasons he is seeking help (Butler & Lewis, 1977).

The conditions discussed above are some of the most prominent psychiatric disorders of old age. There are others, including schizophrenia (a severe emotional disorder marked by disturbances of thinking, mood, and behavior), neuroses, and personality disorders. Despite the gloomy view which is often taken, many of these disorders respond well to treatment.

Self–Esteem

It would be virtually impossible to define any properties of the quality of life for the aged that do not in some fashion impinge on their sense of self-worth (Schwartz, 1974). A drop in income can bring on decreased feelings of self-esteem because reduced income invariably brings a change in the individual's usual style of life. Poor health is another threat to self-esteem. Poor health is the main cause of voluntary and early retirement. Feelings of poor health invariably correlate with low current satisfaction (Streib & Schneider, 1971). However, older people who are in good health, living comfortably, and with their spouses do not experience the same threats to their life-styles as do those older people who are in different circumstances.

Self-esteem is developed in the individual through those innumerable events, large and small, that provide emotional support and psychological reward. Such events range from the cuddling and stroking of the newborn to the public recognition of certificates and other rewards of adult life. All such events mirror back to the individual an image of self that says, ''You belong; you count; you have an impact; you are important.'' Along with this go the internal signals that derive from a growing sense of mastery and control over oneself and the environment which tells the individual, ''You are effective.''

PRACTICE IMPLICATIONS

Social workers, more than members of any other helping profession, work not only with a diverse socioeconomic clientele but also with patients and clients whose functioning ranges from the most maladaptive to quite good (Strean, 1974). Because of this it is imperative that the profession draw on a large body of personality theories (Strean, 1975).

As the social worker studies, diagnoses or assesses, and intervenes in the lives of diverse older clients and client systems (the individual, family, group, organization, or community that asks for help and engages the services of the social worker as the change agent), he must be knowledgeable about what personality theories serve him best at various phases of the process. For instance, Freudian theory offers much assistance in helping the social worker assess psychopathology in certain older clients' lives, but its techniques of dream analysis, interpretation of the unconscious, and free association have limited applicability to social work intervention (Strean, 1975). Carl Rogers' Client-Centered Therapy may be extremely useful for working with the verbal client, but what would the Rogerian counselor do with the nonverbal client? While Lewin's no-tions of life-space and of the person in constant interaction with his environment may be helpful in undergirding certain aspects of social study, Lewin's orientation would, at best, be of minimal help in treatment (Strean, 1975).

When one looks at the "outer," more visible aspects of personality processes, it is fairly evident that they seem quite stable until old age. One's interests; the amount of time and energy devoted to being a worker, friend, volunteer, or spouse; and how one feels generally about life, do not seem to change much from middle age to the mid-sixties or early- to mid-seventies. At that time, social involvement tends to drop off for many people as they retire and become widowed, as their circle of friends grows smaller, and as their health deteriorates. These changes are often resisted by older people, and many healthy people remain involved and happy. Some older adults are very involved in social activities, have lots of energy, and feel quite positive about themselves; others always seem withdrawn, moody, and unhappy; others have a few good friends and live a quiet, happy life. Therefore, age is not a good predictor of changes in the "outer you."

Nevertheless, there do seem to be some normal developmental shifts in the "inner" aspects of personality, beginning in middle age. These inner aspects of personality are not measurable by direct questioning, since the individual may not be consciously aware of his hidden feelings and perspectives. To assess these feelings, psychologists and others have rated personality functioning from long interviews with individuals, analyzing the qualitative aspects of the interview as well as the content.

Another technique for assessing this level of personality is the Thematic Apperception Test (TAT). Respondents are shown a picture with figures in an ambiguous position, and are asked to tell a story about the picture. Since the pictures have no clear "meaning," the story told reflects the person's concerns, perceptions, fantasies, and so on (Huyck, 1974).

SUMMARY

The psychological effects of human aging are a function of a number of variables ranging from genetic through environmental. Each individual possesses a distinctive set of attributes that sets him apart from everyone else. It is this set of attributes that helps to identify that individual or gives sameness to that person in different situations and at different times over the years.

A number of changes appear to occur in the psychological area as individuals grow older. Generally the changes are associated with loss, which may interfere with and delimit competence and mastery, affect well-being, and ultimately diminish the older person's self-esteem.

Age-related sensory changes affect the quality and quantity of an individual's interaction with his social environment. Several aspects of vision decline with age. For instance, far-sightedness increases with age. On the other hand, general visual acuity declines with age. Hearing loss is more prevalent among the elderly than any other age group in the population. Deafness may be the result of a variety of factors. Sensitivity to pain may decrease with age, as may the sense of taste and smell. Reaction time also changes as the individual grows older.

Establishing the relationship between intelligence and aging has attendant difficulties. Cross-sectional measures of IQ indicate that older persons perform less well than do younger individuals. However, longitudinal research yields data on intelligence that suggest that verbal activities show little or no change with age.

Although individuals continue to be creative as they grow older, the quantity of output is less than was the case when they were younger. Major impairment of memory or learning will most likely interfere with the older person's ability to think or create.

The special biological and psychological effects of aging increase the vulnerability of the individual to physical and mental illnesses. Social isolation and emotional stresses often become both more common and less easily dealt with as people age. Social work has a major role to play in helping people adapt to changes and to cope with stressful situations to their maximum capabilities.

The social aspects of aging refer to what happens to people in society as they grow old. How do social gerontologists explain and rationalize how older people adjust to their own aging? What theoretical formulations exist that are useful for understanding the relationship between a society's social system and its older members?

A theory is an attempt to explain, predict, and understand behavior (Crandall, 1980). Theories can provide social workers and other human services workers with explanations and a sense of understanding of events experienced in practice. Although we do not have a unified and comprehensive theory of aging, theories of social gerontology are useful for explaining what happens to human beings socially as they grow old. One well-known theory that attempts to do this is the disengagement theory.

THE DISENGAGEMENT THEORY

The major architects of this theory were Elaine Cumming and William Henry. The disengagement theory first appeared in their book, *Growing Old*.[1] The theory was developed during a five-year study of a sample of aging people in Kansas City. The sample consisted of a total of 275 individuals, ranging in age from fifty to ninety years, who were studied at a single point in time. The subjects were all in good health and were financially self-sufficient.

The essence of Cumming and Henry's theory is that as an individual ages, he begins to withdraw from society by surrendering or giving up some of his social roles. The authors state that this disengagement is an inevitable process in which many of the relations between a person and other members of society are severed and those that remain are altered in quality.

As the individual gets older, he begins to face up to the inevitability of death, and begins preparing for it by gradually withdrawing from active societal roles. Cumming and Henry argue that, once it has begun, the disengagement process becomes self-perpetuating.

The disengagement process may be initiated by the in-

[1]Cumming, E. & Henry, W. *Growing Old: The Process of Disengagement.* New York: Basic Books, 1961.

chapter 5

THE SOCIAL
ASPECTS
OF AGING

dividual, by society, or by both. If both the individual and society are ready for disengagement simultaneously, the result is successful disengagement. If neither the individual nor society is ready, the individual remains engaged. If the individual is ready to disengage before society expects him to, engagement is likely to continue. However, society might expect the individual to disengage before he is ready. In that case, disengagement is likely to result. Cumming and Henry postulate that, of these two latter situations, the first type is more common among women, while the second is more common among men.

The primary function of the disengagement process is the preparation of the individual and his social environment for his death. What is involved is a steady decline in activity to the point of death. Thus, disengagement is seen not only as a normal process but also as a desirable one which leads to high morale and preparation for the ultimate disengagement—death (Dibner, 1975). The architects of this theory see disengagement as a mutual, inevitable, and irreversible process between the older individual and others in the social system to which he belongs.

Since this theory was first formulated, there have been numerous attempts to test it. The findings to date have been contradictory. The major criticism of the theory is that it is too simplistic; there are many individuals who do not disengage and who do not appear to suffer from their engagement (Crandall, 1980). In general, the consensus reached has been that, on both theoretical and empirical grounds, disengagement is one of several alternative life-styles equally capable of producing satisfaction or morale in late life (Maddox & Wiley, 1976).

ACTIVITY THEORY

George L. Maddox has been a major advocate of activity theory. He and other activity theorists assert that the more active an aged person is, the better his morale will be (Maddox, 1963). Happiness is achieved by denying the onset of old age and by maintaining a middle-aged way of life, values, and beliefs for as long as possible.

Thus, successful aging consists of remaining middle-aged (Crandall, 1980).

Activity theorists contend that by keeping active, the older person will remain socially and psychologically fit. Maddox asserts that the more roles that are available to the older person, and the more roles he participates in, the better off he will be when he enters old age.

Maddox examined life-satisfaction in aged individuals in a longitudinal design. He found that increased activity levels over time were predictive of increased morale, and decreased levels of decreased morale (Kalish, 1975). Thus, activity theory emphasizes social integration and involvement as explaining life-satisfaction, while disengagement theory emphasizes withdrawal of affective attachment and withdrawal from conventional involvement in social roles (Maddox & Wiley, 1976).

Further, activity theorists assert that disengagement theory may be applicable only to a small minority of the elderly. They suggest that, if disengagement does take place, it occurs among the very old and the very sick. Further, a low level of activity in old age is no proof of the disengagement process because a low level of activity may be the usual life-style for certain people. Activity level in old age must be measured against each individual's baseline.

Some studies to date support activity theory (Tallmer & Kutner, 1969; Rosow, 1967; Havighurst, 1968) while others do not (Lemon, Bengtson, & Peterson, 1972). The study by Lemon and colleagues (1972) suggested that high morale was not determined by the number of roles an individual participated in, but by an enduring, stable, and intimate relationship with at least one individual. This finding confirmed that of an earlier study by Lowenthal and Haven (1968). These researchers found that individuals who had one highly intimate and stable relationship were not as depressed and had greater satisfaction than those without such a relationship. Even so, many individuals maintain high morale and appear to suffer no ill effects from lack of a confidant (Crandall, 1980).

It appears that activity theory fits the prevailing American ethic of activity, work, and productivity as human ideals, while disengagement can be seen as an appropriate mode for many aging persons—although the process does not fit the society's ideals (Dibner, 1975).

SUBCULTURE THEORY

Cultures are made up of a number of different subcultures. A subculture can be defined as a group or segment within a society of persons of the same age, social or economic status and ethnic background. A subculture has its own interests, goals, and so forth. People belonging to a subculture share similar interests, friendships, and values. Arnold Rose (1965) proposed that the elderly live increasingly within the context of an aged subculture. They interact with each other more often as they grow older, and much less with younger persons.

Subcultures develop when certain members of a given category of the population interact with one another more than they interact with persons in other categories. The more older people are excluded from interaction with other age categories, the greater the extent and depth of subcultural development.

Rose acknowledged that there are some influences which keep older people in contact with the larger society, and tend to minimize the development of an aged subculture. Such influences include (1) contacts with the family, many of which increase as parents get older; (2) the mass media, which cut across all subcultural variations; (3) continued employment, even on a part-time basis, which keeps the older person in contact with younger age groups; and (4) an attitude of active resistance toward aging and toward participation in the aged subculture (Rose, 1965).

Within the subculture of the elderly, two distinctive and related factors have special value in conferring status. One is physical and mental health. Good health is rare among the elderly and becomes rarer with advancing age. The second distinctive factor in the status system of the aging is social activity. This is partly based on physical and mental health (Rose, 1965).

Rose recognized the growth of a new phenomenon—aging group-consciousness or aging group-identification which has expanded the scope (that is, in terms of increasing numbers) of the sub-culture of the aged. Thus, some people have begun to think of themselves as members of an aging group. Although only a minority of the elderly have taken this step, Rose asserts that their number is growing. One of the early manifestations of group-consciousness occurs when an older person joins a recreational or other similar group in which he or she can interact almost exclusively with persons of similar age. Examples of this phenomenon include membership in various senior citizens groups, and participation in multipurpose senior centers.

AGING AND THE SOCIAL PROCESSES

The intent of this section is to examine how society directly affects the individual in age-related ways. In relating the individual to his social surroundings, the concepts of norms, statuses, and socialization take on importance since they all have some bearing on the way in which the individual functions in society.

The sociocultural world is always in a state of change, and everyone is to some degree always behind the times. Although we are never fully socialized and a margin of autonomy always remains to us, we must be substantially responsive to the demands of the social order to function with any stability. These demands are incorporated in norms that proscribe, prescribe, condemn, and condone a vast range of activities (Bensman & Rosenberg, 1976). For the most part, most human beings most of the time do what is expected of them. In fact, culture indicates, sometimes within broad limits, but more often in narrow ones, what is expected of them (Bensman & Rosenberg, 1976).

In some ways aging is socially and culturally determined. In other words, people do not determine for themselves whether they are aged; rather, that determination is made on whether they are perceived by others to be so. A seventy-year-old man may declare that he's a fifty-year-old at heart and that he feels not a day older than he did then. But if he looks like a seventy-year-old, his self-concept is socially meaningless (Rosow, 1974). Society perceives him as age seventy and treats him accordingly. Society is also a powerful determiner of what his social behavior should be. That is, social behavior is related to the socially assigned roles that a person fills—grandfather, retired person, or old man, for example.

Cultural Uniformities and Cultural Variations

There is much uniformity among cultures. Every society, no matter how simplistic or complex, has a division of labor. Institutions having a noticeable similarity to one another govern the economy of every people. Religious rites and feelings, the belief in supernatural powers, and ceremonial acts based upon that belief are universal (Bensman & Rosenberg, 1976).

The list of universals could be extended. All people are sufficiently alike for us to make certain valid generalizations about the whole species. If this were not so, if uniformities or regularities in human behavior could not be discerned, there would, by definition, be no human species—and thus no science of human society (Bensman & Rosenberg, 1976).

But there is also cultural variation. What is deemed beautiful in one culture may be thought to be ugly in another. A crime in one culture may be the law of another. Note the differences in the way people walk and talk, the clothes they wear, their mannerisms, their deportment.

Age Norms

Norms are a set of expectations about behavior that people carry in their heads and use to regulate their own behavior and to respond to others' behavior (Kimmel, 1974). Society has an established set of social norms that prescribe what behavior is expected in socially defined positions. For instance, society has rules of conduct which spell out what is expected of firemen, policemen, fathers, students, and lawyers. Norms are linked to social sanctions, coercive measures that are imposed to bring about expected behavior.

Society imposes varying degrees of sanctions, ranging from humiliation or ostracism to imprisonment or death, for the violation of a norm. In addition, culture provides us with ready-made rules for everyday behavior and with socially acceptable goals. Laws set age limits—beginnings and endings—in various institutional spheres: compulsory school attendance, marriage without parental consent, entry into the labor force, eligibility for Social Security benefits.

Individuals, themselves, have expectations for what behavior is appropriate at different ages. Most people are aware of age norms and govern their behavior accordingly. It would be most unlikely to find a teenager going to school dressed like an aged grandparent, or a sixty-five year old woman walking on the street in a bikini. Some investigators (Bengtson & Haber, 1975) believe that the sanctions society places on conformity to these norms is so great that if one is tardy in living up to life-cycle norms, one will hurry to move toward the norm on the next event. If, for example, one marries late, one will quickly have a first child. It remains to be seen the extent to which such perceptions about life-cycle norms are changing.

Since age norms involve the individual's perceptions of what is appropriate and inappropriate behavior at different ages, it is also possible to measure the amount of constraint that age norms exert (Kimmel, 1974). Neugarten, Moore and Lowe (1965) found that middle-aged and older people see greater age constraints operating in society than do young people. Older people regard age-appropriateness as a reasonable criterion by which to evaluate behavior and believe that to be off-time with regard to major life events brings with it negative consequences (Neugarten et al., 1965). While young people feel that others think age is important in terms of determining appropriate behavior, they do not experience much constraint themselves. (Kimmel, 1974). Nevertheless, the age-norm system creates an ordered and predictable life-course, it provides timetables, and it sets boundaries for appropriate behavior at successive life-stages.

The Social Status of Today's Elderly

Both economically and socially, older people are in a disadvantaged position. They obviously do not command the needed goods and services necessary to enhance their position in society. In addition to having low incomes, many live alone in relative isolation. Their low socioeconomic status reflects their style of life. The socioeconomic position in which the older person finds himself may affect his entire outlook on life. In fact, there is evidence that a person's activities, his attitude toward life, his relationships to his family or to his work are all conditioned by his position in the age structure in the particular society in which he lives (Riley et al., 1968).

Social Role

Role, as a concept, is related both to the individual's social position and to the norms of society. A role is the behavior that is expected of the person occupying a social position. The norms prescribe the expected behavior. Since many social positions have role behaviors associated with them, the social position is often called a role (Kimmel, 1974).

On the stage, it is the script that determines the actor's behavior. However, in real life an individual's behavior is determined by his roles in society. Within a certain range, roles such as father, mother, or school principal all specify certain behaviors that are or are not appropriate. Obviously, there is some latitude in each role played, but the role nevertheless demands certain behavior from the performer. For instance, the school principal is expected to make sure the teachers show up on time for their classes and teach the required content at the various grade levels, meet with the teachers individually and in groups on a regular and ongoing basis, hold PTA meetings regularly (making sure parents have been notified of the time and date), and meet with Board of Education officials as necessary. These are only some of the duties required.

If the roles performed by the individual are not carried out in an appropriate manner certain sanctions can be applied to make certain that he performs his roles according to the standards that have been laid down. If the school principal is lax in his duties and does not meet up to the required standard, then he can be reprimanded, suspended, or fired by the Superintendent of Schools or the School Board.

Most of the time each of us presents the self that seems most appropriate to the situation. For example, if an older person wants to become a volunteer in a nursing home, he will demonstrate an attitude of warmth and good will toward both patient and staff. He will listen to the patient and be as helpful to him as possible. He will smooth the way and report any problems that may arise to the social worker.

Older people have performed many roles in the course of their lives. Some roles, such as spouse, parent, and worker, are quite clearly defined. Other roles, such as retired person and widow are less well defined and it is sometimes difficult to know what is expected in carrying them out. Either the individual has not had any opportunity to become appropriately socialized to the role, or the behaviors for carrying out the role have not yet been determined by society.

Over time, people begin to lose certain significant roles. The work role may be lost by both men and women. Along with the loss of this role goes the loss of other associated activities such as lunch with fellow workers, union or managerial association membership, and recreational linkages (Schwartz & Peterson, 1979). Women lose the motherhood role when their children leave home.

Some older people manage to compensate for role loss by taking on other meaningful roles. Volunteer work is a useful way of filling in time for many older people. A few return to school. Others become active in the community and in local politics. Some older persons spend more time with their grandchildren or become actively involved as teacher aides in elementary schools. More ways of using one's time meaningfully seem to be opening up to older people, including second careers.

Socialization to Old Age

Socialization serves to teach individuals at each stage of the life-course how to perform new roles, how to adjust to changing roles, and how to relinquish old ones. It is the process by which infants learn how to express their human nature and adults learn how to take part in new social situations (Bensman & Rosenberg, 1976).

The infant, a weak and completely helpless human being, is aware of his inner tensions and biological needs and has an innate tendency to reach out for gratification. He is completely dependent upon his environment for his safety and comfort and needs other people in order to have his physical requirements met. Eventually, to join others as a member of society, the child will have to master a complicated range of techniques, beliefs, and values. When this happens, we say that he or she is socialized (Bensman & Rosenberg, 1976). In other words, the individual has learned (and continues to learn) his culture.

Culture has continuity. In every generation the whole of a culture is transmitted to new generations by the process of socialization. It is obvious that society needs new participants; socialization is a major process through which society attracts, facilitates, and maintains participation (Atchley, 1977). The basic institutions —family, school, church, and the polity—have primary responsibility for socializing the individual. But the individual must also learn some things on his own. For instance, he must learn how to use the transportation system, how to negotiate the new shopping mall, what foods are healthy to eat, how weight and excessive cigarette smoking effect health, and so forth.

The individual's environment can either assist or retard developmental processes throughout the life-span. For example, if there are no supports in the environment to encourage older people who are isolated, lonely, and in declining health to channel their emotional energies in positive ways, then mental and physical functioning may rapidly decline. In nursing homes the attitudes toward the possibility of continued growth and/or rehabilitation of the patient population are of primary importance. In line with this, one extreme view considers the elderly as "too far gone and senile to respond to any restorative activities, whether medical, psychological, or social." This view places a premium upon "the needs of the institution to provide efficient maintenance of the institutionalized population." The opposite view maintains that, "although the institutionalized aged are ill, they are nonetheless capable of some level of improved functioning and that proper care and stimulation ought to be provided." (Kosberg & Gorman, 1978, pp. 398–403).

Many societies pay little attention to the needs of their adult members for the maintenance or renewal of either their knowledge or skills. This pattern seriously hampers the ability of some older people to remain integrated in the society (Atchley, 1977).

MAJOR ROLE CHANGES IN LATER LIFE

Retirement

A number of role changes are common to later life. Retirement is one. Retirement on a mass scale is a relatively recent phenomenon. In modern industrial society, it takes only a few individuals to produce enough goods and services for a large number of individuals. Therefore, retirement on a mass scale has become possible (Crandall, 1980). Also, older people are often encouraged to leave the labor force in order to make room for younger workers. Retirement in modern industrial society has been greatly facilitated by the development of Social Security systems and private pension plans that make leaving the work force financially possible.

Retirement has been viewed in a number of different ways. First, retirement can be seen as an event. It is an event that marks a major transition point in the person's life. The retirement even may occur when an individual receives a gold watch and a testimonial dinner for his years of service to the company. In some instances, the retirement event may go almost unnoticed, with little pomp or ceremony accompanying it. At any rate, it is a social milestone marking the shift from the middle years to old age (Kimmel, 1974).

Second, retirement may be considered a status (Kimmel, 1974). That is, following retirement the individual enters into a new and different social position with its own unique roles, expectations, and responsibilities. The individual may assume a number of new roles such as hospital volunteer, teacher aide in an elementary school, part-time worker. The roles that people assume following retirement depend on a number of factors including interest, health, income, and the availability of meaningful roles. Retirement has never been accorded the same value in our society as has work, but as the number of retired people continues to rise and as the amount of time spent in retirement lengthens, it is likely that the retired status may become more positive. A set of role definitions more rewarding than the definitions that presently exist may evolve (Miller, 1965).

Third, retirement may be viewed as a process—that is, the phase through which one goes in anticipating a new status and in working through the difficulties inherent in giving up an old position and being resocialized to something new and different. How effective this process is will depend on the biopsychosocial characteristics of the individual and his own stituation, as well as the nature of the new position into which he is moving.

Grandparenthood

An important family role that is available to older people is that of grandparent. Actually, this is becoming a middle-aged role since it is increasingly common to have grandchildren in one's forties or early fifties (Ward, 1979). Grandparenthood at an earlier age is due to early marriage, earlier childbirth, and a longer life-expectancy. Currently, almost 70 percent of the aged have grand-children and 30 to 40 percent have great-grandchildren (Brody, 1974). With more and more people living to advanced old age, the emergence of four-generation families has become commonplace.

It is safe to say that some grandparents attach a great deal of significance and meaning to the role. Interaction between aging parents, their adult children, and their grandchildren may increase, as may mutual assistance during family emergencies. On the other hand, most of the research on grandparenthood indicates that the role has limited significance for most older people. It is often primarily symbolic and ritualistic, with little meaningful involvement of grand-parents in the lives of their grandchildren (Kahana & Kahana, 1971; Wood & Robertson, 1978).

In one study, Neugarten and Weinstein (1964) explored the satisfactions and styles of grandparenthood among 140 middle-class respondents in the Chicago area. They found that for some grand-parents, the role gave a sense of biological renewal or biological con-tinuity. Others perceived their role as a source of emotional self-fulfillment and vicarious accomplishment (that is, they were able to achieve something through their grandchildren that they and their children were not able to achieve). They saw themselves as resource persons to their grandchildren.

Neugarten and Weinstein (1964) also describe five styles of grandparenting. Of these, the first three are quite common and tradi-tional; the latter two are more newly evolving roles and are perhaps more characteristic of younger grandparents. The five styles of grandparenting are:

1   Formal: clear separation between parental and grandparental functions; grandparents only provide special treats and occasional minor services. However, they are careful not to interfere in childrearing.

2   Surrogate parent: mostly true of grandmothers who assume parental responsibility when mothers work or are incapacitated.

3   Reservoir of family wisdom: mostly true of grandfathers who are dispensers of special wisdom or skills.

4   Fun seeker: participates in an informal, frequently playful relationship with the grandchild. There is mutual participation and authority issues are ignored.

5   Distant figure: has infrequent contact with the grandchild; emerges on special occasions such as on holidays and birthdays, and gives gifts on such occasions.

Styles of grandparenting are related to a number of factors including the personalities of the grandparent and grandchild, the frequency and quality of interactions between them, geographical distance, the ways in which the parents structure the child's time and availability, and the adequacy of income and transportation (Kalish, 1975).

The significance of the grandparent role as one with which an individual can strongly identify has yet to be determined. The role itself encompasses behavior ranging from "diffuse nurturance" to "formal distance" (Ward, 1979), a wide range, to be sure.

Widowhood

Any marriage that survives over the years will almost certainly end with one of the spouses, usually the woman, widowed; it is very rare that both spouses die simultaneously. The loss of one's spouse can be devastating, especially since the roles associated with being a spouse—friend, lover, companion, housekeeper, financial manager—are no longer available, and a source of interpersonal need fulfillment has been lost (Ward, 1979).

Widows comprise by far the largest category of older persons living alone; they number about 10 million in the United States or slightly over 12 percent of all women over the age of fourteen (*Bureau of the Census,* 1973). Their large numbers derive from the differential longevity of the sexes (Rogers, 1979); life-expectancy for women is seven years greater than it is for men.

There are many problems associated with widowhood. One is the difficulty of finding a new mate. Women are limited because society does not sanction their marrying a younger man. Another common problem is money. Six out of ten elderly widows have incomes below the poverty level, and only 2 percent of those whose husbands were covered by a pension are receiving benefits (Rogers, 1979). Several of the widows in Lopata's (1973) study had little knowledge of financial matters; traditional role specialization within the family had not prepared them (Ward, 1979). As a result, some widows are extremely vulnerable and open to exploitation by fast-talking swindlers.

Widowhood may also have its positive effects. This is especially the case if the marriage has been one of constant bickering and unpleasantness, or if the spouse's death comes after a long, protracted illness. In such instances, the remaining spouse frequently expresses relief over the death and may well look forward to living a peaceful life alone.

The burden of adjusting to widowhood is placed squarely upon the shoulders of the widow herself, although children and other relatives are usually important souces of support. Most widows live alone after the spouse's death, either because they do not wish to impinge on their children's lives or because they wish to maintain their own status and independence. When widowed persons live with one of their children, it is more likely to be with a daughter than with a son.

Social interaction with friends may decline somewhat. Sometimes friends are uncomfortable about knowing what to say to the new widow or widower, or in knowing what to do for them. This is unfortunate because contact with friends is a meaningful and gratifying source of support.

For the widow, new roles must be filled, old roles must be reassessed, and social relations must be redefined by the people with whom she interacts. Most relations undergo a change, some to be terminated, others to be adjusted (Kennedy, 1978). In ceasing to be a wife, a woman can no longer function as her husband's nurse, confidant, sex partner, or housekeeper; moreover she may have to assume unfamiliar roles like financial manager, handyman, or worker (Kennedy, 1978). Lopata (1973) notes that widows are especially likely to feel lonely at dinnertime. Not only must they eat alone, but the entire rhythm of the housewife role is disrupted when there is no "object" for one's tasks.

There are problems in adjusting to widowhood that are unique for men. Among these is the probability that the loss of a wife will produce a marked change in the home-living pattern for the surviving husband. Generally, the man is not experienced in maintaining many of the household responsibilities. Preparing meals can often produce problems for the newly widowed husband; cleaning and numerous types of general domestic care are not familiar to him (Kennedy, 1978).

Despite the problems experienced by both men and women, many of the widowed make a relatively good adjustment. They seem more content than single or divorced people, and they report the least stress and pressure of any other grouping despite their generally low incomes (Campbell, 1975).

Some communities extend assistance to those widows and widowers who might be experiencing difficulty adjusting to widowhood. This is frequently done through widow-to-widow programs and group therapy programs for those who have lost a spouse. The literature is contradictory on whether men or women make the "best" adjustment to widowhood (Crandall, 1980).

Grief.   Almost universally, the role transition from spouse to widow or widower involves grief. The remaining spouse must go through a period of grief and begin to accept the loss. During the acute period of mourning, it is essential for the bereaved person to tap painful feelings, to face and experience loss both emotionally and intellectually, and to realize that every relationship has some ambivalence in it. Pain, irrespective of source, produces anger. The reaction of "How could the death of my loved one happen to me?" may be a defensive maneuver against any anger which could read "How could you be so cruel as to die and leave me all by myself?" This, in turn, may produce the guilt connected with the idea "Had I done enough, this would never have happened." The grieved widow or widower feels as if he or she had the power to prevent the death but failed to utilize it.

The older person grieving over the death of a loved one can be greatly benefited by the family physician, a member of the clergy, an older child or other relative, a neighbor, or a close friend who, by his very presence, can help him or her during and after the working through of grief.

The length of time involved in bereavement may vary from six months to a lifetime. It is not unusual for widows and widowers to idealize their late spouses and to feel that a part of them has died also. In time, however, they must begin to emancipate themselves from their preoccupation with the deceased.

Volunteer Work

Elderly people are eager to be useful and to spend their time in meaningful activities (Ward, 1979). They like to feel that they have something of value—usually in the form of a service—to offer to someone else. Therefore, few activities can rival volunteer work as a source of "good feelings" about oneself (Ward, 1979). The decision of service providers to utilize the "knowledge, skills, experience and maturity of the older adult in a meaningful volunteer role is a strategic and useful means for enabling him to retain his sense of self-fulfillment and adequacy" (Feldman & Feldman, 1974, p. 185).

Despite the nation's efforts to deal with problems of poverty, education, housing, transportation, and health care, the problems still persist and proliferate. Helping professionals have long recognized the shortage of service personnel to deal with such problems. Historically, the social work profession has relied on the efforts of volunteers to fill in the manpower gap. However, the efforts of older adult volunteers have not been utilized as frequently as have those of younger volunteers.

Studies indicate that 35 percent of those eighteen to sixty-four, and 22 percent of those sixty-five and over engage in volunteer work. Although participation in such work does, in fact, decline with age, approximately one in five persons sixty-five years and over engage in some type of volunteer activity, and another 10 percent would like to do so (Harris & Associates, 1975).

The primary reasons why some older people do not engage in volunteer work are poor health, lack of transportation, family responsibilities, absorption in work, lack of opportunities, procrastination or lack of energy (Harris & Associates, 1975). It appears that volunteer participation is greater among older whites and those who are employed or have a relatively high income (Ward, 1979).

However, older blacks have volunteered their services in the community for years. Their contribution to the betterment of younger generations has been well documented in the literature. Older black women, in particular, have taken into their homes younger people who were experiencing difficulty living in their own homes. They have also cared for young children while their parents worked, taught vocational Bible School classes, and provided a variety of volunteer assistance in the church. The volunteer activities of older blacks have been mostly confined to their own communities. The worker needs to gain special knowledge of minority communities, as well as of the type of volunteer activities that minority elderly provide or engage in.

The talents of older people must be tapped and utilized in a more meaningful way than at present. This may mean that society will have to experiment with new options, inventing or upgrading positions of leadership and service (Ward, 1979). Older people want to engage in meaningful and fulfilling activities. As Ward (1979) points out:

> There is room for optimism. Future cohorts of older people will have more education and money, and better health, making them more capable and resourceful, as well as more demanding of meaningful involvement in community life. (p. 263)

THE COMMUNITY

Community is an elusive concept. By "community" sociologists refer to the area that an individual lives in and the people that he lives near and interacts with. Other meanings of the term stress the condition of living with others in a particular area (district, city, and so on). "Community" has also been defined as a group of people living together as a smaller social unit within a larger one, and having interests, work, and so forth, in common.

Regardless of how the concept is defined, it goes without saying that the type of community in which an individual lives can have a tremendous impact on that individual's life. Communities characterized by high crime rates and by lack of facilities and resources such as hospitals, transportation, nutritional services, churches, libraries, senior citizens centers, banks, grocery stores, legal services, day care centers, medical and dental centers, and leisure time facilities, are disadvantaged and preclude fullest participation by the older individual. Such lacks also lower morale, increase isolation, and reduce independence and self-sufficiency. In fact, high crime rates coupled with inadequate transportation can virtually make older persons prisoners in their own homes.

MINORITY GROUP AGED

The elderly are not a homogeneous group. Like the general population, the elderly can be differentiated by race, ethnic group, religion, social class, level of education, and a host of other variables. It was not until the early 1950s that a number of factors that make the elderly a heterogeneous population began to be noticed. Even so, research on minority aged did not appear until the mid-1960s (Crandall, 1980).

A number of reasons have been offered for lack of research on minority aged. First, there has been greater interest in other areas in gerontology. Second, older people are suspicious of researchers who are of different racial or ethnic groups (Crandall, 1980). [For instance, Ransford (1976) found that white researchers trying to complete studies on blacks frequently observed that, as soon as they start asking questions, blacks assume they are from the police department and refuse to answer.] Third, language may be a problem for the gerontologists who want to study Spanish-speaking (Hispanic) elderly or older Asian-Americans. Geography and inability to reach distant places where certain groups of older people (for example, Native Americans) are located, may be a fourth reason. Fifth, there are relatively few gerontologists who are also minority group members.

The pluralistic society in which we live is composed of a number of different racial, ethnic, and socioeconomic groups. These minority groups are distinct from the majority group. As Crandall (1980) vividly states:

> Each minority group has a unique history, has suffered discrimination and stereotyped images, has developed a subculture, has evolved certain characteristics within that subculture to help it cope with the larger culture, and has been in a state of constant change. (p. 377)

Wirth (1945) has defined a minority as ". . . a group of people who, because of physical or cultural characteristics, are singled out from the others in the society in which they live for differential and unequal treatment" (p. 347). Minority status carries with it exclusion from full participation in the society. In addition, minority groups are characterized as having limited access to power and unequal access to certain opportunities in society (Crandall, 1980). Minority groups can be formed on the basis of a number of criteria, including race, ethnicity, religion, sex, marital status, and age (Streib, 1965; Rose, 1965).

Women as a Minority Group

Historically, the patriarchal order cast females into fixed family roles: daughters, sisters, wives, mothers. They could also be distant love objects or, at a progressively lower level, household servants, harlots, or slaves (Bensman & Rosenberg, 1976). Man's superior status was powerful and unquestioned. In 1848, in Seneca Falls, New York, during the first woman's rights convention, the cry arose for the emancipation of women and slaves. Feminists demanded the franchise, greater protection on the job, property rights, better education, and more occupational opportunities. Finally, they sought equal access to jobs. Although feminism lapsed for decades, it reappeared with more vigor and increased militancy in the late 1960s (Bensman & Rosenberg, 1976).

This more recent women's movement, with its emphasis on equality and justice for women, has focused on issues such as day-care centers, abortion, and education—which are of little concern to older women (Crandall, 1980). Although strides have been made in the educational, employment, and, to some extent, political arenas, women are still not equal with men.

Older women are even more disadvantaged than younger women. The negative stereotypes that abound picture the older woman as an old maid, a hag, or a mean old witch. Older women are described as "old bags." When their husbands die, their chances of remarrying are limited. Those older women who have never worked may experience difficulty in managing their financial affairs when a spouse dies. They may fall easy prey to certain nonviolent criminals, such as those who practice bunco or confidence games.

Since women have traditionally held lower paying jobs than men, when they retire their Social Security benefits are generally lower than most men's. For instance, the average Social Security payment in 1977 was $268 per month to men and $213 to women (U.S. Bureau of the Census, 1978). Older women are more likely to live below the poverty line than are older males.

Native Americans

Native Americans constitute one of the most deprived segments in our population. It is difficult to provide an accurate figure on the number of Native Americans in the United States, but the most recent figures place their numbers within the range of 792,730 to one million.

Though Native Americans are scattered throughout the land, nearly half live in the West, primarily in Oklahoma, Arizona, California, and New Mexico. A significant number also live on reservations in North Carolina, New York, Washington, and South Dakota.

Life-expectancy among Native Americans is low—forty to fifty years, more than twenty years shorter than that of most white Americans. Only about 5 percent of Native Americans are sixty-five years of age or more, less than half the percentage for whites (Crandall, 1980).

Native Americans are one of the most economically deprived minorities in contemporary American society. The sole source of income for many of the elderly is welfare, with only the minimum level of Social Security at age seventy-two. It is safe to say that most never participated in retirement programs such as company retirement plans, insurance plans, and investing in income property. Apparently, the Bureau of Indian Affairs (BIA) has made little effort to inform them of the social service benefits to which they are entitled.

Housing.   Housing is so substandard that the National Indian Conference on Aging, in 1976, named housing as the number one priority issue for aged Native Americans. Most of the aged live on reservations where housing is often inadequate and unsanitary.

A large percentage of elderly Native Americans do not have sufficient income to cover housing and the utility costs of existing programs. Nursing homes or sheltered care facilities are urgently needed by some chronically ill elderly. However, some states refuse to license nursing homes on reservations due to a question of jurisdiction (i.e., territorial range of authority between Native Americans and the Federal Government through the BIA), and at the same time Federal funds are not authorized unless the facility is licensed by the state.

Transportation.   Lack of public and private transportation is a problem and frequently denies the elderly Native Americans the opportunity to obtain medical services, food, and clothing. In addition, "poor road conditions, lack of communication systems, absence of public conveyances, and isolation compound the problem" (*Toward A National Policy on Aging,* 1971, p. 201).

Health.   Native Americans generally suffer deplorable health conditions when compared to other races in this country. They suffer more chronic limitations and disabilities than whites and malnutrition is a major problem. In addition, there is a lack of funds for dental prosthetics, hearing aids, eyeglasses, and psychological services.

The Spanish Speaking (Hispanics)

The Spanish-speaking aged compose a particularly vulnerable class of needy persons within the larger population of elderly Americans. Currently Hispanics represent about 60 percent of the Spanish-speaking population in the United States. The Hispanic minorities are Puerto Ricans, Cubans, South or Central Americans, and others (U.S. Bureau of the Census, 1976).

After blacks, Hispanics are the second largest minority group in contemporary American society. There are currently approximately 6,545,000 Hispanics in the United States (U.S. Bureau of the Census, 1978).

Language.   Perhaps the most pervasive handicap the Spanish-speaking elderly person has in this society is his inability to speak and communicate in English and his lack of understanding of the "system" (Harbert & Ginsberg, 1979). There appears to be a high correlation between an inability to speak English and a lack of awareness of existing and rightfully accessible programs and services.

Health.   The mortality rate of the Hispanic elderly is above-average. At forty-eight years of age, the health of an Hispanic is equivalent to that of an Anglo-American of sixty-five. Inadequate nutrition affects all elderly Hispanics. Surplus commodities offer some relief, and although they are not designed to provide a complete meal, for many they do so.

Transportation. In rural areas, transportation is either unavailable most of the time or too expensive. In the past, where transportation was available, Hispanic elderly had difficulty communicating with the drivers and understanding routes and time-schedules. In most instances, this situation has been remedied by printing schedules in Spanish.

Housing. Many Hispanic elderly poor own their own homes. For the most part, these homes are below-standard and do not have modern facilities (running water, indoor plumbing, furnace, and so on). One study (Carp, 1969) found that most elderly Hispanics take pride in home ownership and have strong community ties and close relationships with other family members who live nearby. The study also found that many aged Hispanics had no desire to move into housing units that had not been designed with their needs and culture in mind.

Family. It is possible that the family structure of Hispanics has been changing over the years. Earlier studies indicated that the extended family prevailed among this group. In the extended family (two or more nuclear families living together in the same household), the aged were held in high regard and were cared for by a variety of relatives. The family bonds were kept intact because of poverty and discrimination. Poverty forced family members to rely on one another for goods and services (Crandall, 1980). A later study (Crouch, 1972), however, found that the economic realities of membership in the lower class had truncated the extended family's obligations to its aged members. The majority of elderly Hispanics apparently did not expect to receive any support from their families.

Asian-Americans

Chinese, Filipinos, Japanese, Koreans, Vietnamese, Cambodians, and Samoans make up the Asian-American population. For years it seems that the Asian-American elderly have been handicapped by the myth that aged Asian-Americans do not have any problems, that Asian-Americans are able to take care of their own, and that the Asian-American aged do not need or desire aid in any form. Such assertions are false. A quick look at the two largest Asian-American groups may help to dispel that myth.

Chinese-Americans

"There are currently about 432,000 Chinese-Americans in the United States" (Crandall, 1980, p. 396). More than 90 percent are located in metropolitan areas. The majority live in California and Hawaii as a result of immigration directly to those areas. Only 6 percent of the Chinese-American population is sixty-five or more years of age. (Crandall, 1980). Older males outnumber females, reflecting pre-World War II immigration laws that prohibited women and children from accompanying men to the United States.

Health.   Elderly Chinese-Americans have health problems similar to those of all older persons. When asked to rate their health, 63 percent of the aged Chinese who were sampled rated their health as no better than fair, and 29 percent said that their health was poor or very poor (Carp & Kataoka, 1976). Over a third of aged Chinese-Americans who were studied had never had a medical or dental examination. This could be related in part to cultural and language differences which make access to health care services difficult.

The suicide rate among aged Chinese-Americans is three times the national average (Kart, 1981). This is especially the case among aged Chinese bachelors (Crandall, 1980). One study (Lyman, 1974) found that the suicide rate among aged Chinese-American women is also high.

Income.   Limited and fixed income levels for older Chinese as provided by Social Security, pension funds, and savings has been inadequate to meet needs, especially health and housing costs (*Toward A National Policy on Aging,* 1971). Furthermore, many aged Chinese have no source of income whatsoever, other than welfare, since they were employed in occupations which were not covered by Social Security or private pensions. They were often self-employed, worked on farms, or as domestic help.

Kinship. Traditional patterns of kinship and community responsibility have been damaged by the experiences of immigration and forced disruption of normal family life. Many of the elderly speak little English, thus increasing their difficulties in an alien culture.

Most non-Asian workers currently serving the needs of elderly Chinese are not aware of their needs and concerns. They are not able, therefore, to communicate effectively with them and in some instances have actually alienated them.

Japanese–Americans.

There are currently about 591,000 Japanese-Americans in the United States. Like Chinese-Americans, the vast majority live in California and Hawaii. About 8 percent of Japanese-Americans are sixty-five years of age or more (Crandall, 1980).

Family. Japanese-Americans appear to have been able to provide their elderly with greater family support and economic security than have Chinese-Americans, since they were not so severely restricted from bringing their families with them when immigrating.

Economic and Health Characteristics. One-fifth of the elderly, in areas outside California and Hawaii, are poor. Over half (58 percent) live alone, and the majority of these are widowed females. Elderly Japanese men usually speak at least broken English; older women tend to speak only Japanese. Health surveys have found that many of the elderly of this group are physically healthy.

Aged Blacks

The Census Bureau projects 3 million blacks sixty-five and over for the year 2000. This projection, if borne out, would increase the older black population by 46 percent in the next two decades, 21 percentage points more than the older white population over the same time-span (Soldo, 1980).

Aged black Americans are our largest racial minority. Despite this, there is little in the scientific literature about the process of aging among blacks. In 1977, there were 25,112,000 blacks in the United States. This figure represented 11 percent of the population of the

United States. Aged blacks make up between 7 and 8 percent of the total black population (U.S. Bureau of the Census, 1978).

Historically, the black population has been concentrated in the South. About 52 percent of blacks still live in the South; 40 percent live in northern states, and the remainder in the western states (Crandall, 1980). When blacks do move to metropolitan areas they tend to concentrate in central cities.

Health.   Generally, blacks can anticipate shorter life-expectancies than whites. At birth today, whites can anticipate an average of 5.1 more years of life than blacks. However, it should be pointed out that the differences in life-expectancy between blacks and whites are narrowing. Between 1950 and 1976, black men and women added about nine years to their life-expectancy, while white women added five years and white men three years (Crandall, 1980).

Those who survive to age sixty-five tend to suffer from chronic illnesses and disabilities (Benedict, 1972). They are less likely to receive medical care for their problems because of a variety of barriers, such as low income, scarcity of services where they live, and discrimination (Ward, 1979).

Blacks are said to suffer from chronic illness at twice the rate of whites. Why this is so has yet to be determined. Some suggest that it has to do with their socioeconomic circumstances. Discrimination in the area of employment and lack of sufficient money to purchase quality medical care, food, and housing, may be contributing factors.

Poverty.   Income is the most serious problem confronting many aging and aged blacks. Census Bureau figures show that two out of every five blacks sixty-five years or over lived in poverty in 1980. An estimated 783,000 elderly blacks were considered below the poverty line in 1980, as compared to 662,000 in 1978, an 18 percent increase. The poverty rate among older blacks rose from 33.9 percent to 38.1 percent in those two years (Davis-Wong, 1981). Another 310,000 older black Americans are marginally poor. People are considered marginally poor if their income is above the poverty threshold, but not more than 25 percent above it.

A significant proportion of blacks have worked full time for minimal wages and in menial jobs generally lacking adequate fringe benefits related to retirement. Thus, when blacks leave the labor force, for whatever reason, they must frequently subsist at or below the poverty line. Black aged women are especially vulnerable economically (Crandall, 1980).

Family Ties.   Strong kinship bonds among blacks exist well into old age. Rober B. Hill, research director for the National Urban League, points to statistics that reflect great family strength in the majority of black families. He describes the strength of most black families as coming from strong kinship bonds, a strong work orientation, adaptability of family roles, strong achievement motivation, and strong religious orientation (Hill, 1971).

It is not unusual to find children and younger persons residing in black families headed by an elderly couple. These children may be their own, grandchildren of friends, or relatives whom they have taken in. At any rate, this nurturing role appears to be a dominant one, particularly among older black women.

It is rare to find older blacks in nursing homes or in homes for the aged. Less than 3 percent of nursing home residents are black. The reasons advanced for this situation are (1) the cost factor, that is, older black families are unable to afford the cost of nursing home care; (2) racial discrimination; and (3) the reluctance of the black community to seek institutional care for its older members.

STEREOTYPES ABOUT OLDER PEOPLE AND AGING

The fact that in terms of sheer numbers more people than ever are reaching old age has been thoroughly documented. Nevertheless, there is a collection of negative beliefs that seems to accompany the experience of aging, and attaches to the aged themselves. Atchley (1977) points out that old people are seen by society in general as valuing companionship more than sex; being old-fashioned; not caring much about their appearance; suffering neglect; being in only "fair" health; and being narrow-minded. If the general population believes these characteristics to be true, it will react to older people as though they did, in fact, possess these characteristics. This statement also applies to older people who may believe these things about themselves, regardless of the truth of the matter.

Stereotypes such as those described by Atchley emphasize the negative images of growing old. Such images tend to be insidious, pervasive, and generalized. There are some stereotypes that may apply to all older people whereas others may apply to only some of them. Some stereotypes contain insufficient evidence or no evidence at all to document their veracity. Other stereotypes are factually untrue. For instance, one of the findings of Louis Harris and his associates, in their study, *The Myth and Reality of Aging in America* (1976), was that 52 percent of the persons eighteen to sixty-four felt that the best thing about being over sixty-five is "having more leisure," that is, more free time to enjoy life, to do the things the individual has always wanted to do. However, only 43 percent of those persons sixty-five years of age and over felt that way.

Harris and his associates (1976) also pointed to the discrepancy between the problems attributed to most people over the age of sixty-five by the public at large, and the problems personally experienced by the elderly themselves. For instance, 23 percent of those elderly people interviewed said that "fear of crime" was a very serious problem for them personally, while 50 percent of the general public felt that this must be a concern for elderly people. For years, loneliness has been assumed to be a problem for the elderly. However, the Harris study found that only 12 percent of those over sixty-five felt that loneliness was a very serious problem for them personally, while 60 percent of the public felt that it must be. Another concern was the issue of feeling needed. Fifty-four percent of the general public felt that "not feeling needed" was a very serious problem for those sixty-five and over, while only 7 percent of the elderly indicated that this was a serious problem for them. These findings suggest that younger people exaggerate the problems associated with later life and tend to think that getting old is worse than it apparently is.

It may well be that early theoretical formulations that focused on development during childhood and adolescence have had a negative impact on perceptions of growth and change during the adult and later years of life. All too often we have assumed that once an individual reached adulthood there was little growing left to do.

Everything from that point on was "downhill." However, as Butler (1979) points out, although the stability of the adult character structure is remarkable, old people are more open to change than is generally realized. Apparently, we as a society have been operating under a set of beliefs about the elderly that are not in line with reality.

The negative views that are held about the elderly (and the process of aging) are reflected in the rewards and reinforcements (or lack of them) that are made available to them. For instance, the institutionalized elderly may be indiscriminately treated as "frail," "sick," and/or "too weak" to do anything for themselves. As a result, they may be discouraged from exercising their skills because to do so might interfere with the efficient management of the particular setting. This kind of response to institutionalized older people is frequently based on biased attitudes and expectations about the sick role of the elderly.

The myth of aging has carried with it the stereotype of the helpless, hopeless, incompetent, and dependent oldster (Eisdorfer & Wilkie, 1977). The physical picture frequently portrayed is that of a person with gray or white hair, wrinkled skin, stooped posture, slowness of gait, weakness, and physical dependency. In contrast, youth conjures up images of firmness of body, smooth skin, physical attractiveness, boundless energy, flexibility, productivity and independence. The older person is thought to have reached a state in life where his most productive years are behind and decline and deterioration lie ahead. Thus feeble, uninteresting, the old person awaits his death, a burden to society, to his family and to himself (Butler, 1975). The truth is that older people vary more in personality than any other age group, and become increasingly diverse as they grow older. There are very young seventy- and eighty-years-olds, as well as old ones.

The effects of ageism (that is, the prejudices and stereotypes that are applied to older people solely on the basis of their age) are often subtle, but always damaging. As with any prejudice, ageism affects self-image—in this case, older peoples' views of themselves. Thus, they tend to adopt the very stereotypes that serve them so poorly; in so doing they reinforce them. In the meantime, younger people try to avoid old people, who remind them that their day, too, will come (Rogers, 1979).

STRESS AND AGING

It is a well-known fact that older people are vulnerable to in-numerable stresses. Some of the most salient of such stresses are acute and chronic illnesses, isolation, loneliness, loss of spouse, loss of social relationships (especially of work associates), loss of social roles, declines in mobility, declines in physical health, life-style transitions such as retirement and children leaving home, relocation, and loss of opportunity for meaningful work and for recognition. Often these stresses overlap; in most instances, they are cumulative. The cumulative effects of loss experienced as stress may lead to breakdown in individuals where normally none would have been predicted (Lowenthal et al., 1967).

Naturally these stresses have a tremendous impact upon the aging process. Schwartz (1974) contends that, left untouched and un-modified, they signal an increasing loss of control over one's environment and with it an increasing subjective sense of loss of impact upon and effectiveness within the environment'' (p. 10). Although relatively little attention has been paid to the cumulative effects of stressors, there is enough evidence that indicates that the frequency and variety of stresses that occur as the individual moves toward advancing old age is related to decrements in physical and mental capacities (Schwartz, 1974).

The way in which an older individual reacts to a stressful event depends upon a number of factors, such as personality, the capacity to compensate for and adapt to the current social environment, the availability and quality of personal supportive relationships, and concrete social and health supports (Brody, 1977).

In spite of the general decrement that accompanies aging, older people have the capacity to enjoy life to maximal levels of functioning. They also can still adapt to changes. Pfeiffer (1977) defines adaptation as the ''process of meeting an individual's biological, psychological, and social needs under recurring changing circumstances'' (p. 650). This is not always easy, especially for those older individuals who experience one loss after another.

It has been suggested that the task of the older individual is two-fold. The first part of the task is to replace some of the losses which have occurred with new relationships—new friends; remarriage; new roles such as second and third careers; volunteer work—and to retrain lost capacities, for example through speech therapy and/or physical therapy after a stroke. The second part is to make do with less (Pfeiffer, 1977).

Butler (1977) sees another important task in late life as the "life review." He has postulated that reminiscence in the aged is part of a normal life review process brought about by approaching dissolution and death (Butler & Lewis, 1977). The "life review" can be described as an evaluative backward glance at one's life. The individual weighs his accomplishments and failures, satisfactions and disappointments, seeking to delineate a final identity which integrates the diverse elements of his life and allows him to come to a reasonably positive view of his life's worth (Pfeiffer, 1977). The process is characterized by a continuous return to consciousness of past experiences and the resurgence of conflicts not completely resolved which can be reviewed again and, it is hoped, reintegrated. If the reintegration is successful, it can give new significance and meaning to one's life and prepare one for death, by mitigating fear and anxiety (Butler & Lewis, 1977).

Another major task facing the older individual is to remain active for as long as possible in order to retain function. Essential areas of function include the maintenance of physical activity, social interaction, intellectual and emotional stimulation, and the capacity for self-care (Pfeiffer, 1977). If the older individual does not maintain regular and vigorous physical activities, preserve extensive social contacts, and pursue intellectually and emotionally stimulating activities, then decrease of these functions through disuse can lead to unnecessary physical limitations, social isolation, disorientation, and apathy (Pfeiffer, 1977).

OLDER PEOPLE SEEK HELP

Older people seek help for a variety of reasons; they may be having difficulty adjusting to retirement; they may be experiencing depression after the loss of a loved one; they may be troubled by feelings of inadequacy, loss of self-esteem, or self-confidence; or there may be deep strife in the marriage. Whatever their reasons, they are likely to be people who are deeply troubled and who wonder what the future holds. They are looking for hope and some assurance that things will get better.

Nevertheless, attitudes about working with older people have frequently taken on negative overtones. For instance, in a well-known demonstration project conducted at the Benjamin Rose Clinic in Cleveland, Ohio, Blenkner and colleagues (1971) reported the tendency of workers to form a therapeutic alliance with younger responsible others at the expense of the older client. Human service personnel, in general, perceive younger clients as more open to improvement by the techniques at hand. In work with the aged the perspective is different. There is a look backward. There is a tendency for human service personnel to dwell on past rather than on future accomplishments of the older person.

Practitioners must not become entrenched with the view that old age is a static period, and that the older individual is incapable of effecting change in his life. To believe that one is powerless and under pressure from inescapable and inexorable forces, is to believe that one is no longer self-determining or responsible for one's life.

The view offered here is that optimism is a good thing. However, optimism must be tempered with the realities of the world in which the older person finds himself. What good does it do for the worker to give enthusiastic support to the plan of a seventy-three-year-old retired teacher who is in relatively good health and thinking about beginning a second career as a paid employment counselor, if economic conditions are such that people half her age are not being hired for such jobs? Is it appropriate to encourage a sixty-five-year-old man to go back to school for a doctorate when most graduate and professional schools refuse to consider applicants over the age of forty? Where is the propriety in helping people to expand their options if the world is going to close doors in their faces? Such action requires a combination of ability and energy beyond what most people possess (Schlossberg et al., 1978).

Social work is and has always been an essential ingredient of the health and social care systems and should have a major role in the identification of problems, whether crisis situations or on-going, long-term ones. At another level, social work must begin to place more emphasis on preventive rather than remedial services. A preventive perspective focuses on the impact of environmental systems on the development of human problems (Fischer, 1977). The goals of preventive intervention include attempts to build strengths into individuals and systems as a viable means of avoiding problems.

SUMMARY

In order to function smoothly, every society must have some structure. Age is used as a prime criterion for access to the more desired positions in society. Age-grades are institutionalized within the fabric of our society. Societies also have age norms. Age norms are a set of expectations about required or accepted behavior that people carry in their heads and use to regulate their own behavior and to respond to others' behavior. Both economically and socially, older people are in a disadvantaged position. Older people do not command the goods and services necessary to enhance their position in society.

Social role is related both to the individual's social position and to the norms of society. Older poeple have performed a number of different roles throughout their lives. Over time, people begin to lose significant roles. Some older people compensate for role loss by taking on other meaningful roles including the volunteer role.

The problems of the elderly in America are largely the problems of women. Far more older women are widowed, live alone, and on less income than older men. Although widowhood can be particularly devastating and requires many adjustments, it may also have its positive effects.

American society is characterized by ethnic and racial diversity. Research on minority aged has only recently begun to appear in the social gerontology literature. A number of reasons have been advanced for the lack of research on minority elderly. There is no way of generalizing ideas about the aging process across cultural groups until or unless systematic research of minority elderly is undertaken. However, the research that has been done reveals that there are commonalities such as deprived income status, unequal access to certain opportunities in society, and unequal treatment that cut across various racial groups. There are also unique differences that characterize each racial minority.

chapter 6

THE SERVICE CONTEXT

By now, it should be obvious that the elderly are a heterogeneous population that exhibits a broad range of problems and needs. Older people differ appreciably among themselves in their expectations, their living arrangements, their financial or social resources, their mental and physical health, their coping abilities, and their subjective sense of fulfillment. Some are managing extremely well; some could do far better with modest changes in their environment, changes in self-confidence, or social opportunities; some are fragile and floundering, but too independent to seek help; and some are barely able to sustain themselves outside of an institutional setting (Rosenfeld, 1978).

Characteristics of the elderly indicate that increase in age lends to increase in disability. For instance, persons seventy-five and over are more likely to require assistance with the daily tasks of living such as dressing, bathing, eating, and toileting. The situation is aggravated by the fact that the longer the individual lives, the greater is the likelihood that he will develop a degenerative illness that will require even more expensive care. In recent years, the number of persons at risk for some type of ongoing, long-term health and social care has greatly increased.

Surveys of elderly people have found that the great majority prefer to remain in their own homes rather than enter institutions. It has been widely asserted that many people who have entered institutions would not have needed to do so if certain supports had been available to them in their own homes. If adequate home care and community supports were available, an "unknown proportion of nursing home patients could live in the community" (Leviton, et al., 1982, p. 212). A limited amount of federal support has been available to states to create home-delivered services under several programs (Glasscote et al., 1976).

More research studies are needed to gain a realistic picture of how well the elderly are faring, how effectively service agencies are reaching their intended targets, and where there is a need to develop new services or make existing services more accessible to those who need them (Rosenfeld, 1978).

The composition of the aging population changes continuously, with each cohort of older people constantly bringing new identities, life-styles, and experiences into old age. Consequently, values, orientations, and expectations will continue to change within the older age group (Beattie, 1976). It goes without saying that planning and service delivery systems need to be designed to assure flexibility in response to the ever-changing nature of the aging population.

Older people in contemporary society probably experience more changes in the physical, social and psychological realms than other age groups. Weg (1975) makes the point that the aged in contemporary society experience

> ...change in living arrangements, loss of job, decrease in income, loss of status, loss of friends and relatives, loss of identity, and often a decline of physical capacities. It appears conceivable then, that these multiple changes represent mounting stress that finally taxes homeostasis and coping abilities to the limit, leading to the breakdown of adaptability and to disease. (p. 245)

When we look closely at the individual and the social environment in which he lives, it is obvious that his ability to cope and adjust to his situation depends upon a number of factors. Such factors include financial resources, health and mobility, living arrangements, family relationships, and formal and informal social networks. Some people are more outgoing and gregarious than others and exhibit a great deal of resiliency in coping with their problems. Others are less open and less successful in meeting the challenges of everyday life and may become extremely depressed, isolated, and lonely.

SOURCES OF SUPPORT FOR THE ELDERLY

The nature of aging is shaped by its social context, a critical part of which is the network of services available to the aging individual. Most Americans have traditionally thought of themselves as independent people, capable of self-help. If help is needed, then assistance from friends, neighbors, relatives, and other natural helpers is generally sought and accepted prior to seeking outside help.

For many years, primary assistance for the support of the elderly came from the family. However, soaring inflation and the high cost of living have exacted a financial strain on most families. Thus, adult children and their families cannot continue to be relied upon to assume full responsibility for their aging parents without support or respite from outside sources. Because of shifts in the structure and function of social institutions such as the family and church, older people today are having to rely more heavily upon extra-familial social supports in the community to meet their needs.

With a few exceptions, the role of the federal government in the provision of social services since the 1930s has been profound. However, as a service delivery system, the federal approach has been increasingly under fire; it has been described in Congressional hearings as characterized by fragmentation, duplication, and total lack of coordination. As the system now functions, it is the responsibility of the older individual to determine what kind of services he or she needs, where they are available, and how to orchestrate a comprehensive service package. Older people in need of help must often struggle through a maze of independent applications for Medicaid, Supplemental Security Income (SSI), Title XX, and Title III programs. Often this means trips to several different state and local social service departments scattered all over town. This lack of coordination, coupled with limited program funding, helps explain why many elderly in need go without services. There is no question that the current service delivery system must be more responsive to the individual needs and conditions of older persons and their families (Beattie, 1976).

Care–Giving Settings

Emphasis today appears to be on providing those kinds of services that will maintain people in the community for as long as possible. To that end, a number of major public and private programs are now working to help the elderly.

In many communities a range of services is offered through departments of public welfare, mental health and community mental health, public health, and others. Many services are funded or coordinated through United Funds and Welfare Councils. Other services may be under the jurisdiction of area-wide human resource commissions, councils on government, housing authorities, public transportation departments, libraries, or school districts. Still others are provided under an informal structure of religious or sectarian auspices.

The formal welfare structure is complemented by an infor-

mal, quasi-institutional structure. Bridging the gap between professional care-giving and lay services, it is composed of a network of civic
organizations, service groups, fraternal associations, church groups,
social action groups, and so forth.

The complex of public, private, and voluntary services is often
very confusing to the inexperienced planner; it is difficult to identify
and to categorize its various components. One approach to identifying the many programs and services currently available is to review
briefly the major pieces of federal legislation and government programs to benefit the elderly.

THE OLDER AMERICANS ACT (OAA)

The OAA was enacted in 1965. Under this Act, a variety of programs
were authorized and funded for older people, as well as projects for
researchers, educators, social service personnel, and administrators,
among others (Hess & Markson, 1980). The Act, which has been
amended several times—most recently in 1978—lists ten major objectives. These objectives declare the right of the elderly to:

1   An adequate income
2   The best possible physical and mental health
3   Suitable housing
4   Full restorative services
5   Opportunity for employment with no age discrimination
6   Retirement in health, honor, and dignity
7   Pursuit of meaningful activity
8   Efficient community services
9   Immediate benefit from proven research knowledge
10 Freedom, independence, and the free exercise of individual
    initiative.

The Administration on Aging (AOA), located within the Department
of Health and Human Services, is responsible for carrying out these
objectives and for providing coordination among federal agencies
that have programs for older people (Soldo, 1980). The AOA is an

advocacy agency which channels funds to states, communities, and non-profit organizations in order to promote the development and coordination of services for older persons.

Under the comprehensive Older Americans Act of 1978, federal funds are authorized under the following sections, or titles, and administered by AOA:

1   Title III for social services, senior centers, and nutrition services
2   Title IV for demonstration projects
3   Title V for community service employment programs (administered by the Department of Labor)
4   Title VI for the development of services to older Native Americans by tribal organizations.

Although emphasis is on maintaining older persons in the community, in 1979 Congress also designated OAA funds for long-term care. The delivery of services under the OAA is channeled through the "aging Network," a system of State and Area Agencies on Aging which, in turn, coordinate the delivery of needed services in their communities (Soldo, 1980).

Social Services

Social services attempt to facilitate the social functioning of people who are experiencing problems in daily living. Thus, social services have physical, psychological and social components. The aim of these services is to allow the older person to remain in the community, and be a part of it, for as long as possible. Social services are also intended to help people achieve, maintain, or support the highest level of personal independence and economic self-sufficiency.

Services may include the following: information and referral, transportation, crime prevention and legal assistance, outreach, and in-home services. All of these social services are available under Title III of the OAA of 1978. Coordination of social services is essential. A smoothly functioning network of services must be available to ensure that the individual receives exactly what is needed at the time it is needed.

Information and Referral.   Information and referral services are designed to provide older people and their families with information of the availability of the services that exist, as well as how to use them. It is well documented that those older persons with the greatest service needs are often also the least likely to have information concerning available services (Beattie, 1976). Of particular concern are those people of advanced age who are socially isolated, living alone, and on reduced incomes. Such people are probably more in need of existing services than anyone else. The two basic functions of information and referral are:

1   The linking of older people with the opportunities, services, and resources designed to help them meet their particular problems.

2   The collection and reporting of information about the needs of older people and the adequacy of resources available to them as aids to the evaluation, planning, coordination and resource development efforts required of state and local agencies. (Gelfand & Olsen, 1980)

Information and referral service systems thus link individuals to requested and/or needed services, and link services to each other. These systems identify and evaluate existing services; follow up on referrals to ascertain whether the client got the needed services and whether the service was useful; identify gaps in available services by keeping an accurate record of requests made; and make continuously updated resource files available to agencies needing service information, so that such information may be used as part of an ongoing planning process.

A casework approach is often utilized. Using this approach, the information and referral worker explores the individual's problem and the alternative services available. As needed, the older person is referred to a specific service (Gelfand & Olsen, 1980). Thus, when the individual calls, the basic purpose of the program is to provide information. Information and referral generally receives calls from elderly persons and/or their families who are faced with an immediate problem.

A case in point is described in this brief example:

Mrs. W., a mild-mannered and soft-spoken lady of seventy-one
years, called the information and referral service in her community.
She seemed rather shy about calling as she haltingly told the worker
she heard of the service through an advertisement on television.
Mrs. W. went on to say that since her husband died nine months
ago she hadn't been her old self. She mostly kept to herself because
she didn't want to burden anyone. However, three days ago she
had a fall and sprained her ankle. She thought the pain would
disappear in a day or so, but it hadn't. Mrs. W. became concerned
when the pain did not disappear and called her doctor. The doctor
advised Mrs. W. to arrange to come in to have the ankle checked as
soon as possible. The major difficulty was that Mrs. W. had no
transportation and did not think she would be able to manage on
the local public transportation system.

After getting the necessary factual information, and to
facilitate the referral, the worker arranged transportation for Mrs.
W. through Magic Carpet. (Magic Carpet is a para-transportation
system in the area that is designed for handicapped people; it
provides transportation to places of employment, medical facilities,
schools, shopping areas, religious services, and so forth.) The
worker called the service provider directly, giving information
about the client. Following this call, the worker called Mrs. W.,
advised her that the necessary contact had been made, and told her
when the transportation service would pick her up in the morning.

The afternoon of the next day, the worker called Mrs. W. to
inquire if she received the needed services. Mrs. W. said she had
and expressed relief that everything had gone off so well. In talking
to the client further, the worker discovered that Mrs. W.'s ankle
was expected to heal within the next few months and that the doctor
had equipped her with a cane to assist her in her recuperation.
Mrs. W. also expressed a need to be more active and around other
people her own age. The worker told Mrs. W. about the nearby
Multipurpose Senior Center and about the services they provided.
The worker arranged to make a home call to Mrs. W. to discuss
this information in more detail. The worker also felt that a home
call would enable her to make a more accurate assessment of Mrs.
W.'s situation and her need for services.

Information and referral services are crucial. Inadequate
assistance can result in people not getting the service they need or in a
"bouncing around" of the client from one agency to the next. These

kinds of non-service efforts must be avoided because they deter the very people who need the services from actually getting them. As Guttmann and Gueller (1982) point out,

> dependencies of old age, even for the most needy among the elderly, are often camouflaged by excuses for not using a given service despite the obvious need for it. Thus, for example, a number of elders with unmet needs in health care, transportation or housing refused to seek aid mainly to avoid a damage to their self-image. (p. 32)

Obviously, an inadequate approach to services can be detrimental to those elderly persons whose very lives depend on them.

It is essential that the service to which the individual is referred be accessible to him; that older people be aware of available services; and that they be assisted in making appropriate use of the service. Following up on clients receiving information from the information and referral program can indicate how effective the service response has been. This information is important for future service planning (Gelfand & Olsen, 1980).

Multipurpose Senior Centers

Multipurpose Senior Centers are the focal points for a variety of services to the older adult. Generally, these programs operate from a separate facility, and have their own boards of directors who establish policy. The executive director is directly responsible to the board for program operation. These centers are perceived as community facilities for the organization and provision of a wide range of services. Older individuals have an opportunity to become involved voluntarily in the variety of activities provided by the center.

The 1973 amendments inserted into the OAA the new title of Multipurpose Senior Centers, rather than Senior Centers. The programs and services provided by these centers are comprehensive in scope. Some centers can be identified according to whether they provide primarily services, activities, individual services and casework, or a combination of the three. Another way of categorizing centers is by their administrative structure. As Gelfand & Olsen (1980) point out:

The center administrative care may either be centralized (everything in a central facility), decentralized (located in several neighborhood facilities), combined (central location, with satellites), or a multiplicity of operations with some linkage. (p. 145)

There are two major ingredients for a successful senior center. The first is a recreation-education component, the second is the service component. Recreation-education activities include cards, table games and other games, bingo, bowling, parties and excursions. Services likely to be available through senior centers include information, counseling, and referral; housing and living arrangements and employment; health programs, including screening clinics for a variety of health problems; specialty services such as podiatry, dentistry, and hearing and speech programs; nutritional programs, that is, congregate meals and meals-on-wheels; legal and income counseling; day care services; transportation programs; in-home services; friendly visiting by center participants; service management; protective services; pre-retirement programs; and a variety of related volunteer opportunities. Participants coming to these centers have an opportunity to select their own activities, meet others, and find meaningful ways to use their leisure time.

INCOME–MAINTENANCE (SOCIAL SECURITY)

The Social Security Act was enacted on August 14, 1935. The law established two social insurance programs on a national scale to help meet the risks of old age and unemployment: a federal system of old-age retirement benefits and a federal-state system of unemployment insurance. Since that time, the Social Security program has undergone a number of significant changes. For instance, amendments in 1939 provided benefits for insured persons, dependents, and survivors under Old Age, Survivors, and Disability Insurance (OASDI). In 1965, amendments eased the eligibility requirements for people aged seventy-two and over who previously had not been eligible for benefits. A transitional insured status was introduced, under which people aged seventy-two who had no coverage at all, or less than three quarters of coverage, were made eligible for similar special payments under another transitional provision (*Social Security Programs in the United States,* 1973). In 1965, with the enactment of Medicare, a health program was added, Old Age, Survivors, Disability, and Health Insurance (OASDHI) (Crandall, 1980). OASDHI has been broadened over time to include many more persons.

The Social Security Act was a belated gesture, made in the light of the Depression. It was inadequate in some respects in meeting the nation's needs, for its benefits did not extend to the entire labor force. The adoption of the program it embodied was, nevertheless, a significant milestone in the economic and social progress of the United States. And in spite of inevitable diehard opposition to any such new departure, and much sound criticism of certain administrative shortcomings, there was never any question of the popular acceptance of social security (Dulles, 1959).

The original Social Security Act required that workers reach the age of sixty-five before any retirement benefits could be paid. This eligibility age was lowered to sixty-two for women in 1956, to sixty-two for men in 1961, to sixty for widows in 1965, and to sixty for widowers in 1972 (*Social Security Programs in the United States,* 1973). With the 1972 amendments, a worker's benefits were increased in those instances where retirement was delayed beyond age sixty-five.

The benefit structure has improved several times since 1950. In 1950, the average benefits were $45 a month. In 1960, a retired worker and his wife were paid an average of $124 a month; in 1970, $199 a month; and in 1976, $347 a month (U.S. Bureau of the Census, 1978). In 1981, payments were made to 20.5 million people sixty-five years and older.

Certain groups in the population (black men and other minorities) are disadvantaged under social security. Their age at retirement, and their inequitable benefits under the social security system, reflect their shorter life-expectancy and racial discrimination in the work force.

Although benefits are increasing in adequacy, the amount received will inevitably fall short of what many people will want or need in their retirement years (Gelfand & Olsen, 1980). Many older persons work in order to supplement their retirement checks. It is to the advantage of the older worker if his Social Security is supplemented by a private pension, but this is not always the case.

Supplemental Security Income (SSI)

The Social Security Act introduced three main programs. The first was social insurance, consisting of a federal old-age insurance system and of a federal-state system of unemployment compensation. The second program provided for public categorical assistance supported by federal grants-in-aid for three groups: the aged, the needy blind, and dependent children. A fourth category, aid to the permanently and totally disabled, was added in 1950 (Friedlander & Apte, 1980). The third program introduced was health and welfare services. This program provided for maternal and child health services, services for crippled children, child welfare services, vocational rehabilitation, and public health services.

The state-administered programs of aid to the aged, blind, and disabled were replaced in January, 1974, by a federally administered and funded program: Supplemental Security Income (SSI) (Weaver, 1977). This program guarantees every older American a certain income per month. If social security payments and other income add up to a figure below the specified amount, the individual will receive the difference through SSI (Crandall, 1980).

Supplemental Security Income payments totalled $8 billion in the fiscal year 1982, and were received by 4.2 million aged or disabled people. Many other older people are eligible for the program, but, for whatever reasons, do not participate in it.

Health-Related Programs (Medicare and Medicaid)

Prior to World War II, it was largely left to city and county governments or to private charities to care for the indigent aged, and generally to provide for those who could not meet the costs of physician and hospital services (Weaver, 1977). However, immediately following the war, serious attempts were made at the federal level to enact legislation for a national health insurance program. The medical establishment tenaciously fought these efforts, fearing that such a program—resulting in socialized medicine—would be a blow to the free enterprise system. President Truman characterized the American Medical Association (AMA) as ''the public's worst enemy in the efforts to redistribute medical care more equitably'' (Marmor, 1973, p. 14).

There were a number of objections to passing a national health insurance program. Among those objections were the following: (1) medical insurance was a ''give-away'' program which made no distinction between the deserving and the undeserving poor; (2) too many well-off Americans who did not need financial assistance in meeting their health needs would be helped; (3) utilization of health care services would increase dramatically and would exceed capacity; and (4) there would be excessive control of physicians, constituting a precedent for socialism in America (Marmor, 1973). As long as the objections remained, there was little hope of passing a national health insurance proposal.

Obviously, another strategy had to be developed. Instead of focusing on a national health insurance program that would benefit the general population, emphasis was placed on creating the kind of program that would benefit the elderly. The elderly were perceived as being both deserving and needy. Many older people were concerned about the high cost of medical care. A long-term major illness could wipe out a lifetime of savings. Something had to be done to allay the insecurity and the burden of medical costs with some type of national health insurance program. Those who approved of this new strategy waged a public war of sympathy for the aged and a private war of pressure politics from 1952 until 1965. Still the opponents were unyielding and continued to wage a tough battle. However, their efforts were finally defeated in 1965, when the Eighty-ninth Congress, in a single session, enacted legislation dealing with the health needs of the nation, including what must be regarded as the most important piece of social welfare legislation since the New Deal itself: the Medicare and Medicaid amendments to the Social Security Act. Medicare was enacted as Title XVIII of the Social Security Act amendments of 1965, Medicaid as Title XIX.

Medicare is a basic hospital insurance program for persons aged sixty-five and over, financed through a separate earnings tax and trust fund that provides protection against the costs of hospital and related care. The amendments also established a voluntary supplementary medical insurance plan financed through monthly premiums paid out of the current income of the elderly and a matching federal government contribution from general revenues. This insurance covers part of the cost of physicians' services and other related medical and health services not covered by the hospital plan

(*Social Security Program in the United States*, 1973). The 1972 amendments extended Medicare coverage to certain severely disabled persons under age sixty-five, including disabled workers, disabled widows and widowers, and childhood disability beneficiaries.

Under Medicare, a patient still pays a significant part of his medical bills. The total can run to about one-third of both hospitalization and medical costs. A major reason for this is that Medicare does not cover certain expenses of the ill elderly person. For instance, Medicare does not pay for such things as visiting nurses, home health aides, and homemakers. Because Medicare does not pay for many in-home services, older people are often forced into hospitals and nursing homes. In addition, Medicare does not cover prescriptions and prosthetic devices such as eyeglasses, canes, hearing aids, and false teeth (Hess & Markson, 1980).

Medicare is, in many ways, a remedial program. Emphasis is placed more on hospitalization (treating acute conditions) than it is on prevention (teaching people how to stay well). For instance, the basic package of benefits, Part A, is directed to hospital care. Although an extended benefit is provided, it is available only as a follow-up to an in-hospital stay. Need for other long-term institutional care is not met.

Although Medicare has eased much of the financial anxiety associated with chronic or prolonged illness in old age, the costs of health care are nevertheless exorbitant for most Medicare recipients. Medicare does not cover the first $160 of a hospital charge, the first $60 of most doctors' bills, or daily charges for lengthy stays in hospitals or skilled nursing facilities. Thus, the aged individual's higher expenditure for medical care—more than double that for younger persons—further restricts discretionary purchases.

There is supporting evidence from Medicare records to indicate that the individual sixty-five to sixty-nine years of age has requirements for both hospital care and physician services between two and three times greater than those of individuals forty to fifty-nine years of age. The elderly's need for services is even more disproportionate when compared to that of younger adults and children (Duffy, 1975).

Medicaid is a joint federal-state program that pays doctor, hospital, nursing home and other related health costs of the poor. The federal share ranges from 50 to 70 percent, with the highest proportion going to the states with the lowest per capita income. Within broad federal guidelines, states set rules for eligibility, covered services and payment rates. Eligible persons are entitled to have their bills paid, whatever the total cost. Spending rose more than 15 percent a year, primarily because of higher health care costs. The program cost more than $18 billion in the fiscal year 1981.

Medicaid necessarily affects many of the aged, but is intended for the health care of the general population. It generally requires no premiums and is correctly classed as a welfare program, with a means test in most cases. Medicaid supports long-term nursing home care and pays fixed amounts for specified benefits.

Cost of Health-Care for the Elderly.   In a single month, more than 500,000 persons aged sixty-five and over are admitted to hospitals and another 960,000 elderly persons are residents in 23,000 nursing homes or extended care facilities. Rising aggregate expenditures and rising unit costs—the cost of a physician's visit, the cost of hospital stay, the cost of a prescription—are a chief focus of health policy concern today.

Title XX

Title XX of the Social Security Act, passed in 1975, incorporated all the previous public welfare provisions of the Social Security Act—Title I, Old Age Assistance; Title IV, Aid to Families with Dependent Children (AFDC); Title X, Aid to the Permanently and Totally Disabled—into a single social service entity. A $2.5 billion annual ceiling was authorized at that time that gave considerable latitude to the states. The states had to describe what their programs were expected to achieve in terms of increasing the economic self-support and self-sufficiency of clients, preventing neglect and abuse, reducing inappropriate institutional care, and assuring referrals for institutional care when other forms of care were inappropriate (Murphy, 1977). The original $2.5 billion annual ceiling has since been raised; it reached $3.1 billion in fiscal year 1980-1981.

As a result of the funding limitations, social services in individual states must compete for monies from the same limited pool of Title XX funds. States that have declining populations are placed in a particularly difficult position since the amount of money allocated to any given state is based on population rather than on social service needs.

As Title XX was formulated, community-based preventive and rehabilitative services were identified as having priority. A second goal was the prevention and reduction of inappropriate institutional care. The final goal concerned referral to institutional services as appropriate. This ranking of goals clearly supported the concept of deinstitutionalization.

Under Title XX, eligibility is restricted to low-income families and recipients of AFDC, SSI, and Medicaid. Nevertheless, within the basic outlines of the federal law and the ceiling on appropriations, states have wide discretion as to which services will be provided and how they will be organized and delivered.

Where We Currently Stand.   The consolidation of services provisions into a new title recognized social services as a separate component of the social security system, rather than an adjunct to public assistance. Moreover, although the services programs still carry a "residual" or welfare connotation, federal law has extended eligibility to a population far broader than the recipient caseload. For instance, states can extend eligibility for services on a fee basis to individuals with incomes of up to 115 percent of state medians. Thus, the separation of SSI from the adult social services, and the enactment of Title XX, can be seen as significant steps toward the goal of a free-standing and universal system of social services to individuals and families, whether financially dependent or not.

Today, with emphasis on cost-cutting and less federal involvement in welfare, it is difficult to predict how social services will fare. The overall reduction in financing proposed by the Reagan administration will undoubtedly diminish social services.

COMMUNITY-BASED SERVICES FOR THE ELDERLY

Emphasis is now placed on keeping older people in the community for as long as possible. As an objective, this is not intended to mean that institutional care must be done away with. Instead, it conveys the idea that were more services available to older people in the community, they might remain in their own homes for a longer period of time.

The negative effects of institutionalization have been well documented, and so have the wishes of older people to remain in their own homes. Home is symbolic of security, mastery (in that the individual is in personal control), and familiarity. Butler and Lewis (1982) point out:

> One of the obvious advantages of home care is that most older people prefer it. Care at home offers better morale and security as long as proper services are given to provide comfort, support, and direct treatment of physical and emotional ills. (p. 256).

In order to determine which individuals can benefit from what services, a careful evaluation of the person and the nature of his home situation must be made. Any decision to provide treatment in the home is influenced by what the individual both needs and wants, his family situation, and the services available to him in the community (Butler & Lewis, 1977). A variety of skills are required if older people are to maintain themselves in the community. Some of the elderly are more proficient at these skills than others. Butler and Lewis (1977) identify the following as being essential for independent living: orientation to time, place, person; cooking and feeding oneself; bathing, dressing, grooming and toileting; continence; transferring from bed to chair; standing, walking, and climbing stairs; fire and accident security; ability to shop and manage money; ability to follow instructions—for example, those concerning medication; ability to seek assistance when needed; and social participation. Of other considerations, one of the most important relates to whom, if anyone, the individual is living with and relying upon. Some older people may be living with and relying upon a spouse, an adult child, some other relative, or significant other. Others may be living alone. Particularly in the latter situation, services must be available in the community if home care is to be provided.

Ward (1979) has developed a typology of four types of community-based services that are necessary for maintaining the dignity, independence, and integration of the elderly. They are: (1) preventive services, (2) treatment services, (3) protective and support services, and (4) linkage services.

Preventive Services

Prevention implies a stopping or keeping something from happening, as by taking some prior action. This means that certain programs are needed in the community to prevent the development of human problems. For instance, consumer education programs can be used to generate information about the importance of regular physical exercise. Making regular exercise an integral part of everyday life is now accepted as a prudent thing to do. Studies have documented that continued use and exercise of many physiological capacities prolong retention of those capacities (Freeman, 1965; Bierman & Hazzard, 1973; deVries, 1970, 1974).

The same is also true of diet and nutrition. Changes in one's diet toward a low to moderate caloric intake and an increase in minerals, proteins, and vitamins may have multiple benefits in prevention or modulation of a number of age-associated disorders (Weg, 1975). Proper diet and nutrition may also play a key role in preventing the loss of teeth and the periodontal disease that frequently plagues many elderly people.

In the design of environments for the elderly, sufficient attention must be paid to environmental barriers that prohibit or impede the effective use of physical and social space. For example, in designing housing for the elderly it is important that the number of steps that must be climbed be substantially reduced. In case of fire, the older person's chance of escape or getting to his neighbor's house for help is limited if he has a number of steps to negotiate.

In essence, a preventive perspective focuses on the impact of environmental systems on the development of human problems (Fischer, 1977). The basic aim of preventive intervention is to build stengths into individuals and systems as a means of avoiding problems. The environment must be responsive to the needs of the individual, particularly since the individual is in constant interaction with his environment.

Treatment Services

The kinds of programs that have so far been developed to deliver treatment to older people while they are still living in the community include outreach efforts, visiting nurses or physician assistance, and various outpatient programs and day hospitals.

Outreach services such as homemakers, home health aides, and friendly visiting[1] are needed to obtain health-related, demographic, and social information about certain community-based older people. Such information is invaluable to the psychiatrist, social worker, nurse, or paraprofessional who can put it to use in finding the most effective treatment strategies for meeting needs.

Some conceptualizations of treatment, such as Ward's (1979), focus primarily upon health aspects. However, the social component must also be included. For instance, when social workers visit an older person in the home, they may be providing an invaluable service that helps to alleviate stress around physical illness. A home visit helps the worker get a better understanding of how the older client is functioning in relation to physical or mental illness. Senior companions and friendly visitors can also provide a range of social services in relation to an illness.

Protective and Support Services

These services are intended to maintain and assist older people to continue relatively independent community living. Such programs include legal services; friendly visitor and telephone reassurance programs; consumer education; housekeeping and personal maintenance; meals; home repair; and fiscal management (Ward, 1979). Such services may have physical, psychological, or financial components. For example, income counseling is centered on helping people get the maximum use of their financial resources. As Atchley (1977) points out:

> Income counseling often includes such things as how to buy consumer goods at the lowest prices, how to take advantage of seasonal sales, the cost of credit buying, how to form consumer cooperatives, how to save on rent or get into low-rent housing, ways to save on auto insurance, ways to save on building repairs, and so on (p. 265).

It has only been in recent years that legal representation for the elderly poor has been available. In 1975 the Legal Services Cor-

[1] Friendly visitor programs are characterized by the training of volunteers to visit isolated individuals. Volunteers are trained to listen, and to know how to recognize problems or situations to which their supervisor can be alerted. They have been increasingly viewed as part of the helping team of professionals and paraprofessionals.

poration (LSC), authorized under federal legislation, came into being. The LSC services all individuals who fall below the federal
poverty level (Gelfand & Olsen, 1980). Legal issues about which
older people frequently need help relate to questions about social
security, SSI benefits, food stamp certification, Medicare claims, and
wills and probates.

Older people who are found to be neglected, abused, or at
high risk because of some deficiency or malevolent activity in their
situation, require protective services from the community and its
social agencies. Harbert and Ginsberg (1979) point out that "there
are times when due to physical changes, mental functioning, and extreme stress, older adults may not be able to make decisions about
their own well-being" (p. 223). Thus, protective services are initiated
in response to symptoms which seem to put the older person at risk
and in need of care or protection. Older people who are gravely
disabled as a result of mental disorder or chronic alcoholism, or people who are a danger to themselves or others because they are so
mentally impaired that they cannot provide for themselves, are prime
candidates for protective services.

Many groups are becoming aware of the problems confronting incapacitated older people. These include lawyers who are involved with questions of guardianship, trusts and commitment;
medical and social work professionals, who observe the effects of illness, neglect, and exploitation at close range; and labor unions, insurance companies, and the police (Follett, 1977).

Linkage Services

Information and referral services (discussed earlier in the
chapter) are the primary means for bridging the gap between people
with needs and appropriate service agencies (Atchley, 1977). In order
for the older person to take advantage of existing services, he must be
provided with information about what is available. A variety of agencies such as public health and welfare departments, religious
organizations, visiting nurse services, departments of vocational
rehabilitation, and multipurpose senior centers include information
and referral as part of their overall service delivery system.

Area Agencies on Aging are frequently responsible for providing and coordinating services for older persons within their areas.

The older person is encouraged to call the Area Agency on Aging for information about programs for the elderly. If, for instance, the older person needs details about a particular benefit program, wants to know how to sign up for Medicare or Medicaid, or would like to know which services he may receive, he is advised to call information and referral services.

INSTITUTIONAL CARE FOR THE ELDERLY[2]

Slightly over one million adults in the United States live in institutions, with about 80 percent in nursing homes and old-age homes and 20 percent in mental or chronic disease hospitals. For many of the chronically mentally and physically ill, institutional living has long become familiar through many years of hospital residence. For most, however, institutional living is an unfamiliar style that was adopted relatively late in life when, for a variety of reasons, they could no longer manage well as independent community dwellers.

Overall, among those sixty-five years of age and over, only 5 percent live in institutions, but the chances of institutionalization rise appreciably with age. Thus, only 2.1 percent of those sixty-five to seventy-four live in institutions, compared to 9.2 percent of those seventy-five and over. Hence, any significant discussion of aging and institutionalization is addressed particularly to the well-being of a small but substantial population of our older members, often the oldest segment.

Nursing homes are the major providers of long-term care for the chronically ill in America. These homes typically provide room, board, and various levels of nursing and medical care. In addition to caring for the chronically ill, some homes provide post-hospital rehabilitative care following acute illness. Seventy-five percent of nursing homes are proprietary.

Nursing homes are often confused with homes for the aged, which are mainly sectarian or fraternal non-profit institutions (Kosberg, 1977). Homes for the aged serve a more affluent clientele

[2] The author is indebted to Science Monographs, National Institute of Mental Health, from which most of this material comes. See Rosenfeld, A. H. *New Views on Older Lives.* Rockville, Maryland: U.S. Department of Health, Education, and Welfare, 1978, pp. 108–109.

and those who have community persons actively interested in them.

Long-term programs are more easily discussed than defined. One possible definition is made in terms of the type of facility involved; it states that long-term care is provided in nonprofit homes for the elderly, county homes, and proprietary nursing homes (Cohen, 1974). However, this definition leaves something to be desired because it does not describe in any way the range of services offered.

Another categorization sometimes used is one based on the level of payment which is received by the facility. Cohen (1974) points out that "most state programs of payment for care are arranged hierarchically with those facilities presumably furnishing highest skills receiving the highest payments" (p. 19). Thus, there are extended care facilities, skilled nursing homes, intermediate care facilities, and boarding care facilities.

The cost to the nation for institutional care of our elderly is in the billions of dollars annually. It is also rising, due both to inflation and an increased population receiving institutional services. Concern has arisen in many quarters that this large investment has not resulted in appreciable improvement in the quality of life for the older dependent population. Indeed, some would argue that it has merely reinforced the use of an unsatisfactory solution to the many complex problems faced by these individuals: failing physical and mental health and the absence of an adequate system of social supports.

Unquestionably, there are some individuals whose service needs could be met effectively outside of an institutional setting. In many instances, we are just beginning to discover who these people are and to provide other arrangements so that they can remain community dwellers. Nevertheless, there will always be some elderly people too sick and feeble to remain at home, even with the support of many helping services.

SERVICE PROVIDERS

Just as a range of services is needed to meet the needs of the aged, so a variety of trained personnel to provide services to older people is also a necessity. Thus, manpower to care for the needs of the elderly comes from a variety of disciplines, professions, and organizations.

Helping personnel include those who are professionally trained (for example, physicians, psychiatrists, social workers, nurses, and psychologists), paraprofessionals (for example, homemakers, home health aides, paramedics, and friendly visitors), and volunteers.

If there is to be an effective utilization of skills, those who work with the elderly—particularly professionals—must *want* to work with them. That is, they must be highly committed to work with them, and deeply interested in their well-being. Butler and Lewis (1977) write vividly about professional discrimination against the poor and the old. Many private psychiatrists prefer to work with young, verbal, well-educated, and successful patients. (Psychiatrists, like many other helping persons, like success stories.) Human service personnel, in general, perceive younger clients as more open to improvement by the treatment techniques at hand. Thus, older clients are often rejected because of their poor treatment potential.

This negative attitude among helping professionals is reflected in their interactions with older patients and their families. It is not unusual for doctors to tell patients and their families, ''Don't call me directly. I'll deal with your problems through the nurse'' (Butler & Lewis, 1977). The clinical picture that the doctor gets from the nurse may not be as accurate as it would be if he were making the diagnosis in person.

Nurses have provided services to the elderly in a variety of health care settings. Nurses perform health care functions in hospitals, nursing homes, in the person's own home, outpatient clinics, and community mental health settings.

Social workers have also provided services to older individuals, but not on as large a scale as those provided to younger people. It has only been since the late sixties and early to mid-seventies that accredited schools of social work began to offer courses in gerontology. Social work was slow to take advantage of the scientific knowledge about older life and to recognize the potential of older people for personal growth and successful adaptation. As a result, the profession set low priorities on the needs of the elderly (Morris, 1969).

Today that situation has changed considerably and most schools of social work are offering courses in gerontology at the graduate and undergraduate levels. Social workers provide counseling services to older people and their families in family service agencies, supervise semi-professional personnel engaged in service provision, and provide a variety of services in general and psychiatric hospitals. They work as consultants to nursing homes, as case management specialists in public welfare agencies particularly in protective services, as directors of meals-on-wheels programs, in program planning, and as administrators of Area Agencies on Aging. An increasing number of multipurpose senior centers are employing people with social work backgrounds to provide group services in their recreational, occupational and educational programs. Day care programs have been developing for the impaired elderly, and the need for social work expertise in this area is self-evident.

In order to raise the quality of life for current cohorts of elderly, and to enrich the lives of present and future cohorts, serious efforts must be made to recruit and train various levels of staff. Professional manpower in this area is unable to keep up with services demands. Paraprofessionals are being used to take up the slack. According to a citation made by Butler and Lewis (1979),

> Nonprofessionals are providing such therapeutic functions as individual counseling, activity group therapy, milieu therapy; they are doing case finding; they are playing screening roles of a nonclerical nature; they are helping people adjust to community life; they are providing special skills such as tutoring; they are promoting client self-help through involving clients in helping others with similar problems. (p. 150)

Although paraprofessionals do and should play key roles in the provision of services to the elderly, they are not there to take the place of professionals. They must be provided with adequate training and supervision, and there must be some uniform set of criteria by which to evaluate their performance and ensure proper treatment capabilities.

Although volunteer work should not be limited to older people, frequently they are the major resource for voluntary services. Older people often have time on their hands and many of them want to use their time in meaningful ways. Where volunteer efforts are needed, social workers can be hired by churches and various organizations to develop an agency-wide volunteer program. For those organizations that decide to use volunteers, there must be systematic and planned recruitment, training and placement of older persons as volunteers.

SUMMARY

Services and programs for the elderly must be viewed within the larger social context. The social context shapes and stipulates the range of options available. The emphasis today is on limited federal funding and involvement in social services programs.

The major influence on programs of older adults has been the Older Americans Act (OAA). The basic purpose of the Act was to help older persons by providing funds to the states for services, training, and research. All three of these activities are coordinated through the Administration on Aging (AOA). The AOA is an advocacy agency that channels funds to a number of communities and non-profit organizations to promote the development and coordination of services for older persons.

A number of programs developed to improve the quality of life for the elderly have been identified in this chapter. The reader must be cautioned, however, that the proliferation of aging-oriented programs requires very careful and comprehensive planning, better integration and coordination of a wide variety of services, effective casework supervision and viable advocacy efforts. Advocacy efforts should be focused on helping older people find their way through the bewildering maze of services and financial entitlements. As it now stands, there is far too much duplication, overlapping and fragmentation in the actual delivery of services. Increasing emphasis should be placed on forging links among the various services and creating methods of connecting them with those older persons they are designed to reach.

chapter 7

PRACTICE WITH INDIVIDUALS

The person who aspires to help others must have developed an awareness of who he is, his strengths, and any limitations in his own personality that impede his working effectively with others. Brill (1973) points out that man is endowed with both the need and the capacity to relate meaningfully to others of his own kind. To be free to relate effectively to others, the individual must be aware of his own imperfections and be willing to try to change.

Individuals develop certain attitudes and behavior that are strongly influenced by their culture. Human behavior is shaped by values. The child is born into a universe where right and wrong, good and bad, the true, the beautiful, and the false and the ugly are all defined for him. These values will be internalized by the individual to a very considerable extent.

A large part of the culture is transmitted directly to children by their parents. Besides parents, there are other influential agencies of socialization. Socialization is a lifelong process—one may be socialized, asocialized, and resocialized (Bensman & Rosenberg, 1976). Human beings are never perfectly socialized and so must constantly adapt or readapt to the constant changes.

Older people are often viewed as rigid, cranky, uncooperative, senile, and unwilling to change. Society has for centuries attributed negative stereotypes to growing old. Even though evidence contradicting these negative stereotypes exists (Beauvoir, 1972), they persist. Nevertheless, as people have more exposure to the realities of aging, some of the negative stereotypes will disappear. However, Keller and Hughston (1981) believe that these stereotypes serve a useful societal purpose and that as long as society has unemployment problems, tight promotion tracks, and difficulty in transferring power from the old to the young, we will continue to have negative stereotypes about the old.

The elderly face a variety of problems for which counseling can be useful. Children leave home and start families of their own, a transition with which older parents often have difficulty. Friends die. Spouses become ill or die. Chronic illnesses develop. Retirement may bring serious psychological dislocation. Financial maintenance problems are typical. Roles and expectations are in transition (Keller & Hughston, 1981). Given that older people have to face such serious problems, one wonders why so much effort has been devoted to childhood and adolescence—stages which add up to only about one-fourth of our life span.

An individual brings into old age the same characteristic ways of responding that he exhibited during earlier years. Difficulties that developed in childhood and were reinforced in adolescence, early adulthood, and middle age, often present themselves in the aged (Keller & Hughston, 1981).

The key concept in responding to change is adaptation. As people get older, there are a number of areas with which they must come to grips: loss of a spouse, energy and reserve capacity decline, loss of employment, and lowered expectations by others. Thus, adaptation to loss is one of the principal tasks facing individuals in later life. While losses can occur at any age, they are ubiquitous in old age.

THE SOCIAL WORKER'S FUNCTION

Social workers are called on to assist all manner of persons who present a broad range of human needs and problems. These human needs and problems cover the entire spectrum of life, from birth to death. As a result, social workers are found in a variety of settings including preschools, day care centers, child guidance clinics, juvenile detention facilities, residential treatment centers, outpatient clinics, hospitals, emergency rooms, adult day care centers, service management, protective services, nursing homes, and countless other places that exist to serve people. Social workers practice as planners, community organizers, service management specialists, directors of programs for the aged, and in health and welfare agencies. Those who work with the aging and the aged have as their goals the improvement of the quality of life and the maximization of their clients' independence and well-being.

Social work is by no means limited to the solution of problems that have already arisen. Many social workers are also engaged in efforts to prevent problems and human suffering. Others endeavor to enhance personal satisfaction and well-being, either through working directly with persons seeking to further their own self-development or through modifying social conditions that adversely affect certain individuals and groups (Briar & Miller, 1971).

What makes the social worker's function unique is the disciplined way he employs himself and his techniques. The social worker is not "just another person." He must be informed, disciplined, and skillful in carrying out his special role. Experience is another essential characteristic. His manifest objective is the improved social functioning of the client or patient. Whatever he does in helping will be dependent upon his ability to mobilize events to this end.

Social workers must acquire effective techniques and ways of working with people. Currently, there are several models of social work practice (Gilbert et al., 1980). There are the so-called traditional models of practice, which include the psychosocial approach, the problem-solving model, crisis intervention, behavior modification, and task-centered casework. Most of these approaches have been developed within the social work profession and are useful for working with people of different ages who are experiencing a variety of problems. There are also a number of other methods which have been developed outside of the profession and have been used primarily with the elderly. Such methods include reality orientation, milieu therapy, and ecological intervention.

Social work can be described as a multimethod practice based on borrowings from many disciplines. Flexibility in the selection and use of techniques and skills is highly important to students working with the elderly. However, students must learn how to make critical choices in the use of any theory or model.

Values and Purposes of Helping

The ultimate value that guides the social worker's practice is the belief that each individual should have opportunities to realize his potentialities for living in ways that are both personally satisfying and socially desirable (Northen, 1969). Human beings are constantly engaged in a search for personal adequacy, potential, or fulfillment. The basic striving of individuals for fulfillment has been called the "growth principle" because the effect is to move them continuously, and for as long as possible, toward health and growth (Combs et al., 1971).

Underlying this ultimate value of realization of potential or fulfillment are other specific ones that elaborate on its meanings

(Northen, 1969). Professional social workers are dedicated to service for the welfare of mankind; to the disciplined use of a recognized body of knowledge about human beings and their interactions; and to the mobilizing of community resources to promote the well-being of all without discrimination (*National Association of Social Workers,* 1963). It is these values that guide the worker as he undertakes his role of providing services to individuals, groups, and communities.

The purpose of social work, then, is to improve the objective and subjective functioning between individuals and their environment. "Objective" refers to readily visible physical and social functioning; "subjective" refers to feelings or states, including morale. To this end, the social worker does not seek to control the individual. Instead, he seeks to understand him in all his complexity as he interacts with his environment. Moreover, only if the worker understands to some extent his own motivation can he leave the client free to establish himself securely, first with the social worker and later with others (Hamilton, 1954).

Social workers must eschew conditions that humiliate and degrade the client and strive to bring about those conditions and opportunities that are essential to his fulfillment. This may be accomplished by working with the environment of the client or through the unique relationship established between the worker and client.

When working through the environment, the worker's efforts may be directed toward changing the environment so that it provides the client with greater freedom to explore and realize his maximum potential. The social worker may do this by helping a retired businessman find part-time employment as a consultant, or assisting an older woman to find meaningful volunteer work, or placing a chronically ill seventy-seven year old man in a nursing home.

The second way in which the worker can contribute to the improved functioning of the client is through the professional relationship. There is no question that the essence of professional social work is the effective use of oneself. Professional social workers must be thinking, problem-solving people; the primary tool with which they work is themselves. If social workers and other human services workers are to be successful in their work with clients, then they must combine knowledge and skill in a way that will facilitate growth and client betterment.

THE OLDER PERSON AS CLIENT

The older person is, by definition, an individual who has lived to be at least sixty-five years old. He has a life-time of experiences behind him. His sensory processes are probably not as sharp as they once were. His muscles are probably not as strong or as coordinated as they were when he was young. His bones have lost their calcium and have become brittle. They are quick to break when he falls. His once erect posture has become stooped and bent because the connective tissue (the substance that binds together and supports other tissues and organs) has hardened and contracted. His skin has become stiff and thin and prone to wrinkles. Fat has accumulated around the midsection. His once dark hair has turned gray and started to fall out.

There are also a number of changes that have taken place within the various organs of the body. For instance, Jones (1977) points out the following:

> Organs function more slowly. The heart pumps less efficiently. Blood doesn't move as fast as it should through the body, and the kidneys filter the blood more slowly. The lungs breathe in less and less oxygen. The bladder's capacity is similarly diminished. The brain shrinks, 100,000 of its cells die each day. The flow of hormones from the ovaries, testes, adrenals, and pituitary glands diminishes. Sludge accumulates in the cells, impairing their functioning. The yellow-black sludge called lipofuscin may make up 30 percent of the volume of our cells in old age. (pp. 25–26)

These biological or "natural" changes have been fully documented in the gerontology literature, but there are a number of culturally determined and circumstantial changes which also mark the passage of time (Schwartz, 1974). Social and interpersonal networks decrease as friends and loved ones die. Children leave home. Retirement becomes a reality for many, and this, in turn, brings about changes in social status and roles. With retirement, the older person's income may be reduced to half of what it was when he or she was employed. Naturally, reduced financial circumstances will have an impact on the individual's style of living. Many older persons in such circumstances reduce their contact with friends, and cut back considerably on a number of valued activities such as card games, attendance at social clubs, or various community activities. It is not difficult to understand how these various losses, regardless of how gradual, have important psychological consequences for the older person.

The reader should be aware by now that there are no characteristics that apply uniformly to old age or old people. Each older individual must be perceived as unique and different in his own right. However, he is also very much like other older people of his own sex, social class, race, and ethnicity.

The older person as potential client can be characterized in general terms as having a certain amount of wisdom gained through years of experience; as having lived through a span of history different from that of younger persons and with different socializing influences; and as wishing to maintain his own independence for as long as possible.

Older adults have an identity, a history, a long-range perspective on time. During their lives, they have probably passed through various transitions and role changes, learned certain coping skills and experienced and observed many things (Schlossbert et al., 1978). Most have already retired from their jobs and have made a relatively satisfactory adjustment to retirement. Many are grandparents or great-grandparents. Some have lost loved ones, have moved from their previous residences, and are beginning to experience declines in their physical health. Poor physical health may be restricting the mobility of some older people around the house and in the community.

Poor health may be compounded by serious financial problems. Many are lonely, apathetic, and depressed. Older people in these circumstances have little to look forward to unless they are provided with financial, social, and emotional support from family and friends or from more formal sources, such as social agencies.

People generally come for help because there is a problem in their intrapersonal system, or in their interpersonal relations, or in their environment. If the problem is in the intrapersonal system, there may be a personality problem. Some people are extremely withdrawn and shy; others are argumentative and hostile; some have set impossibly high standards for themselves and cannot understand why they continue to fail; other lack confidence and have poor self-images. Some older people are laden with anxiety and apprehension as they worry about what the future holds. Some of the elderly have experienced so many personal losses that depression pervades their whole personality. However, Butler (1963) reports that mild depression even among healthy aged respondents appears to be fairly common. When depression does exist, the worker should be supportive and demonstrate genuine concern, warmth, and caring for the client.

When there are problems in the older person's interpersonal relationships, the difficulty could be with a spouse, an adult child, other members of the family, an employer, the landlord, a neighbor, and so forth. When the older client presents problems such as these, it is the worker's responsibility to listen carefully and try to sort out what the difficulty is, what has brought it about, what can be done to alleviate it, what the client has tried to do about it and with what degree of success.

Many environments are characterized by economic deprivation, substandard housing, lack of available or accessible transportation, high crime, and poor health care systems. These, in turn, exert a considerable amount of distress and hardship on the lives of older people who experience them.

In such cases, the worker may find himself engaged in a variety of roles such as advocate for the client, locator of a resource, consultant/educator, and/or broker. Each of these roles encompasses a wide range of functions and services which are centered around the notion that it is the primary responsibility of the social worker to work in the older client's behalf.

Older persons who are experiencing psychosocial problems that are exacerbated by declining physical health frequently have limited resources to which to turn for help. Medical personnel are reluctant to refer older persons with even minor physical health problems for consultation, even when such referral would be appropriate (Hess & Markson, 1980). Other helping professionals prefer to work with younger clients for whom success in therapy appears to be more likely. But in addition to this, older people in general are hesitant to define any of their personal problems as suitable for professional help (Hess & Markson, 1980). Today's older people were socialized throughout life to be self-sufficient and independent (Harbert & Ginsberg, 1979), to rely on themselves, and to carry their own load. Moreover, many refuse to seek out services such as SSI and Medicaid, even when they are entitled to them, because they feel that to accept such services is like accepting charity or a ''handout.'' This is intolerable and unacceptable to them.

An Outreach Program was recently established in Y County, and an all-out effort was made to reach all low-income rural elderly sixty-five years of age and over. The agency sponsoring the program felt that large numbers of elderly people in the county were not part of the existing service system. Although names of older people had been obtained from various agencies in the county that customarily provided services to the elderly—the Red Cross, the Salvation Army, Social Security offices, and so on—the agency decided to locate the target population through a door-to-door canvass of the community.

Mrs. A., a seventy-two-year-old widow who lived alone in a small one-story house in a relatively isolated area, was one of the first persons to be reached. Prior to this face-to-face visit, the worker had contacted Mrs. A. by phone to inform her of the visit. Mrs. A. appeared to be receptive to the visit and expressed an interest in knowing about the various services in the community. The worker discovered that Mrs. A. had a lot of deep concerns on her mind. She told the worker that she was worried about financial security and frustrated by ill health. These two factors climaxed when she was hospitalized recently; she had reacted by becoming very depressed and withdrawn. She spent a lot of time explaining to the worker why her family was unable to help her, and why she, with a heart condition, needed help. Her anxiety over finances and her physical complaints were very much interdependent.

The worker discovered that Mrs. A's only daughter lived in another part of the state and was rarely able to visit. Nor could she provide financial help since she was struggling to make ends meet with her own family. Occasionally, a neighbor would come to look in on Mrs. A. to see if she was all right. A couple of other neighbors had been providing meals for Mrs. A. since her return home from the hospital, but not on an everyday basis. In assessing the situation, the worker felt that a number of services were needed including visiting nurse services, meals-on-wheels, transportation to the doctor's office, friendly visiting, telephone reassurance, and financial assistance in the form of SSI.

Mrs. A. was agreeable to all of the services, except SSI. Mrs. A. said that this ''smacked of welfare to her'' and that she didn't want any ''handouts.'' The worker informed Mrs. A. that she understood how she felt but told her that, like the other services, this was one for which she appeared to be eligible. The worker told Mrs. A. that SSI is a federal program designed to increase the income level of certain older and disabled people who qualify for assistance. In other words, she would be given a subsidy from public assistance funds to make up the difference between her social insurance benefits and the amount of money she needed for food, clothing, and shelter. Mrs. A. appeared to be relieved by this explanation and told the worker that if SSI would help her situation, then she would like to see if she qualified.

If social workers and other helping professionals are to meet the needs of older persons, special efforts must be made to reach them and explain to them what services are available and why. Often a clear statement can take the onus of "charity" out of a program, and help to make the older person feel more comfortable about using it. Sometimes a person's reluctance to use a service is based on his fear or misunderstanding of it. Once this has been explored and misunderstandings dealt with, the individual is free to accept or reject the service. However, the older person should be left with information (a card or phone number) on where to find the service in case of a later change of mind (Harbert & Ginsberg, 1979).

Many older people undergoing stress in their interpersonal or intrapersonal lives—including widows and widowers, retired persons trying to adapt to their new status, those undergoing the stress of relocation, and those isolated psychologically and geographically from family and friends—do not know where to turn for appropriate help. Some may be unwilling to admit that they need help and fail to take advantage of the services available. Others may have a negative image of outside help, seeing it not only as charity but as an admission of their inability to maintain independence. Still others are reluctant to ask for outside help because they are afraid they will not make themselves understood. In some cases, the service may be unavailable. Thus, many of the elderly must cope with stress on their own and make decisions in a vacuum, deprived of the kind of help that they desperately require.

A final point is that those who work with the elderly must rid themselves of negative and debilitating stereotypes about older life. Older people can still change; they continue to grow. Older people bring with them wisdom, the accumulation of experience, and the capability to cope with a variety of situations (Schlossberg et al., 1978).

THE PROFESSIONAL RELATIONSHIP

All helpers must, at one time or another, carry out some part of their functions in a face to face relationship with another person. The social work relationship is the medium through which direct work with clients takes place. It is through this medium that an exchange of thoughts, ideas, and feelings takes place.

When the client seeks help he is usually deeply troubled. If the client is an older person, he may recently have retired, his spouse may have died, an adult child may have moved without leaving a forwarding address, or he may be worried about not having enough money to live on. The older person may feel that he has little to look forward to. Whatever the reasons, the older individual is deeply troubled and needs someone he can trust. When people come for help, their need is not necessarily for information, despite the fact that this may be the tenor of their original request. Generally speaking, people in trouble want not so much to be told as to be understood (Combs et al., 1971). Therefore, emphasis must be placed on developing an effective relationship with the person who needs help. The following case illustrates this principle.

Mr. Richmond was hospitalized two weeks ago for cancer of the prostate which spread to his penis. As a result, the penis was surgically removed. Mr. Richmond is sixty-five years old; his wife is the same age. Mr. & Mrs. Richmond moved to the area from some distance about two years ago. They have no family members living in the local area. The Richmonds are financially independent and able to pay for all medical care required. The physician has recommended that the patient be discharged home, as he can manage there medically. However, Mr. Richmond wants to remain in the hospital. Mrs. Richmond is at the patient's bedside from 10:00 a.m. until 8:00 p.m. daily. Mrs. Richmond comes to the social worker frequently with small, seemingly unimportant requests. She doesn't want to be burdened with the physical care of her husband when he is discharged, and has refused to help with his care while hospitalized. Mrs. Richmond has been told everything regarding the patient's diagnosis, prognosis (he has a five-year life expectancy) and medical treatment. The social worker has not yet ascertained what the patient has been told regarding his diagnosis, prognosis, and medical treatment.

The couple has been married for twenty-five years and has a daughter living in another state. Prior to her husband's hospitalization, Mrs. Richmond never had to do anything on her own—according to her statement, her husband ran the household and took care of everything. Mr. Richmond refuses to talk to the social worker, or anyone else. He either pretends to be asleep or turns his head and body toward the wall whenever the social worker enters the room.

Most of the social worker's interventions have been with Mrs. Richmond. The worker recognizes that Mrs. Richmond is currently facing many anxieties due to her husband's rather sudden illness, which is forcing her out of a dependency role which she has filled throughout their marital relationship. Thus far, she has been unable to verbalize her anxieties directly and instead has come repeatedly to the worker with seemingly insignificant questions that in reality represent bids for structure, attention, and an opportunity to ventilate.

In thinking through the current situation and the many complexities it presents, the worker decides that as part of the treatment process, there are certain feeling areas that must be dealt with. She will encourage Mrs. Richmond to verbalize some of her unexpressed feelings of anger, anxiety, and guilt. These are most immediate and pressing for her and the least difficult to verbalize. The worker will demonstrate empathy. This is communicated by nonverbal means—nodding the head, moving close, maintaining direct eye contact, and so on—and also verbally: "I can understand how you feel." The worker will also offer interpretation: "That must make you very angry. . . ." or, "It must be difficult to see your husband this way. . . ." She will give approval and withhold any judgment regarding what the client has to say. She will let her cry if she needs to and be available when she needs to talk, keeping in mind that previous contacts regarding "silly little things" could be guided into the in-depth discussion that the client needs and is actually seeking. The worker will gather past history regarding Mrs. Richmond, Mr. Richmond, and their life together. As Mrs. Richmond relates these facts, there will be opportunities for her to open up and share feeling content as well.

As the worker provides a facilitative atmosphere for the

client, her relationship with Mrs. Richmond deepens. A feeling of rapport is established between the worker and Mrs. Richmond. Mrs. Richmond thanks the worker for allowing her to get so many things off her mind: "I really didn't know where to turn, and if it hadn't been for you, I wouldn't have known what to do."

In the relationship, the older person has an opportunity to be accepted, feel comfortable enough to permit personal disclosure, and receive positive feedback from the worker. The relationship should be developed in such a way that it permits the client the maximum expression of feelings, attitudes, and problems. In addition, the client's right to manage his own affairs must be respected. Some older clients may be unwilling to enter into a relationship with the worker because of their own past experiences. Combs et al. (1971) point out that:

> In the past, the efforts of the client in reaching out to others may have met with hostility, indifference, and misunderstanding. Consequently, he may become mistrustful of others and maintain an attitude of distance that will prohibit others from approaching him. (p. 154)

Some older people are ashamed to ask for help, particularly at this stage of their lives. Asking for help often brings on feelings of failure, some degree of helplessness, and feelings of dependency. A major task of the worker is to help the older client deal with a value system which implies that asking for help is a sign of weakness and inadequacy.

The goal of the helping professions is to produce some change in individuals. Even change in society can only be brought about in the final analysis through changes in individual people (Combs et al., 1971). Any helping person engaged in a face-to-face relationship with the client must learn to use himself optimally. The worker must engage in a balancing act—careful not to dominate the situation and thereby stifle growth; not so aloof that he appears distant and uninterested. The worker engaged in a helping relationship with the clients needs to develop skills in listening, empathy, self-discipline and patience (Combs et al., 1971). The relationship is dynamic, ongoing, and constantly changing because people change and grow. In addition, new feelings and attitudes are constantly being integrated and fed into such a relationship, which must in turn be able to encompass these changes if it is to continue to exist (Brill, 1973).

Acceptance

A basic ingredient of the casework relationship is acceptance. Acceptance implies an attitude of interest, understanding, concern, and the ability to respond to the client in a positive way. From the experience of acceptance should come freedom to be oneself—to express one's fears, angers, joy, and rage; to grow, develop and change —without concern that so doing will jeopardize the relationship (Brill, 1973). Acceptance is not a wishy-washy attitude that goes from one extreme to another depending on the "rightness" or "wrongness" of the client's behavior. Rather, it means an ongoing feeling without reservations, without evaluations (Rogers, 1979).

> Acceptance also involves the recognition of the uniqueness of the individual as a person who possesses the need and right to participate in matters relating to his own welfare. The extent to which the person is able to exercise this need varies among individuals, but the need is there. (Brill, 1973, p. 48)

The worker must perceive each older person as different from every other older person and recognize his own values in relation to aging and the aged. There must be an ongoing attitude of positive understanding toward the older person as client.

Self-Determination

Older people have a tenacious desire for independence; they must be closely involved in any decision-making about themselves (Butler & Lewis, 1977). In fact, the more the older person can make decisions about his own life the better, and the less the worker assumes or tries to take over these responsibilities the better.

The worker's behavior implements the belief that the client has the right and capacity to direct his own life. He works with the client in problem-solving, and communicates confidence in the client's ability to achieve his own solution in his own way (Kadushin, 1972). Clients are aware of when they are free to work on their own problems in their own way. They often express the feeling, "She made me feel as though my solution was a good one"; "He didn't seem to think it was necessary for me to accept his advice or opinion about the matter''; ''I felt free to disagree with her without being afraid that it would interfere with how she felt about me.''

The couple of case vignettes below are followed by a series of possible responses from the social worker, some illustrating an attitude respecting self-determination and some illustrating an inappropriate violation of this approach.

Client: female, fifty-one, white, school teacher, family service agency.

CLIENT: I'm just not certain about this. My mother just hasn't been herself lately. She wanders around the neighborhood all the time and can't find her way back. The last time she got lost, a policeman brought her back and suggested if she keeps this up, maybe I should put her in a nursing home. I hate to think about doing that, but maybe that would be the best thing for her. I don't know.

Appropriate Worker Responses:
1   You're puzzled about what to do.
2   It's hard to know what would be best.
3   It's particularly hard on you.

Inappropriate Worker Responses:
1   Well, if you'd take the policeman's advice the problem would be solved.
2   My own feeling is that you'd have more peace of mind if she were in a nursing home.
3   A nursing home wouldn't be so bad for your mother.

Client: female, sixty-six, part-time stenographer, medical social work agency.

CLIENT: I know I should have this operation, but I would rather not talk about it or even think about it.

Appropriate Worker Responses:
1   It's hard to talk about.
2   Thinking about it makes you anxious.

> 3   Okay, perhaps there is something else you would rather talk about.
>
> *Inappropriate Worker Responses:*
> 1   But I was supposed to discuss this with you.
> 2   Not talking about it won't make the problem disappear.
> 3   Well, it has to be discussed sooner or later, so we might as well do it now.

In practice, self-determination cannot necessarily be applied as an absolute concept. That is, there are certain limits imposed on all persons. No one can do exactly as he wants. Society would never operate efficiently, nor for the good of all, if everyone did so.

In the case of the older person, illnesses (physical and/or mental) may invalidate the capacity to make choices. This capacity is also invalidated in the case of legal commitment, when the older person is a danger to himself or to others, or is in clear and present need of immediate care or treatment (Butler & Lewis, 1977). Nevertheless, where possible, the worker must strive to increase the older person's capacity for self-direction, to provide him with viable options from which to make choices, and to respect his ability to think things through himself. To illustrate this point consider the case situation of Mr. and Mrs. Hunt.

> Mr. and Mrs. Hunt are in their eighties. Several months ago, Mrs. Hunt, who has a history of poor health, was hospitalized with complaints of severe pain, some mental confusion, and weight loss. She was found to have metastatic cancer. After several weeks of hospitalization, in which it was tried at least to get her stabilized, she became ready for discharge. The physician recommended nursing-home placement.
>
> Mrs. Hunt is on a catheter and requires tube feeding. She is not alert mentally and is for all practical purposes comatose. She is completely bedridden. Her skin is breaking down and prevention of bedsores is nearly impossible. She requires full nursing care. As Mr. Hunt is himself an elderly, rather frail man, it is not felt that he could possibly care for his wife at home. Thus, nursing home placement seems the obvious and most humane plan for all concerned.

Mr. Hunt, however, absolutely refuses nursing home placement. He and his wife have been together for almost sixty years, and he refuses to "desert" her now. He insists on taking her home, where he will care for her in their one-bedroom apartment. He feels that this is what his wife would want and he won't consider any other options. He seems fully alert mentally, though very unrealistic in his plans. It is obvious that Mrs. Hunt's death will be hastened by this plan, and her condition could deteriorate in a most unpleasant manner. A certain amount of physical strength and exertion will be required to provide the physical care needed. The physicians and floor staff feel that Mr. Hunt couldn't even lift his wife.

The worker is asked to see Mr. Hunt and try to find out if he understands the realities of his situation. The worker is prepared to offer him at least outpatient nursing services if he won't accept anything else, but has been warned by the floor staff that he won't allow any strangers into the house. He maintains, "I will provide personally all the care my wife needs." The worker must decide on a realistic approach.

According to the worker's impressions, it is obvious that Mr. Hunt has strong feelings about allowing out-patient nursing home services for his wife. He feels responsible for her and is afraid to desert her now. Part of Mr. Hunt might wish he could accept help in meeting his wife's needs, but the other part rejects this as letting her down. Mr. Hunt needs to feel that even in this situation he is still able to provide adequate care for his wife and he is afraid to trust anyone else to do that for him. By taking care of his wife himself, Mr. Hunt is avoiding unacceptable feelings of guilt, anger and rejection of his wife. If anything were to happen to her while she was in someone else's hands, this would probably kill him. However, the reality of trying to care for his wife alone, particularly with her serious illness and his own fragile health, poses problems.

This situation is potentially one for protective services. Protective services seek to protect the older person from physical, emotional, or mental harm (whether to himself or to others) by stabilizing his situation in order to maintain him in the least restrictive setting, or by providing institutional care where needed.

Before offering any kind of services, the worker feels that it is essential to establish a meaningful relationship with Mr. Hunt. She is able to do this by respecting his wishes to provide care for his wife himself. He tells the worker that this means a lot to him because he had promised to love and to cherish his wife in sickness and in health for the rest of his life. He says that he thinks he has the strength to do it, and wants to at least give it a try. The worker discusses with Mr. Hunt his plans for feeding, bathing, and dressing his wife, and so forth. Mr. Hunt informs the worker that he has thought about all these things and that they present no problems for him.

The worker's evaluation and assessment of the situation is that Mr. Hunt, while frail, is still competent, and that he is able to carry out normal everyday personal functions without help from others. Besides, he is still able to make decisions on his own and to take independent action in behalf of himself and his wife. Nevertheless, the worker advises Mr. Hunt to call her if anything changes in his situation. She tells him that she will keep in close contact with him by making home calls on a regular basis, and gives him her card with her name, phone number, and place of work on it.

Once a week, the worker telephones the Hunts and once a week makes a home call to see how the situation is progressing. At the end of three weeks, Mr. Hunt makes his first call to the worker and requests that she make a home call to see him and his wife. Mr. Hunt appears exhausted. His wife had had a couple of bad nights and he has gotten little sleep. He wonders how long he can keep this up, especially since he doesn't feel too well himself. The worker informs him that there are services such as visiting nurses, homemaker, meals-on-wheels, and transportation that could be useful to him. Mr. Hunt expresses relief at the thought of getting some help, especially since he has tried himself and found it to be too much for him.

Protective services pose a dilemma for social workers, who are often called on to decide if an older person is a risk to himself or to others. Protective-service measures remove many of the rights an individual has to make his or her own decisions. In those instances in which an older person can make decisions for himself, social workers have a corresponding duty to respect that right, recognize that need, and activate that potential for self-direction by helping the client to use the available and appropriate services of the community.

In the case of the Hunts, the worker was able to help the client see his problem clearly and in perspective, to establish a relationship in which the client could grow and work out his own problem, and to acquaint him with the pertinent resources that could be brought into the home. A couple such as the Hunts could obviously benefit from many forms of assistance, including medical and social services.

Communication

Another important element in interpersonal helping, and one that is essential to the relationship, is communication. Communication constitutes the basis of social interaction. Hertzler (1965) points out that without communication there are no interstimulations between people; no common meanings and concepts; no action which provides information, instruction, and provocative imitations. In a sense then, communication is the giving or exchanging of verbal and nonverbal information.

It has been suggested that in some helping situations the words used between the person to be helped and the helper may be of no consequence whatever. The fact of communication, of engaging in human interaction with another person, may itself be the important facet of the helping relationship (Combs et al., 1971).

Verbal and Nonverbal Cues. The messages that are sent through the communication channels are roughly divided into verbal and nonverbal messages. Verbal messages tell the social worker a great deal about the client. The client's choice of words can reveal his socioeconomic status, his ethnic group, his religious orientation, his feelings about himself, and his feelings about other people. The language of a well-read and/or highly educated elderly individual reflects the social and economic setting to which he has been exposed.

Ethnic group language is frequently intertwined with the speech mannerisms characteristic of a particular socioeconomic status. Such words as "macho," "chutzpah," and "soul food" are now included in the dictionary. However, Hispanics, Jews, and blacks originated these words (Schulman, 1974). People from different racial and ethnic groups have their own vocabulary which is not only similar for the group, but is also individualized. This vocabulary is rich in meaning for them and unless the worker understands the meaning of the words used, then little is communicated.

Nonverbal messages are more various than verbal messages; they include the language of the body, gestural language, facial language, and the language of objects. Nonverbal cues are a part of behavior many people neglect, perhaps because they are so obvious.

The importance of bodily communications is shown by the frequency with which expressions referring to the body are used metaphorically. A number of terms in common use describe behavior and feelings in bodily terms. Such terms include: chin up, grit your teeth, pain in the neck, sink your teeth into, tight-fisted, knuckle under, choke up, shrug it off, itching to do it. We talk of "tight-lipped," to indicate secrecy; a "stiff upper lip" suggests fortitude; and we associate dejection with being "down in the mouth" (Kadushin, 1972).

Nonverbal cues often come from the person's body movements. The comfortable client is physically relaxed and seated with a natural posture. Some clients who are listening closely cross their legs; other keep their feet flat on the ground. Leaning slightly forward and moving the body slowly backward and then toward the worker accents certain points that the worker makes and reassures the worker of the client's attentiveness.

Gestural language includes pantomimic and nonpantomimic gestures of the hands and fingers (Schulman, 1974). Pantomimic gestures are actions that substitute gestures for words. The game of charades is an example. Nonpantomimic gestures are actions that accompany words and modify or regulate the meaning of words. Some pantomime is formal and has specific meanings that are known to most people in a particular culture—waving good-bye, making two wavy lines in the air to demonstrate the form of a well-proportioned female, putting one's thumb to the nose with the remainder of the fingers extended to signify extreme distaste and annoyance, and so on.

The wrinkled brow, the smile, the blink of the eyes, and the gaze or stare of the eyes all regulate, communicate, and express ideas and feelings. Eye contact may be so intense that it annoys one; eye movement may start or stop a conversation. Wearing sunglasses makes the individual less available to others; this makes the removal of sunglasses a significant sign of becoming available. While hands may be hidden in one's pocket, placed on one's lap, or sat upon, and legs and feet may be concealed behind a desk, the face is constantly exposed. Unless hidden behind a hand or mask, the face cannot conceal the feelings communicated.

Personal adornments such as clothes, hairstyle, makeup,

jewelry, and tattoos are expressive extensions of the self. Home furnishings also have this significance. It is not unusual for older people to have an elaborate collection of objects on display in their home. For instance, on her initial visit to the home of a seventy-four-year-old widower, the worker observed his train collection. There were replicas of trains from the oldest to the most recent. While visiting a sixty-nine-year-old single woman, the worker was struck by the many varieties of plants the client had. Each plant became a conversation piece, as the client fondly shared with the worker what was involved in their care. Another elderly client had an extensive record collection that included many of the early classics.

Much of what transpires between caseworker and client will be dependent upon the nonverbal aspects of the relationship in which they are engaged. Artifacts, clothing, and the body itself are rich sources of communication. Workers must become sensitive to nonverbal cues. Nonverbal communication has significance for the interview in that it provides additional content regarding the relationship (Kadushin, 1972). Nonverbal factors determine in large measure the nature and effect of what is communicated in the helping dialogue (Combs, et al., 1971).

Listening

What mother has not scolded a disobedient child with the words, ''I thought I told you not to do that. Didn't you hear what I said?'' It has been said that an individual may hear, but he does not listen.

Effective listening is built on the cooperation of both the speaker and the listener in advancing toward better understanding (Schulman, 1974). To be an efficient listener it is necessary for the worker to be actively engaged in receiving, recording, and getting the meaning of the client's message. Good listening requires following carefully both what is said overtly and the latent undertones. It requires being expectantly attentive and receptive. Listening is a selective process in that we pick out from the many stimuli surrounding us those most fitted to our needs and purposes (Keltner, 1973). The task of the worker, then, is to observe and to record in his memory thousands of little signs and to remain aware of their delicate effects upon him (Reik, 1971).

Schulman (1974) stresses that "competent listening presupposes a receptive state in which the client's glances, muscular twitchings, gestures, and other bodily reactions as well as his tone of voice, his pauses, and his words are noted" (p. 121). In this state the worker is in tune to what the client is saying. There are occasions on which the worker may anticipate what a client is going to say, and in reality may miss what is actually said. Consider the following example.

Client: male, seventy, black, retired steel worker, medical social work agency.

MR. B.: Since my wife hasn't been feeling well lately, I'm reluctant to leave the house even for a short time. You see I worry about her even though—

WORKER (interrupting): I can understand your concern Mr. B, especially since she's all alone and you've no way of knowing how she's doing when you're away from home.

MR. B.: What I was going to say is that we recently took in a boarder—a very nice woman—who is willing to sit with my wife whenever I have to leave the house.

A review of the worker's retrospective comments indicated that he "felt ashamed about interrupting Mr. B." The worker went on to say, "I had anticipated that Mr. B. would say one thing and instead he said something else. I can see how such a remark might have negative effects on the client because he must sense that I am not being totally attentive to him."

According to Schulman (1974), the empathic listener develops large eyes, big ears, a small mouth, and positive actions that reveal his interest and acceptance of the client" (p. 121). Listening is the bridge between hearing and understanding. The worker's choice of words tells the client that he is listening to what the client is saying.

SUMMARY

If the social worker is to help others attain their maximum potential, he must first develop those personal qualities that are essential in helping people to utilize their own strengths and resources.

Older people, like those who are younger, are still able to grow and develop. By the time they reach old age, many people experience a number of successive losses for which treatment can be useful. Social workers can assist people in maximizing their independence and well-being.

Older people are reluctant to seek help for a number of reasons, one of which is that they have been socialized throughout life to be self-sufficient and independent. To accept help is akin to accepting a handout. Social workers may have to make special efforts to reach the elderly to inform them of services that are available as well as to explain why they are entitled to such services.

The social work relationship is the medium through which direct work with the client takes place. When the older client seeks help, he is not so much looking for advice as wanting to be understood. It is through the relationship that the older person has an opportunity to be accepted, respected, and understood. It is also through the relationship that growth takes place, as the worker strives to increase the older person's capacity for self-direction.

Communication is an essential element in the relationship. Communication gives meaning to interpersonal interactions. The messages that are sent through the communications channels include both verbal and nonverbal ones. Effective listening is a basic element of interpersonal exchange.

chapter 8

GOALS AND TREATMENT PLANNING WITH INDIVIDUALS

CONTENT AND FOCUS OF THE INITIAL INTERVIEW

The central concern of the social worker in the initial interview will be the client's presenting problem. The client who comes for help must be given the opportunity to begin with what seems most salient to him. The social worker must provide a situation in which the client feels free to talk to another human being, and be sure of that other person's interest, attention and concern (Dewald, 1964). Garrett points out that "sometimes the client can quickly be put at ease by letting him state his purpose in coming, sometimes by giving him a brief account of why he was asked to come" (1966, p. 36). Whichever approach is used, it is essential that the client be encouraged to talk and the worker to actively listen. While the worker is listening he must also make observations about the client's nonverbal behavior, thereby expanding his understanding of the client.

The primary purpose of the helping or therapeutic interview is to obtain an understanding of the problem, of the situation, and of the client who has come for help (Garrett, 1966). Much of what transpires between the client and worker will depend on what the agency is empowered to give, that is, on the agency's functions. The worker will listen to his client's statement of his need. Need exerts a selective effect on what is perceived. Thus what is communicated to the worker by the client will somehow be related to the client's need or current problem(s). The worker will then guide the interview along those channels that seem most appropriate to the circumstances of the case (Garrett, 1966).

In listening for content, the worker must understand the feelings that are attached to the statements. Subjective feelings are just as important as the objective facts on which they are based. Often feeling tones are indicative of a serious objective situation. The worker must, therefore, understand the person who is troubled and the meaning the situation or problem has for him.

Obtaining Necessary Information

Hollis (1972), stresses the importance of understanding the situation in order to help the person. She emphasizes that the worker must secure the information pertinent to treatment as early as possible. This means that the worker must collect pertinent data, test it, analyze it, and eventually arrive at conclusions. Information-gathering is, however, only part of the therapeutic process. The worker is always trying to put the client at ease, alleviate his distress, and maintain a relationship of trust.

Factual information may be derived from a variety of sources. Many agencies have their own forms in which they request such information as age, working status and occupation, educational status, marital and living situation, referral source, and previous agency contact. This information may provide useful clues as to what is troubling the client. For instance, knowledge about the client's living situation may give useful information about sources of support, or lack of them, as well as about the stress of daily living. As an example, take the case of Mrs. Penn.

Mrs. Penn's responses to the questions on the form indicated that she lived alone, was not in close physical contact with any relatives because none lived in her state, and that she rarely saw her friends and neighbors. The initial interview fleshed out this information.

Mrs. Penn, a seventy-four-year-old retired schoolteacher, had been living with her twin sister for the past ten years. A year ago, Mrs. Penn's sister died. Up until that time, the twins had been very close and active in a variety of social clubs. Since the sister's death, Mrs. Penn had severely reduced her activities and had appeared apathetic and listless. Her neighbors had become concerned, and through their gentle persuasion encouraged her to see a therapist. Mrs. Penn was very reluctant to seek treatment of any kind and felt distrustful of outside help.

In this case of an older person living alone with minimal contact with family, friends, neighbors, the worker was interested in obtaining as much information as possible about her living situation and how she managed on a day to day basis.

It is also useful to gather information about the client's family, social, and medical background, and previous agency contacts (Zaro et al., 1977). Such background information is essential to assessing the severity of the problems, evaluating the client's coping skills, and understanding how the problems came about. The information collected relates to problems that affect the individual, his immediate social situation, and the interaction between the two.

The primary souce of information is the client himself. However, in the case of an elderly client with debilitating physical and mental problems, an adult child may be the primary source of information. The following is a summary of a social worker's interview with a client's oldest daughter and a first cousin.

The seventy-five-year-old patient is described by her daughter and cousin as being "slow." She has led a very sheltered life with her family and has had little formal education, but whether she has any actual organic retardation is unknown. She is a very passive, dependent person, but her life-situation has undoubtedly been a factor which has contributed to this. She is very childlike in her affect. She is open, friendly and at times easily frightened and upset. She is a widow, but evidently knows little about her economic situation or whether she receives social security benefits.

It is my impression that she will not be subject to the emotional stress that normally results from having had major surgery and intractable illness because she is unaware of the implications of her prognosis. (I was informed by her physician that she is terminally ill. Her exact prognosis in terms of time left to live is not known.) It is my feeling that at this time, or unless she indicates a desire to know, no useful purpose will be served in relaying this information to her.

The patient's needs, aside from her physical care, will predominantly be in the area of support and reassurance. Since she is such a dependent person, she has not developed the internal strengths which serve to counteract the episodes of depression, frustration, and emotional upset which she experiences.

Ongoing treatment for this patient should include continued supportive counseling with her and her family. Her physician has advised that visiting nurse services are indicated on a daily basis for her during the first week after her discharge; therefore, discharge planning for this will be necessary. An effort to have the patient and her family contacted by a friendly visitor would be useful, and an investigation into the patient's possible eligibility for social security benefits is also indicated.

Whenever possible information should be obtained from the client himself. The client knows how he feels, what he is concerned about, what he has done to try to alleviate his situation and the results of these efforts, that he wants relief from his discomfort, and how he would like to go about getting it (Brill, 1973).

Assessment of information is an ongoing process. The worker is constantly evaluating the data, trying to discern how the pieces of information fit together. He is cognizant of the client's attitudes and feelings, his strengths and his weaknesses, the support systems in his environment, the problems that are currently troubling him, the client's potential to deal with the situation, and the community resources that can be utilized in meeting need.

Diagnosis or Assessment

The client has presented herself to the worker, has related her concerns to him and has tried to respond to the range of questions asked. Now she waits eagerly for the worker's opinions about her problems and for some decision about treatment. The client wants to know how the worker perceives her problems, what the goals of treatment will be, what steps may be involved in the treatment process, and what potential risks and gains are involved. In other words, the client requires some feedback from the worker.

The basic task of the worker at this point is to think through the facts that the client has presented in order to offer the client his professional opinion. This process in social work has been labeled diagnosis or assessment.

In the illustration below, the worker presents a descriptive diagnostic impression to the seventy-year-old client.

Mrs. Lake, you have suffered a brief but severe emotional reaction during which you were very confused and lost contact with reality. However, you quickly began to improve, and I feel you are now functioning much more effectively. There is every reason to believe that your functioning will return to its previous level.

There is one form of diagnosis about which there is considerable difference of opinion among workers—that is, clinical diagnosis. Hollis (1977) points out that

many workers have become disenchanted with this form of diagnosis
because of the difficulty both psychiatrists and social workers have found in
arriving at agreement on specific diagnoses and of misuse of this form of
diagnosis through carelessness and stereotyping. (p. 1304)

Turner (1978) states that diagnosis applied in this manner is a
derogatory way of classifying human behavior and of putting clients
into categories.

   Nonetheless, it is the worker's responsibility to decide what the
client needs and wants, what are the strengths and limitations of the
person and the situation, what resources are available, and what
knowledge can be brought to this situation from other similar or dis-
similar experiences (Turner, 1978). The worker is thus collecting
relevant information—that is, the amount of information necessary
to reach the conclusion demanded by the situation (Turner, 1978)—
and testing and analyzing it so as to arrive at certain conclusions.

   Diagnosis need not be a time-consuming undertaking. The
whole process may be completed in a single interview. This is not to
say that the worker ignores other questions the client may ask, questions that are seemingly unrelated to the current difficulty. However,
it does mean that the worker is constantly assessing what he is learning and observing so as to arrive at a better understanding of the
situation. That is, the worker is carefully thinking through the facts
and making decisions about the most appropriate interventions
needed to help the client to modify either his situation or his feelings
and actions or to change his environment through the worker's interventions on his behalf (Hollis, 1977).

   Although the primary source of data is the client himself,
other information may come from significant people who are a part of
his social network. These include both those with whom he has personal relationships, such as family and friends, and those within the
more extended systems of which he is a part (Brill, 1973) such as
social club, church, employment and volunteer programs, and so on.
To the extent possible, the client has a right to know what information is needed and which person(s) might be contacted in providing
information. For instance, medical information is always essential in
the case of the elderly; contacts with other agencies such as Social
Security and multipurpose senior centers may also have to be made.

An assessment of the older person's social environment is essential. Such an assessment provides information about losses of intimate persons, income, independence, and social roles; the attitudes, feelings, and behaviors associated with those losses; and an understanding of how the individual has adjusted to the changes. In addition, the worker needs to gather information about family structure, housing, work or retirement, friendship patterns, income, social roles, leisure activities and interests. Butler & Lewis (1982) point out the following:

> Interviews with the older person and members of his family can provide valuable insight into the contribution of social factors to the patient's problem and into potential assets that can aid and support treatment. An assessment should include the amount and quality of love and affection that exists between the family and the older person. (p. 236)

Race and ethnicity cannot be overlooked during the assessment process. Elderly black clients, for example, have experienced a lifetime of discriminatory practices and prejudices that are bound to affect their decision to accept help from a white worker. The structure and cultural patterns of the older black client, his social class, value system, and style of life often differ markedly from the social worker's own. Further, older black clients bring to the therapeutic relationship a history of humiliating and abrasive contacts with whites, and this past is not easily shrugged off at the consultation room door. Much of this also applies to people of other ethnic origins. Many of the elderly are immigrants, who, when they came to this country, were treated like second-class citizens. Social workers must develop a healthy respect for, and understanding of, cultural and ethnic pluralism.

As the worker gathers information he is constantly assessing the client's strengths and weaknesses, interrelationships in the family, the family's feelings and attitudes toward the client, the availability of help from significant others, and the causes of the current situation. Even though primary emphasis is on current interacting forces, treatment of interpersonal disturbances can be strengthened by a recognition of the salient antecedents of current behavior (Hollis, 1977). Knowledge of prior events can be used to understand and to change the present.

The worker is engaged in a diagnostic process throughout his contact with the client. Diagnosis is always tentative and subject to change as new aspects of the client's situation emerge, but at every point it guides the worker in the selection of what help to offer the client (Hollis, 1977).

Hollis (1972) stresses that

> The knowledge made available by the psychological study and the diagnostic assessment is used in two ways. First, it supplies the basis for major decisions concerning the general direction of treatment and for details of its early stages. Second, it provides a fund of information that the worker will continue to draw on in treatment planning and treatment throughout his whole association with the client. (p. 283)

In thinking about the best way to help a client, the worker must first envisage tentative goals of treatment and then assess the technical means by which the client can be helped to reach them (Hollis, 1972).

SETTING OF GOALS

Out of the diagnostic process should come a definition of the problem about which the client is most concerned; the difficulty with which the client wants immediate help. It is the problem as the client perceives it, feels it, experiences it, that must first be worked on. Sometimes there is variance between what the client sees as the problem and what the worker sees. For instance:

Miss Sims, age sixty, had been taking care of her mother, age eighty-six, prior to the latter's hospitalization for chronic heart trouble. The mother is about to be released from the hospital and returned to the daughter's second-story apartment. Since her mother's hospitalization, Miss Sims has found employment as a secretary for a law firm. She likes her job a great deal and is torn between keeping it or giving it up to take care of her ailing mother. The worker believes the immediate need is to find a home health aide to come into the home while Miss Sims works. Miss Sims has

become increasingly concerned about the effect her absence from
the home during the day will have on her mother's recuperative
process.

Clearly, Miss Sims' immediate concern about leaving her mother in
the care of someone else must be dealt with first if any progress is to be
made in this case. Miss Sims must be given the kind of feedback that
accurately sets priorities as she sees them.

Often the worker's assessment of appropriate and attainable
goals will fit closely with the client's, even though they may not be
identical or carry the same priorities. The more similar the worker's
goals are to the client's, the less discussion and negotiation will be
necessary to arrive at a mutually acceptable agreement.

After the worker has presented his impression, it is up to the
client to decide whether to accept what has been said and agree to proceed with treatment (Zaro et al., 1977). When the problem has been
thoroughly explored, the worker and client can more specifically
develop goals and objectives for the relationship. The important
point is that both parties agree to the goals and objectives, whatever
they may be (Okun, 1976). It would certainly not be in the best interest of the client if the goals met the worker's needs only. Developing a set of treatment goals is a major step in establishing an alliance
between the worker and the client. Clearly defined goals give direction to efforts and provide some means of measuring progress as
therapy continues.

Goals have a tendency to shift and change over the course of
therapy. They must frequently be reassessed. When clients first come
for treatment they often state their goals in broad, vague terms. The
lack of clarity in defining goals may be part of the difficulty the client
has in coping with problems. During the feedback sessions, the goals
must be clearly presented to the client, together with the priority of
each and the order in which they should be approached. The worker
can make a significant therapeutic contribution by simply stating
goals in a concrete, specific manner. For example:

A recently retired sixty-five-year-old client summed up her
complaints by saying, "I want to feel better. I don't want to feel
depressed." During the feedback interview the worker stated, "An

important goal is that you become less depressed. You want to feel happy more of the time, have more energy, see people more frequently, and feel a greater confidence that you can cope with the everyday matters that come your way.''

It is possible that the goal of the relationship is to develop the relationship further, so that the client's self-concept is enhanced, or to provide a vehicle for self-understanding. Or it may be that the goal is to make some kind of decision or to seek some alternative form of behavior. The point is that the worker and the client need to know why this relationship is occurring and what the goals are (Okun, 1976). One of the things that distinguishes a friendly talk from a therapeutic or helping relationship is the setting of goals. Goal-setting gives the relationship a purpose as both the worker and client move toward the desired end.

If several different goals and objectives are formulated, it is a good idea to decide which has priority and where the focus will be for how long. Sometimes a logical sequence is clear; at others, worker and client decide arbitrarily. The following excerpt illustrates some goal-setting at the end of an initial session.

Mrs. Frye, age sixty-six, has come to see the social worker at the Outpatient Mental Health Clinic. She wants to arrive at a decision about what to do about her seventy-six-year-old chronically ill husband. She is feeling torn between keeping him at home or placing him in a nursing home.

SOCIAL WORKER: It's really important for you to decide one way or the other what to do about your husband.

MRS. FRYE: Yes, it is. It's really not easy to decide what to do. I've struggled so hard and so long to keep him at home. I've tried everything. I had a homemaker come in, the people from the Visiting Nurses Association have been helpful. My pastor and friends from the church have come by to visit or to bring meals. All that was fine as long as he was only physically ill. But then Harold began to have mental problems. He started roaming around the

	house at night and began talking to himself, and he got to be verbally abusive with me and would forget who I was. Still, the idea of a nursing home bothers me.
WORKER:	So, you're still caught between home care or nursing home care for your husband.
MRS. FRYE:	Yes, but at this point, I find myself leaning more in the direction of a nursing home. If only I could find the right one. I mean one where the staff is pleasant and really care about the patients and don't keep them on medication all day long.
WORKER:	It seems to me that it would be helpful if we find out more about the kinds of nursing homes that are available to you and your husband, places that would meet your needs as well as your husband's.
MRS. FRYE:	What do you mean? Is that possible? Where can I get that information?
WORKER:	I have a resource book that lists all of the nursing homes in this area as well as in the entire state. We could go over that list together and check the names of the ones that we wish to explore further. We could do that next week, if you'd like.
MRS. FRYE:	Yes, I would like that very much. In the meantime, my pastor mentioned a few that I'd like to find out more about. Maybe I can bring in the names of them when I come next week.

It is clear in this situation that the objectives of the relationship became focused on an exploration of suitable or appropriate nursing homes. Both the worker and Mrs. Frye participated in the goal-setting.

Some goals appear to be long-term and far-reaching matters. However, the client may be overwhelmed by the situation and feeling a need for immediate relief. Clients need the reassurance that relief from troublesome problems will come in the immediate future. Although there may be a long-term goal that is in keeping with the particular helping services undertaken, for goals to seem manageable they should be relatively short-term. Goals can apparently be most meaningful when they have a circumscribed focus and are prescribed in a stepwise fashion, allowing the client to move to new goals as earlier ones are met (Zaro et al., 1977). For example:

> A seventy-three-year-old extremely depressed man was referred to therapy by his physician who could find no serious physical problems despite his age. His wife of forty-seven years had suddenly died from a heart attack. He was distraught and repeatedly stated he did not know what to do. The worker presented the goals as she saw them, essentially preparing the agenda for therapy. "It is important that you overcome the sadness and depression you are experiencing. You will also have to put your current life in motion again by taking care of yourself, deciding on how you're going to use your time, and maintaining your apartment. Once you have put these things back on some even keel we will take stock of your new life without your wife and decide what to do with it."

The ordering of priorities for depressed older persons in a stepwise approach is the first move in helping the client begin to cope with his situation. The client feels less overwhelmed when he can deal with goals one at a time. After presenting the goals, it is critical that the worker actively seek the client's reaction to them and to the proposed order of priority.

Statement about Process

Older clients who find themselves in treatment may have very little understanding of what is involved and the kinds of information that will be sought. It is essential, both from a therapeutic and ethical standpoint, that the client have at least a basic understanding of what the worker plans to offer, the treatment alternatives that exist, what will be expected of him, and the potential gains and risks.

What the Worker Plans to Offer.   Unless the client is relatively sophisticated and has a clear understanding of the process of therapy, describing the treatment in great detail would serve no useful purpose. However, it is important that the client be given some general explanation regarding the therapeutic process. The following example may help the reader to get a better understanding of this point. The worker is speaking to the client:

> During our sessions together we will be discussing your concerns about your day-to-day living that have brought you to our meetings. This will give us an opportunity to focus on those concerns that are most important to you. In the process we will examine how you approach problems, any difficulties you may be experiencing in dealing with them, the attitudes you hold, and the feelings you experience. I hope that I can help you examine this material, gain new perspectives on it, and assist you in finding new ways of coping with those areas of your life with which you are experiencing some difficulty. (Zaro et al., 1977, p. 86)

This explanation touches briefly on the focus of therapy, the manner in which it will proceed, a few client expectations, and, in a limited fashion, the role of the worker.

It is the worker's responsibility to provide the kind of therapeutic atmosphere in which the client feels free to talk, to express himself, and to respond and interact with the worker. The worker must feel a sense of respect for the client as an individual in spite of any physical or mental health problems.

Choice of Treatment Alternatives. The worker clearly has the responsibility of choosing those solutions and interventions which possess the greatest chance of producing the desired results. In deciding among alternative methods, the worker must think in terms of what is possible and attainable, what resources are available to carry out the plan, what is the strength of the client's motivation, and what are his physical, intellectual, and emotional capacities (Brill, 1973).

Hollis (1972) points out succinctly that

> No treatment step should be taken without the worker's being attuned not only to the goals but also to the personalities of people with whom he is working, their immediate states of mind and feeling, the quality of the relationship between worker and client or collateral, and the nature of the various ways of helping among which the worker can choose. (p. 301)

The worker's capabilities must also be considered. What knowledge and skill does the worker have to deal with the kind of problem presented by the client? Does he believe he has something useful to offer this older client? Is he personally committed to work with this older client and the particular problem he brings? Does he have a negative view about old age? Are there any community resources that can be drawn on to facilitate the individual's social functioning?

What is Expected of Clients.   Clients are individual persons who come directly or indirectly (as through a referral) to an agency for help with some problem in their psychosocial functioning. When the client comes to an agency, he or she is expected to share with a professional social worker the problem(s) that he or she brings. The client is also expected to continue in casework treatment voluntarily. Thus, the client's continuance in casework can be construed as an important indicator of his or her motivation for treatment.

Briar and Miller (1971) point out that

> although much of the social casework literature is written as if the object
> of treatment is an individual person, the social worker works only with
> persons (either unattached individuals or members of family groups) in
> the sense that they present themselves to the caseworker as individuals
> with individual, personal problems. (pp. 93–94)

Clients come to social work settings by a variety of pathways and vary in terms of what they want or expect. It is impossible for the worker to decide in advance of treatment what the client wants or expects. This decision is made only after the client has had an opportunity to share his request with the worker, and after the worker and client arrived at mutually agreed-upon goals.

Gains and Risks (Prognosis).   What can the older client expect from therapy? Not all clients have the same expectations. Some may expect that their preoccupation with death will disappear; that their waning energy will be given a new boost; that their decreased feelings of self-esteem will be augmented; and that a confident, self-assured, and wiser person will emerge. The client's degree of discomfort and his desire for change require that he be given some reasonable hope and expectation that the therapeutic efforts can be successful, since without this there would be little reason for him to enter into the therapeutic procedure. But therapy, like any major undertaking, involves some risks.

The worker cannot promise that the client will not experience depression during the course of treatment, or uncomfortable feelings, an exaggeration of symptoms, or even new symptoms. For instance:

A well-groomed and recently retired man, age sixty-six, sought treatment because of his feelings of dissatisfaction with the way he was running his life. He began to explain in the early sessions that instead of feeling better he was feeling worse. During the sessions the worker would try to draw him out in an effort to deal with his discomfort. The worker was aware that her client missed his job very much, and that he was experiencing difficulty in filling his time with meaningful activities. He seemed to be drifting and uncertain about what to do with himself and his time. But he avoided discussing his feelings about retirement and what it meant for him to give up his job. After each session with the worker, he would experience headaches, and prior to sessions he would experience high levels of anxiety.

The client, who had gotten into the habit of avoiding thoughts about his problems, was experiencing the discomfort that comes when focusing on uncomfortable issues. It is not unusual for such clients in such situations to terminate treatment early because they may feel that they are getting worse rather than better. No client, particularly an older one, wants to feel that he is wasting his time. When the worker anticipates that emotional discomfort may occur, it is important to prepare the client for it. The client may then begin to view the discomfort as evidence of progress rather than of failure.

There seems to be no question that elderly people, like the young, can gain from therapy. Butler and Lewis (1982) point out the following:

> The elderly, if not brain damaged, are greatly receptive to therapy and can in no way be considered poor candidates. Older people often exhibit a strong drive to resolve problems, to put their lives in order, and to find satisfactions and a "second chance." . . . Any evidence pointing toward older people as untreatable is usually found to be in the minds of helping professionals rather than in empirical studies. (p. 321)

Client's Competence

While working with the client, the worker must constantly assess the client's competence. To what extent can the client do things for himself? Is the task beyond the client's power? Does the individual understand the realities of the situation with which he is confronted? Consider the following example:

Client, sixty-five-year-old retired steel mill worker. Mr. M. is a very robust man and apparently in good physical health, wanting to find meaningful part-time work to fill in his hours during the day.

WORKER: Mr. M. you've mentioned wanting to get back to work so that you can do something with all those hours you have during the day.

CLIENT: You're not kidding. My wife and I have been looking in the papers and talking with friends, but we just haven't come up with any leads.

WORKER: Well, if it's of any interest to you, I have been advised that the Vocational School is looking for a teacher's aide to help out in their auto repair shop. Would you be interested in such a job?

CLIENT: I sure would. Who do I talk to? I mean what do I have to do to get the job?

WORKER: Well, if you'd like, I can call the school principal and tell him something about you and your interest in the job, but you might have to go in for a face to face interview. Is that all right with you?

CLIENT: That's no problem with me. I'm just itching to do something worthwhile.

In this case, the worker had to decide to what extent the client was able to intervene in his own behalf, and to what extent he should. The worker had knowledge of the job, the principal, and some other people at the school who had been advocating for competent teachers' aides. The worker believed that input from him to the principal would at least lay the groundwork for Mr. M. to be successful in his job-seeking effort. However, the worker supported Mr. M's strengths by encouraging him to be interviewed by the principal, the teacher, and any others involved, himself. A general rule in treatment is that whatever the client can do for himself, he should be encouraged to do.

However, there are times when the client needs to be helped to deal more effectively with his own environment. In making this decision, the worker turns to his diagnostic impression of the client's personality, evaluating his capacity in relation to the particular task at hand (Hollis, 1972). Is the client physically, emotionally, and intellectually able to deal with the situation? Is his perception of what the situation requires sufficiently clear? Is he immediately ready to handle the situation, or are his feelings so deeply involved that he first needs to ventilate them as an initial step to clear thinking?

When the client's feelings are so deeply involved in a situation that they preclude wise action on his part, then the worker needs to help him to ventilate them. A brief illustration may help the reader grasp this idea.

Three months ago, Mrs. Taylor placed her eighty-eight-year-old mentally disturbed mother in a nursing home. Prior to the placement, Mrs. Taylor had strong negative ideas about nursing homes in general. However, through the help of family and friends, she was able to select one that did not seem to have the negative characteristics that she had feared finding, such as overly medicating patients, keeping patients in bed all day, talking down to the patients by staff, and discouraging patient and staff interaction.

However, on her last couple of visits Mrs. Taylor said her mother appeared to be very listless, lethargic, and more confused than ever. She felt that the doctor was giving her mother more medication than she needed; and she thought she should call the director of the home and ask that the doctor be dismissed. The worker said she knew how Mrs. Taylor felt and that it must have been difficult seeing her mother under those conditions. Mrs. Taylor agreed that it was and hoped that things would get better at the nursing home for her mother. The worker wondered if Mrs. Taylor might find it helpful to discuss her mother's situation with the doctor first before she decided to take any drastic action. Mrs. Taylor said, on second thought, that that would be a good idea, and she thanked the worker for letting her air her feelings.

The worker did not criticize Mrs. Taylor for her angry feelings toward the doctor. Instead, she allowed Mrs. Taylor to verbalize those angry feelings because she sensed that her emotions had reached a high level of intensity. This ventilation was followed by a supportive comment from the worker.

Sometimes the worker must work with collaterals. A collateral is someone who knows the client and may be willing to share pertinent information about the client with the worker. Sometimes the worker may seek out a former employer, a friend or neighbor or business associate of the older person. The worker listens carefully as he tries to gain an increased understanding of the older person in as many aspects of his life as possible.

When the worker works directly with the older client, he may notice during the early sessions that the client may be so depressed or grief-stricken that treatment at first is very heavily weighted with sustainment (that is, sympathetic listening, acceptance, reassurance about the client's feelings of guilt and anxiety), ventilation, and some direct influence (suggestions and advice). But characteristically there is soon some movement into thought about the details of everyday living and an accompanying effort on the worker's part to expand the client's awareness of his own feelings beyond depression and grief to other emotions (Hollis, 1972). The worker cannot proceed in the treatment sessions too rapidly, however. To proceed at too rapid a pace might only result in losing the older client. The worker should instead proceed at a pace that is comfortable to the client. The worker must permit the older client the opportunity to "talk out" the many facets of his problem(s) and examine whatever alternatives are available to him. Social work students and beginning practitioners, in their genuine desire to ameliorate the clients' distress, too often rush to solutions without first obtaining a sound understanding of individuals and their situations (Strean, 1978). Such a procedure can actually be destructive. To advise a recently widowed man to not take too long before he gives serious consideration to remarrying—without first obtaining knowledge of his wishes, interests, anxieties, abilities, and relationships—will in no way help him. To advise adult children to place their chronically ill, seventy-five-year-old mother in a nursing home—without making a comprehensive assessment of their personalities, values, interactions, anxieties, resentments, and expectations—can only exacerbate their distress.

The worker must begin where the older client is. This means that the worker must listen carefully to the client's requests, his wishes, and his ideas for alleviating the situation. Only after listening to the client can the social worker suggest a possible type of intervention such as family or marital therapy, group treatment, or a community clinic (Strean, 1978).

Although treatment is a collaboration among the worker, the older client, and the family, the worker will need to determine the most appropriate level of intervention—that is, with an individual, a family, a group, or a community. At times, the worker will intervene on more than one level in order to help the client. However, the worker must bring to each of these levels of intervention the knowledge and skill that will ultimately bring about the desired result for the client.

THE TREATMENT CONTRACT

A treatment contract is an agreement that involves a common understanding of the goal of the work, an agreement on method of procedure, and a definition of the roles and tasks of the worker and his client (Brill, 1973). Although the term "contract" has a legalistic connotation, in social work it evolves from the dynamic interaction in interviews where the client is helped to talk and the social worker tries to understand and help (Strean, 1978).

The contract need not be strictly formal, but should be verbalized and should serve as a framework for the therapeutic venture. Therapeutic contracts are basically mutual agreements between the worker and client regarding the goals of their work. Neither the client's responsibilities nor the worker's need be comprehensively discussed and consented to. A contract is reviewed frequently. A client's needs may change as his requests are explored, and worker and client may then agree to renegotiate their contract (Strean, 1978).

When a contract is negotiated and renegotiated, it helps bring a focus to the interviews; client and worker are less likely to get sidetracked by extraneous issues, and the interviews' productivity can be sustained.

> When the Rogers family came for a group interview it became obvious to the worker, and eventually to each of the family members, that they were all out for themselves. Each family

member recounted how difficult it would be for him or her to allow their elderly father to live with them. They all talked in terms of their individual dissatisfactions, and the problems they anticipated in having their father in the home. However, nobody in the family considered the other family-members' needs, conflicts, and miseries. They talked as if they paid little attention to each other. After this theme had been noted several times by the worker, she suggested a contract be made: in the interviews she would help the family members see how they avoided each other, neglected each other, and were insensitive to each other as well as to their elderly father. But the Rogers would have a responsibility too. When some member felt slighted, he would be singled out to express his hurt and anger, with everybody listening and thinking about how to help the injured person. They would also find out from their father what he wanted and try to involve him in as much of the discussion as possible. The Rogers agreed to follow this procedure at home as well as during the sessions.

Much progress occurred as a result of this agreed-upon contract. Each member of the family became more sensitive to the needs of each other as well as to their father. The result was that each family member felt more valued, with self-esteem enhanced. They also began to see that perhaps their father would not be such a problem to them at all—if he chose to live with one of them. Although increased family harmony was observed among the Rogers family, another conflict later emerged. The family seemed to be setting up teams, with two of the adult children, Jack and Jennifer, listening more to each other than to the other two. The two youngest children, Evelyn and Wanda, felt slighted. When this phenomenon was remarked on several times by the worker and then later noted by the Rogers themselves, a new contract was formulated. Whenever this collusion was detected in the interviews or on other occasions when the family got together, the dyads (Jack and Jennifer - Evelyn and Wanda) were to discuss what they could do to overcome it. Although this new contract was more difficult to carry out, with the worker's help the Rogers were eventually able to become more sensitive to each other as well as to their father. (See Strean, 1978, p. 60).

Contracts also involve questions of time, money, absences, and termination. Each of these factors will be briefly discussed.

Time

The time factor is generally broken down to include the total length of treatment, frequency of visits, and the duration of each session. The total length of treatment will be determined not only by the complexity of the problem, but by the approach the worker uses in treating the difficulty. For instance, task-centered casework can last up to eight weeks, crisis therapy can last from one to six sessions, and the kind of work leading to clarification or insight development may continue for a year or more.

There are no set rules as to the frequency of sessions. The optimal frequency will vary from client to client. However, sessions should be held on a regularly scheduled basis, generally weekly, and the time set should be mutually agreeable to both the client and worker. Older clients may have difficulty coming to an agency for their appointment with the worker. Therefore, some arrangements will have to be made for seeing the client in his or her own home. The worker must be flexible about the setting and sensitive to the needs of older clients who may have difficulty negotiating public transportation, whose funds may be limited, and who may fear crime in their neighborhoods.

At times when resistance (that is, reluctance to receive help from the worker) is high, the older client may prefer not to come or may have the feeling he has nothing to say.

An hour before her regularly scheduled appointment, Mrs. Leeds, a sixty-eight-year-old divorced woman, called to say she would not be able to keep her appointment. She gave the receptionist no reason, but asked to have the worker return her call. When the worker returned the call, Mrs. Leeds had difficulty expressing herself. The worker was aware that Mrs. Leeds' resistance to coming for therapy was quite high, and encouraged her to express whatever was on her mind. Mrs. Leeds finally broke down and said she thought she was wasting the worker's time especially since she felt that she had nothing to say. The worker encouraged Mrs. Leeds to come anyway and maybe they could explore together why Mrs. Leeds felt that way.

The optimal length of sessions seems to be from forty-five minutes to an hour. Some older clients may want to talk for more than an hour, especially after they have become familiar with therapy. However, the client should be given a polite reminder that the time is up, and that these things can be discussed during the next session if he so desires.

Fees

One of the most important elements in the therapeutic contract is the setting of a fee (DeWald, 1964). Not all agencies charge fees for treatment; when they do they are generally based on the person's ability to pay. The client should know at the outset—during the initial contracting meeting—how much treatment will cost.

In deciding on a fee, the worker should consider the frequency of visits and the probable duration of the treatment. The same fee schedule cannot be imposed on older lower-income clients as on more affluent clients because of their frequently precarious economic situation. Many older clients have limited funds and this must be taken into consideration when setting fees. One fair rule in fee-setting is to set the fee at an amount that the client can pay without jeopardizing his or her financial resources.

The matter of charging fees has always been a sensitive issue to the student in training. However, the student must grapple with his own feelings and biases (often with the help of his field instructor), and deal with the client in a sensitive, thoughtful, and fair manner.

Absences and Cancellations

Workers' attitudes about missed appointments have tended to be negative and inflexible. Workers have perceived client absences as a wish to avoid treatment, a form of acting out, or a way of manipulating treatment. When appointments have been missed, workers frequently convey to the client that the time has been set aside for the client and it is expected that he or she will make the arrangements necessary to keep the appointment (Zaro et al., 1977). Some therapists convey the attitude that the client is financially responsible for all scheduled sessions, whether he attends or not (DeWald, 1964).

However, these same attitudes cannot be imposed on older clients given the nature of their physical, social, and environmental situations. The worker should always first explore the reason(s) why the older client missed a session before charging him for it. A chronic illness may worsen and severely interfere with the older person's venturing out of the house. Lack of transportation, misplaced eyeglasses, or a fall in the house may be other reasons why older clients miss sessions. Forced relocation and lack of familiarity with the neighborhood may leave the older client confused about how to find his way to the agency. Limited income for some of the elderly may mean making a choice between treatment or buying something to eat. For these and other reasons the worker must take time to tactfully ascertain the reason(s) why an older client has missed a session.

What has been said about absences pertains in many ways to cancellations. The client frequently is resentful of his client status, fears what will be revealed in the interview, and feels a loss of power. The client may therefore want to spite the worker by cancelling his appointment (Strean, 1978).

The client is most helped when the social worker does not suggest or interpret the reasons for cancellations but instead tactfully explores the situation through appropriate questions (Strean, 1978). Sometimes the answers are surprising, as the following vignette demonstrates:

> After sixty-six-year-old Mr. King had cancelled two interviews, the worker called him and asked, "What seems to be the trouble?" "It's about time you called me!" Mr. King angrily bellowed over the phone. "I thought you didn't give a damn about me and that's what I almost proved. Do you really want to see me?" "Of course," the worker assured him. Mr. King came for his next interview and succeeding ones on time.

It is not unusual for a client who has experienced real or fantasied rejection in the past to test out the worker. He really wants acceptance and recognition but doubts that it will be forthcoming, so he tries various ploys in order to secure what he so deeply craves (Strean, 1978). Whenever the client cancels an appointment, it is important that the worker get in touch with him as soon as possible and make another appointment.

Telephone Interviews and Home Calls

Sometimes the older client may have difficulty keeping his appointments because of a nagging health problem or a financial setback. He may have difficulty arranging for transportation at the last minute.

     Mrs. L., a seventy-three-year-old client, had been keeping her appointments with the worker on a regular basis. A neighbor had driven Mrs. L. to each of the sessions. However, when the neighbor was called away unexpectedly on business, Mrs. L. had no one else to bring her. She tried to arrange for substitute transportation, but with no success. Finally, Mrs. L. called the worker to see if she could have some time with him over the phone.

     In the case of an older client, the worker may have to be flexible about the use of the phone in conducting therapy. Butler & Lewis (1977) point out that telephone outreach therapy is preferable to denial of therapy for the homebound older person.

     If the client cannot come to the agency, then a home call should be arranged. Workers must be supportive of older clients, accommodating, and sensitive to their situations.

     Many older people would prefer having the worker visit them in their homes. Familiar surroundings are reassuring and the older person does not have to be separated from family members, friends, possessions, and pets (Butler & Lewis, 1977). Individuals and families tend to become intimately involved in treatment when the worker visits at home.

TERMINATION

It goes without saying that treatment cannot go on forever. The final phase of treatment is termination (Kadushin, 1972). Termination of the treatment process is, in a sense, begun in the first interview when the contract is made for an allotted period of time.

When Mr. and Mrs. Gardner were seen during the initial interview, they inquired, "How long will this last?" The worker replied, "Given the difficulties you and your wife have had adjusting to your retirement, Mr. Gardner, as well as your needs,

wishes, expectations, and so on, this should take up to eight
sessions.'' Then Mr. Gardner informed the worker, ''That's a
relief to know. I don't remember anyone telling us at the other
agency how long we'd have to come.''

The general criteria for the termination of treatment are the
accomplishment or near-accomplishment of the goals which were set
when the treatment process was first undertaken (DeWald, 1964).
Another criterion may be the partial accomplishment of the goal. In
this case, the worker may realize that full accomplishment of the
previously set goal is not feasible.

For some older clients, termination may represent loss and
stress. Therefore, it should not coincide with other situations of crisis
or major change in the person's life. For instance, if the elderly client
faces changes in his or her life—retirement, death of a spouse, loss of
a grandchild, forced relocation, for example—he may need the ongoing therapeutic relationship to sustain and help him adjust to the loss
or change. In fact, even if a particular problem has been resolved,
older persons need the reassurance that continuing support is
available and that services can easily be resumed.

Termination by the Worker

It is generally appropriate to bring up the question of termination with the older client when the worker believes either that the
client has reached his or her therapy goals or that further progress is
not possible at this time (Zaro et al., 1977). It is essential that the
worker accept the fact that there will always be some clients with
whom he or she will fail, or whom progress in the treatment situation will cease.

A heavy-set, sixty-nine-year-old woman being seen for
continual somatic complaints including headaches, arthritic pain,
stomach cramps, and hypertensive flare-up, failed to carry out
homework assignments and blamed her lack of progress on the
student worker's incompetence. After six weeks of attempting to
make changes in the treatment format with little success, the worker
confronted the client with her lack of motivation, resistance, and
intellectual defensiveness and suggested the possibility of

termination. For the first time, the client considered the possibility that her own attitude might explain her lack of progress. She renegotiated with the worker to continue therapy for a specified number of sessions to assess whether any change could be made.

If the treatment is no longer helping the older client to change or to feel better, to continue work indefinitely may not be in the client's best interest. If a client is making only very slow progress, he or she may profit from a break from therapy, with the option of reentering later.

As part of the termination phase, the worker should briefly recapitulate what has been covered during the sessions, what decisions have been arrived at, what questions remain to be resolved, and what steps for action, if any, are to be taken (Kadushin, 1972). Since the worker cannot cover everything that has taken place during the treatment process, he must select for his summary those materials that he believes are the most significant. The summary helps the client to get a better perspective on what has taken place during the sessions with the worker.

Often, as termination approaches, clients communicate their separation anxiety and reluctance to leave the worker.

A group of elderly tenants of a high-rise retirement apartment building met with the worker over a period of six months with the goal of improving housing conditions and gaining certain rights. They accomplished all of their planned tasks and even a few they had not anticipated. However, when the worker suggested that the group be disbanded, the members protested. They all felt a commonality of interest and a feeling of kinship, and wanted to continue to see one another and the worker on a regular basis. When the worker pointed out that the group members all lived in the same building and could easily meet, the members protested even more strongly, claiming they needed and liked the worker and that he was their "ally" and "mediator."

It took a couple of months of discussion, in which the group members worked out their fears about autonomy and their "feelings of emptiness," before the worker could appropriately disengage himself from them.

Termination by the Client

Some older clients may terminate simply and finally by not returning for treatment. Some may say, "I don't have anything to talk about anymore," or "I don't see how this is helping me," or "I don't see how that is important to my problems." The worker must accept and recognize the client's privilege of terminating the treatment at any time.

As a general rule, clients want to quit therapy when they feel better. This may mean that the problem situation has been resolved to their satisfaction, that they have learned better coping skills, or simply that external events have changed in the older client's life and his stresses have thus been reduced (Zaro et al., 1977).

When the older client wants to terminate, the worker should listen and ask questions until he understands the reasons behind the desire to terminate. Beginners need to keep in mind that wishing to terminate will not always be directly related to what has occurred in the treatment sessions. It will most likely involve an interaction between (1) progress and goal attainment; (2) what is currently happening in the process of therapy itself; (3) the level of subjective discomfort; and (4) the client's socioeconomic situation (Zaro et al., 1977).

Other factors may precipitate termination prior to its successful completion. Such factors may include a geographical move by the client or worker, prolonged physical illness, interference with the treatment by a spouse or adult children, or the inability of the older client to maintain the financial agreement. In the case of the last factor, the older client may be too embarrassed to tell the worker that he is no longer able to afford the fee. The client's financial situation may then have to be reassessed.

Workers frequently feel that a client's decision to terminate is a personal indictment. They depreciate their own abilities and potential and become angry with the client for reaching his decision independently of them. Such reactions are internalized and inappropriate, and beginning students as well as experienced workers must learn to be objective about such matters.

The worker should maintain an open door policy; the option of entering therapy again should be presented to the client as a viable alternative. It is hoped that the client will first use what he has gained during the treatment process before resuming therapy. However, the availability of the worker in times of need or crisis may be very important to the older client's continuing growth.

PRACTICAL GUIDELINES FOR INTERVIEWING THE OLDER ADULT

Older people who come to social agencies, whether on their own or through referral from family, friends, doctors, lawyers, or police, may be encumbered by social and emotional problems that they are having difficulty resolving. They may resist therapeutic intervention in their lives for many reasons: desire for independence; fear of change; suspiciousness based on past experiences; realistic appraisal of the inadequacies of most "helping" programs for the elderly; clumsy, insensitive, or patronizing interventive techniques on the part of helping personnel; and so on (Butler & Lewis, 1977).

The following are some practical guidelines, presented in summary form, for interviewing the older adult for therapeutic or other change-oriented reasons.

1   The social worker must ascertain the reason(s) for which the client is seeking help—what does he want? What is his purpose in coming? What does the older client expect from the worker? These questions are of primary importance to the worker as he formulates his intervention strategy. In identifying the problem, the worker must also get to know the person who brings it. It is essential that each client be known by his own identifying, biopsychosocial characteristics, by his role and status in his immediate society, by his interaction with those meaningful people around him, by his mode of adaptation and of coping with his world, and by his strengths and his weaknesses.

Some older people may feel that it is somewhat shameful to have to ask for outside help in solving their problems (Schlossberg, et al., 1978). This feeling is heightened by the belief, still prevalent among many older people, that to seek professional help implies serious psychological disorder. The effective worker must be aware of these feelings and begin to assist the older client in overcoming such negative attitudes.

2   In making decisions about what should be done, the worker must be aware of the client as the best possible resource. The client's experience, time-perspective, and view of his own history can be

used as resources, so that client and worker together can build a foundation for dealing with particular problems (Schlossberg et al., 1978). It is important that plans and goals be discussed with the client and that he is in agreement with the goals.

3   In implementing the plan, methods and techniques can be utilized effectively only after certain basic principles are understood and put into practice (Harbert & Ginsberg, 1979). One such principle relates to the ability of the worker to form a positive relationship with the client. The emphasis in social work practice is on the mutuality of the relationship, in which the rights and responsibilities of both the worker and client are recognized. The relationship implies active participation, sharing, and feedback between the client and worker. The worker cannot be socially distant from the client. However, the older client may be reluctant to form a relationship with the worker because of his own attitudes and values. The worker must be aware of this, assume a more active stance, and be patient with the client.

A major task of the worker is to motivate the older client to accept help. Human beings have a natural motivation to grow, to learn, to explore. Most older clients have been coping and dealing with problematic situations all their lives, and to the extent possible, must continue to have opportunities to make their own choices.

Certain tangibles as well as intangibles exhibit themselves during the initial phase of treatment. For example, the worker may provide some concrete services, make a referral, engage the client in an ongoing therapeutic relationship, or offer some general information about agency policy, eligibility, rules, and regulations, and so forth. The worker's attitudes—the spirit in which the service is offered, respect and understanding of cultural and ethnic pluralism, commitment to basic social work values—are all-important during this phase.

Social workers must be cognizant of the fact that older clients often speak more slowly and move more slowly than younger clients. This may be difficult for younger workers to understand and accept. They must learn to listen carefully and respond effectively.

4   Older clients often reminisce while in therapy. Reminiscence may be defined as the act of recollecting or remembering experiences from the past. It may be viewed as a method whereby a person reflects upon past experiences, both positive

and negative, in order to reconstruct and find additional significance and meaning (Keller and Hughston, 1981). Whenever this occurs, the worker must listen attentively and formulate responses that are as nonjudgmental as possible.

Many older clients enmeshed in the priorities of subsistence seek treatment as a last resort, often with a vague sense of what therapy is all about. This is particularly true of the older black client. In addition, the structure and cultural patterns of the older black client, his social class, value system, and style of life often differ markedly from the social worker's own. Further, older black clients bring to the therapeutic relationship a history of humiliating and abrasive contacts with whites, and this past is not easily shrugged off.

The worker must learn to be sensitive to and understanding of racial and cultural differences. The worker needs to help the older client understand that therapy is a mutual endeavor between two active participants, each trying to reach out and touch each other in the giving and using of help. This says that regardless of age, social class, sex, race, or ethnicity that it takes

both participants to do the job—that they are equally important, that they must listen to each other, that they must recognize each other's rights and responsibilities, and that they must respect each other. (Gitterman & Schaeffer, 1972, p. 282)

Harbert and Ginsberg (1979) list several additional practical guidelines that are useful in working with the older client. Some of these guidelines are as follows:

1   Always include the client and significant others in planning and establishing goals.
2   Let the client make his or her own decisions.
3   Gather information about the problem accurately and try to assess the implications of this information for the individual or group.
4   Obtain any additional information needed to understand the problem; speak to other people or groups when appropriate.
5   Explore possible alternatives for solution of the problem with the client or client group.
6   Explore with the client the consequences of the decision, and if a wrong choice is made, help the client with it.

7   Don't misrepresent things; don't give false assurance. For example, if you must send an elderly person to a state mental hospital, don't give a false impression of what it will be like. If you don't know what to tell the client, just say you don't know and deal with the fact that the client is having to leave home. Don't make an elderly person think he or she is going someplace temporarily when you are making a permanent arrangement. It is hard to say to a weeping person, "Your family doesn't want you," but in the long run, this does less damage to the professional relationship than the client's learning you were dishonest.

8   Don't imply you know all the answers and what is best. Listen to the individual; hear out the client's ideas and perceptions of the problem and its solution.

9   It is important to reach out in order to engage those older individuals who can't express their need for help, those who are depressed and feel helpless, and those who don't know the available resources. This involves your being visible, flexible, creative, and sincere in your offer of help.

10 Work with groups of individuals when possible.

11 Obtain community involvement and community support for what you do.

12 Sometimes you will need to be an advocate or broker for the elderly; at other times, a social activist.

13 The timing of what you say or do is of the utmost importance. Don't talk of relocation in a time of grief. Being prompt and keeping appointments is crucial. Some aged, like children, may tend to take what you say literally. (I recall a situation when an older woman got up early and dressed every day for two months, because a relative said she would come and get her in a few days and she wanted to be ready. The relative never came.)

14 Follow through on referrals. Make sure your clients obtain the needed help or resources; don't let them get lost in the shuffle. Be certain the older person doesn't misunderstand directions.

15 Ask open-ended questions rather than ones producing "yes" or "no" answers. For example, "Have you thought about what you might like to do, and would you tell me about it?"

16 Try to guide the individual to a decision by making suggestions rather than giving advice. Bad advice discredits you as a helping person.

17 Don't take over! Give the client a chance to talk.

18 Convey concern, warmth, acceptance, and understanding, and learn to read between the lines of what is said; try to understand unspoken communication.

19 Instill trust and confidence in your relationship with clients or groups by being consistent, honest, and patient.

20 Keep in check your own feelings of anger and frustration toward the client.

21 Reserve judgments.

22 Be realistic. Don't always be bright and cheerful. Don't be afraid to discuss unpleasant aspects of the client's life; you may be the only person who gives the client this opportunity.

23 Exercise judgment in determining if a plan is realistic in terms of resources and/or time. For example, some elderly like to postpone changes in their physical environment as long as possible. You must be the one to set a time limit or help the individual understand one already established. Although a building is to be demolished on July 2, Mrs. Jones may not want to move out until September, when she can go to live with her nephew. She must be helped to understand that this is not a satisfactory plan and something must be arranged temporarily. Similarly, patients who want to remain in the hospital when the physician wants to discharge them must be helped to accept the necessity of change.

24 Learn to assess whether the group or individual has the capacity to achieve the desired goal or will need outside assistance.

These are some practical guidelines you can employ in your helping role. There are others. Direct work with the older client will not of itself solve the problems of the aged, but if you can provide services effectively, it will at least help older people to deal with their difficulties.

As practitioners trying to help the elderly meet the problems of life, we have the responsibility to keep abreast of their needs and problems. We must keep in constant communication with those who best know these needs—elderly people themselves. There must be no ''communication gap.'' In working with the aged, listen to what they say and to what they don't say. Frequently they will spell out their individual needs. Then, too, as you listen to numbers of the aged, you may find several older people with similar needs and no way to meet them. It is only with a clear understanding of such needs that we can best know how to help and the methods to obtain what is needed.

WORKER ACTIVITY IN THE ENVIRONMENT

Social workers mediate between the individual and his environment. The basic aim of this approach has been to counteract those conditions in the environment that are currently—or perhaps potentially—threatening, debilitating, and destructive to the well-being of the individual.

According to Hollis (1977), work directed toward modifying the situational aspect of the client's problem can be conceptualized according to the different roles the worker may assume. At different times the worker may be the *provider of a resource,* an *interpreter* of the client's need, or a *mediator* on behalf of the client with an unresponsive or poorly functioning resource. Inherent in these roles is the linkage function which connects older clients with goods and services and strives to help such clients deal effectively with the complex arrangement of urban structures.

The social worker should be especially alert to the ways in which the physical environment hinders or fosters the delivery of services and links the older person to the point at which the service is delivered (Brody, 1974). For instance, the ambulatory older person may not be able to avail herself of meals served on a congregate basis unless there are ways of transporting her to the site. Similarly, she cannot shop for herself or maintain her involvement in the community without ample means of transportation. Fear of crime in the neighborhood is an important consideration for many elderly persons, and serves to restrict their mobility further. In the situation described above a resource was needed. The worker, acting as a service provider, not only provides transportation for the older person, but also links her directly to the service.

Generally, the major roles assumed by the worker when carrying out the preventive function in the environment are: consultant-educator, advocate, and broker-negotiator. The language of prevention is cluttered with confusing terminology—for example, secondary prevention and tertiary prevention. Prevention is here defined as those activities undertaken by the worker before the manifestations of a problem occur. Fischer (1978) states that "the goals of preventive intervention involve attempts to build strengths into individuals and systems as a means of avoiding problems" (p. 38). The social worker, as consultant to both formal and informal organizations in the immediate environment, can help systems alter their services and procedures to be more conducive to the normal need-meeting activities of older people. Organizations such as churches and clubs, which attend in part to the needs and interests of older people, can use the worker's knowledge and skills in designing and delivering their primary preventive programs for the elderly.

In the role of advocate the worker can help the elderly client wind his way through the bureaucratic maze of private and public organizations. Advocacy includes use of all means at his disposal, from direct action to moral persuasion, to represent effectively the needs and grievances of older people (Butler & Lewis, 1977). The worker can encourage agencies to make effective reforms and provide opportunities for meaningful participation by the older person in paid employment and in creative volunteer roles.

On a case by case basis, the social worker is involved in individualized primary prevention when she works as a broker and/or negotiator in securing the best possible resources from the environment for her client. This role is not new to social caseworkers. Because of the complex impersonal and unpredictable nature of today's society, many of the well elderly need assistance in carrying out certain basic activities. For example, many require assistance in filling out complex and confusing application forms which are required in order to secure rebates, refunds, and other forms of financial assistance. Often the older person needs assistance in negotiating for fair treatment from landlords and realtors. The worker may have to intervene with utility companies to straighten out mistakes in billing and record-keeping which could lead to curtailment of vital services to the elderly client.

This approach views the worker as working no less with the individual than with the environment. Virtually all of the theoretical approaches studied by the writer emphasize a two-fold approach to practice—on person and on situation. Yet the environmental thrust is not given the conceptualization and emphasis it requires. Social workers cannot retreat from environmental concerns when working with the older client.

SUMMARY

Information-gathering is an important aspect of the therapeutic process. Information is essential to the worker because it provides him with cues as to what is troubling the client, what sources of support are available to him, and how he has tried to cope with the situation. The client must always be considered to be the primary source of information. However, there are other useful sources of information: family and friends, neighbors, health records, the church, and other agencies or professionals to which the older person is known. In obtaining information, it is essential that the client's confidentiality not be violated.

Once the worker has obtained the information he needs, it must be carefully thought through so that some decision can be made about treatment. Diagnosis, as this process is called, is ongoing. The worker is constantly assessing what he is learning and observing so as to arrive at a better understanding of the situation. Out of the diagnostic process should come a definition of the problem about which the client is most concerned.

Goal-setting is an essential part of the change process. Goal-setting is most effective when it is a shared process. The goals must be clearly presented to the older client and he must be committed to working on them. It is the worker's responsibility to choose those treatment alternatives that have the greatest chance of producing the desired results.

After the client has been given feedback based on the worker's impressions, it is up to him to decide whether he wishes to continue in treatment. If the client agrees to continue, a treatment contract must be established. Therapeutic contracts are mutual agreements between the worker and client regarding the goals of their work. Questions of time, money, and absences must be worked out as part of the contract.

Termination is the final phase of treatment. Termination takes place when treatment goals have been accomplished or nearly accomplished. Termination may be initiated by the worker or by the client. Both the worker and client may feel that to continue in treatment is no longer in the older client's best interest.

A number of practical guidelines, techniques, and skills for working directly with the elderly client are discussed. When the worker mediates between the individual and his environment he may play a number of different roles including locator of a resource, interpreter of the client's need, or mediator on behalf of the client. Another essential role that the worker can play is that of advocate. In this role the worker functions on behalf of the elderly client to remedy problems stemming from the actions of public bodies.

chapter 9

PRACTICE WITH FAMILIES

FAMILY RELATIONSHIPS AND SUPPORT

The individual obtains the most fundamental information about what it means for him or her to be a social being from early experiences in the family (Keller & Hughston, 1981). Within the family context, the individual is offered an opportunity to develop skills, form an identity, and find avenues of self-expression throughout the course of his life (Kennedy, 1978).

Just as an individual grows and develops new competencies and goals through life, so also the family has a sequence of development. That is, each intact family goes through more or less the same developmental process over time, passing through the same sequences or phases, each usually marked by a critical transition point—marriage, birth of the first child, birth of the last child, the last child's leaving home (the ''empty nest''), retirement and widowhood.

With each developmental phase, the family is provided with new tasks, the need to learn new adaptational techniques, and correspondingly, new risks of family dysfunction. Successful adaptation at any one phase depends heavily on the family's mastery of the tasks required at the previous phase (Goldenberg & Goldenberg, 1980).

Universally, the two most fundamental tasks of the family are to provide care and socialization for the young and a network of interpersonal support and personal identity for adults. Families are composed of interacting and interconnected personalities. The number of persons within the family and the closeness of their involvement varies with various definitions of the family (Kennedy, 1978).

Every family faces a number of crises as it evolves through the life-cycle (Goldenberg & Goldenberg, 1980). Old age is the last transitional crisis for the family. It usually brings with it problems in separation for both the older and younger members of the family.

Those working with the older individual must accept the fact that it is difficult to treat him without taking into account the family of which he is a part. Despite its ever-changing forms and functions, the family remains a crucial reference point for most older persons (Harbert & Ginsberg, 1979).

Older People's Involvement with
Their Families

Most older people have considerable involvement with their families (Kennedy, 1978). The national Harris Poll (Harris, 1975) reported a high degree of family involvement among persons of all age levels. Eighty-one percent of persons sixty-five and over have living children. More than half of those polled said they had seen their children within the last day or so and another one-fourth had seen them within the last week (Kennedy, 1978).

Family interaction among older and younger generations reveals that each generation performs useful services for the other. For instance, older parents often give gifts and money to their children and grandchildren. In addition, they babysit for the grandchildren, give advice on child-rearing, and on business-related matters. Adult children frequently provide monetary assistance, fix things around the house, and run errands for their aging parents.

Some older parents, particularly black parents, have a tendency to take younger children into their homes to live. This finding has been substantiated by Robert B. Hill, research director for the National Urban League. Hill (1972) indicates that many black families take other people's children into their households. In fact, older women tend to take in children and younger persons rather than being taken in themselves.

Rural vs. Urban Family Patterns

Family life is believed to be stronger in rural areas. The family connotes a general understanding of intimate reciprocal helping and committed relationships between generations. This is particularly true of the extended family.[1] In rural areas the family sets behavioral norms for its members, economic problems are resolved through borrowing and lending among family members, home tends to be the house where one grew up, and there is regular face to face communication and contact (Harbert & Ginsberg, 1979).

In urban areas, families may not play the same dominant role.

---

[1] "An extended family generally consists of two or more nuclear families living together in one household. In the extended family, there may be three or more generations living in one household; for example, there may be grandparents, at least one of their adult offspring who has a spouse, and children of that marriage" (Crandall, 1980, p. 412).

This is because family members are often scattered, maintain their own separate households, and have developed other relational networks that play a prominent role in their daily lives. These relational networks include friends, co-workers, and significant others. In addition, "secondary institutions," such as governments, social agencies, and civic clubs, may have greater significance and impact on the lives of people in metropolitan than in rural areas (Harbert & Ginsberg, 1979).

Family Types

There is no typical American family today. It is more accurate to speak of *types* of families—with diverse organizational patterns, diverse styles of living, diverse living arrangements (Goldenberg & Goldenberg, 1980). There are a variety of family types, ranging from the traditional nuclear family to the untraditional homosexual couple with a child. In between are such family types as the dyadic nuclear family, the single parent family, the three-generation family, the middle-aged or old-age couple, the institutional family, the foster family, the kin network, the commune family (monogamous), the commune family (group marriage), the unmarried parent with one or more children, and the unmarried couple with a child.[2]

The most common family form is the nuclear family. The nucleus of the family consists of the parents and their offspring living together in a common household. The nuclear family is seen as isolated from the extended family. Within the nuclear family the traditional role of the husband has been that of breadwinner, while the wife's role has been that of home manager, housekeeper, and child-rearer. Today, neither parent may be strictly tied to either of those roles. Evolving roles within the nuclear family are those of the wife who is employed and the husband who shares in home management and child-rearing.

When a number of nuclear families are conjoined into larger units, they make up the extended or consanguine family (Bensman & Rosenberg, 1976). The extended family is characterized by a network of supportive relationships, generally in the form of emotional and economic support. As America became more urbanized and in-

---

[2] For a more detailed description, see Williams, J. W. & Stith, M., *Middle Childhood: Behavior and Development.* New York: Macmillan Publishing Company, 1974, pp. 80–82.

dustrialized, and as people became more mobile, it was anticipated that the extended family would become obsolete. However, research into family life has revealed that the predicted disintegration of the extended family has not come about (Kennedy, 1978). Sussman and Burchinal (1962) state that the family form most typical of our culture is the "modified extended family" structure. In the modified extended family, family units maintain interrelations between siblings and across generations while also retaining a great deal of autonomy and mobility.

Ethnicity and Families

The term ethnicity implies certain common cultural traits, characteristics, a history, and language. An ethnic group can be defined as people who share distinctive cultural characteristics originating from a common national, linguistic, or racial heritage (Ehrlich et al., 1980). Language is perhaps the most important cultural trait among ethnic groups or families.

Ethnic families have a number of identifiable cultural traits in common. These traits bind families together in a cohesive and unified way. It is not unusual to see Italian, Jewish, Puerto Rican, and Polish groups closely oriented to the extended family (Harbert & Ginsberg, 1979). The same is true of other ethnic groups such as Hispanics, Asian-Americans, blacks, and Native Americans. All of these people seem to have strong ties to the family. In addition, considerable respect, concern, and caring are shown by younger family members toward older members of the family.

THE AGING FAMILY

By the time a couple is in their sixties, the husband (and in many cases, the wife) will have retired or will be anticipating retirement. Once the couple retires, their income will generally be reduced by one-third to one-half, or even more. Frequently, family members begin giving economic and supportive services to their aging parents at this time. In some cases, the giving of financial assistance to older parents may place undue burdens on a family which itself is feeling the strains of inflation and the high cost of living. The economic difficulty is exacerbated as the aging parents' health begins to fail. Failing health may result in a move to a smaller residence or to an institutional setting.

One of the major changes in the family life of the older person is retirement. Retirement is characterized by increased leisure time. If little preparation has been given the use of leisure time, when the person retires this can place a considerable burden on the marriage. Consider the case of Mr. and Mrs. Evans, who were referred to the Family Service Agency by their oldest son.

Mr. Evans, age seventy, recently retired after forty-two years of work with a local manufacturing company. During those years, he devoted himself completely to his work and rose steadily through the ranks. When he retired, he was manager of one of the sections of the company. Mrs. Evans, on the other hand, never worked outside of the home. Her time was mostly spent raising their three children and managing the home. Disciplining the children was also a task assumed by Mrs. Evans. Although Mr. Evans worked long hours, he managed to vacation with his family once a year, play golf with a few male friends on weekends, and attend church with his family on a regular basis, a practice he and his wife have continued. When the youngest child, a son, left the home, Mrs. Evans, who was then fifty-seven, began to devote her time to civic affairs and volunteer activities. Thus, during the day she was frequently away from home. During the early months of retirement, Mr. Evans spent his time playing golf and visiting friends. (Both Mr. and Mrs. Evans appear to be in relatively good health.)

About a month before the couple came to the Family Service Agency, Mr. Evans had become very argumentative with his wife, constantly hurling bitter accusations at her for no apparent reason. He had become extremely bored with his daily routine, jealous and suspicious about his wife's time away from home, and critical of the children who he felt had "forgotten about him." Mrs. Evans insisted on continuing her activities, while her husband insisted she give them up. The arguments continued and became more bitter as the couple reached an impasse. Mrs. Evans, deeply concerned about the seriousness of the situation, discussed it with her oldest son, who in turn discussed it with his sister and brother. They agreed that their parents needed outside help. The oldest son finally referred his mother to the Family Service Agency.

Many older adults encounter marital problems resulting from retirement (Harbert & Ginsberg, 1979). There are several reasons for this, but some of the most obvious are financial problems, lack of meaningful activities, insufficient planning and preparation, and poor health.

Some retired people find it difficult to adjust to having so much leisure time on their hands and have difficulty organizing their time on a daily basis. Social workers can perform an invaluable service to retired persons by helping them identify the things that are of interest to them, make a realistic set of choices that can be used to establish a structure and a routine for life in retirement (Atchley, 1977), and make use of the variety of available leisure-time programs and activities.

Difficulties in adjusting to retirement can place a great deal of stress on a marriage. This is obviously the case in the Evans' situation. Mr. Evans has apparently had difficulty accepting retirement and is at a loss as to what to do with his time. He resents the fact that his wife enjoys her outside activities, and is rarely at home with him. The result is constant quarreling and criticism. The couple is at an impasse as Mrs. Evans insists on continuing with her active and meaningful schedule.

The social worker working with this couple will want to interview both Mr. and Mrs. Evans as well as other members of the family—particularly the son who made the referral. The methodology should include interviews with Mr. and Mrs. Evans, with various combinations of family members (if they are available), and with the total group early in the exploration process. The main reason for family diagnosis is to formulate a plan that will enable the family as a whole as well as its individual members to cope with those stresses that are interfering with satisfactory family relations.

The Focus of Family Diagnosis

Primary focus should be on understanding the main area(s) of difficulty that are interfering presently with the family's (in this case, the retired couple's) relations. This focus should result in a definition of the problem that is understood by the family, and agreement about purpose, method, and goal of treatment. That is, it should result in a treatment contract (*Casebook on Family Diagnosis and Treatment,* 1965). The worker will also want to gain some knowledge about current social life circumstances, how these affect the problem, and the family's ability to work and cope with them. In addition, it is essential to understand family interaction for the purpose of assessing those factors that enhance or impede necessary family and individual operations (*Casebook on Family Diagnosis and Treatment*, 1965). The Committee on Family Diagnosis and Treatment (1965) has defined family interaction as the receiving and discharging of feelings, attitudes, and behavior within the immediate family. With this definition of family interaction in mind, various aspects of family functioning should be examined.

Family Vulnerability and Strength.   With what kinds of stresses can the family characteristically cope? What is its vulnerability and strength in crisis situations? What is its energy level and tolerance for working on the current problem? Are there certain life events such as retirement, the loss of children from the home, or relocation, that overtax coping abilities?

Family Roles.   In what way are the roles that are ascribed to, assumed by, or expected of the family members used or abused in relation to the problematic task? How flexible are the family members in altering or changing roles as family tasks change? What role perceptions and functions should and can be altered by treatment? What is each person's role in the marital conflict?

Family Goals.   What types of changes does the family believe are desirable? Does the means for bringing about such changes exist? Should the ultimate goal be to bring about changes in a particular family member or the family's social situation, or both? Should the goal be to bring about a better marital adjustment?

Family Communication Patterns.   To what extent does the family communicate verbally and nonverbally? Is there concordance between what the person says and how he says it? Does the frowning husband say, "I love you"? Does the old man say, "Doesn't hurt a bit," while his eyebrows move closer and closer into a frown and his jaw and fists become tighter and tighter? How much distance is there between family members? How much closeness is there in the family relationship? To what extent do problems in communication interfere with management of family tasks?

Family Need-Response Patterns. What does each person need from the family and what responses does he get to his needs? How does he perceive his own needs and others' needs? How does he perceive and handle the responses he gets? What balance exists between the need-response pattern of the individual and those of the family? Is individual and family growth promoted or interfered with? What kinds of individual and family defenses are developed and used in relation to needs and responses? What part does failure or breakdown in this dynamic balance or homeostasis play in the problem? How do problems in this area affect ability to meet the tasks of loving and working, dependence and support, competition, and cooperation in the family? How do these problems affect communication, roles and goals?

While each of the components of family diagnosis have been described separately, they are all interrelated in practice. Certain components may require more or less exploration in any situation at any given time (*Casebook on Family Diagnosis and Treatment,* 1965).

FAMILY TREATMENT

One of the key methods for helping older individuals and their families is family group therapy or family counseling (Harbert & Ginsberg, 1979). Counseling services have been offered to families by family service agencies for years (Brody, 1977). The Family Service Association of America (FSAA) is one such agency. The FSAA seeks to interview the total family early in the exploration process. It is quite possible that during a total family interview older parents and their adult children can recognize the importance of interdependence in their relationship.

Interdependence implies mutual giving and taking as well as a balancing of power (Goldberg & Deutsch, 1977). In other words, both parents and children recognize and respect each other's ability to stand alone as well as their dependence or need for help in some form. But interdependence means more than that. It stresses both the parents' and the child's ability to move beyond old roles and patterns of relating and to discover each other as persons relating to each other in the present (Goldberg & Deutsch, 1977). A mother is able to look at her daughter in a different light and say, ''This is my daughter, the

woman'' instead of, ''This is my child.'' The same principle operates
for the daughter who can move beyond her childhood role and begin
to look at her mother, the woman.

One interesting facet of total family interviews is that
adult children have an opportunity to recognize their parents'
strengths and weaknesses as being those of individuals who have had
numerous experiences. As a result, they tend to view their parents in
a different way.

Family treatment is the process of planned intervention
in an area of family dysfunctioning. Since the goal of treatment
requires focus on the family, some form of multiple interviewing is
the major treatment technique. In practice, then, the worker (family
therapist) may choose to work with entire families, subsystems within
the family (for example, the elderly couple, the older parents plus all
of their adult children), or individual family members, in order to
bring about change in the functioning of the overall family social
system (Goldenberg & Goldenberg, 1980). Family therapy is indicated when the family's ability to perform its basic functions
becomes inadequate.

In the case example described earlier in the chapter, Mr. and
Mrs. Evans were referred to the Family Service Agency by their
oldest son. Help is frequently sought not by the older individual
himself but by an adult and member of the family (Harbert &
Ginsberg, 1979). Older people are frequently reluctant to seek help
on their own. Many are reluctant to come to an agency alone because
they do not know what to expect. Some older people are easily intimidated and feel more secure if a member, or several members, of
the family accompany them. To illustrate this point, consider the
following case example:

Mrs. Helms, age sixty-eight, has been living alone ever since
the death of her husband almost a year ago. Shortly after his death,
Mrs. Helms surprised both her family and friends when she decided
to pursue a very active life of her own. She became active in local
politics, volunteered her time at the neighborhood multipurpose
senior center, and began to go on weekend trips whenever her time
allowed. Mrs. Helms' family (which includes two married sons and
a recently divorced daughter) were pleased at how well their mother
had adjusted to their father's death. Mrs. Helms' active pace

continued over a period of about nine months. Then, six weeks ago, Mrs. Helms abruptly discontinued her busy schedule and spent most of her time at home alone—sitting and thinking. Her children were extremely puzzled over the sudden and drastic change in their mother's behavior and expressed concern among themselves over this occurrence. They observed that their mother was eating very little, had begun to lose weight, and had become very apathetic. At the children's insistence, Mrs. Helms saw her physician, who gave her a thorough medical examination. The doctor discovered that Mrs. Helms had lost thirteen pounds over the last two months but could find no physical cause for her problem. He expressed concern about her decreased appetite, decreased weight, and her overall lethargic condition. The doctor felt that Mrs. Helms' problems were basically emotional and suggested that she—with the family's assistance—seek psychiatric help. Mrs. Helms was resistant at first because she said she didn't know of anyone who could help her, and even if she did she didn't want to go by herself—that she would want her family to be with her. The physician advised Mrs. Helms that, with her permission, he would be glad to discuss this further with the other members of the family. He mentioned that with their approval he could suggest the names of certain agencies they might try, and that he could also make a referral to the family service agency.

Some older people are unaware that a service exists. Others are aware that family therapy is available, but they are afraid to go alone. Physicians, neighbors, the local pastor, and others can be very helpful to the older person by sharing with them information about family services—as well as by taking the initiative to make the referral.

Whatever the reasons that the elderly person does not seek help alone, that situation provides the worker an opportunity to meet and work with the total family around those interpersonal stresses that cause patterns of conflict and tension.

Mr. B., an eighty-three-year-old retired railroad worker, had become a source of considerable concern to his wife and family. For six months, Mr. B. had been roaming around the neighborhood at night and getting lost. His usually neat appearance had become slovenly; he had marked shifts of mood; his memory for both recent and remote events was poor. When seen by a psychiatrist, Mr. B. was diagnosed as having chronic brain syndrome, with senile dementia, moderate and of approximately seven years' duration. The major affective disorder was diagnosed as manic depressive illness, depressed. The psychiatrist recommended nursing home care for Mr. B. Mrs. B. concurred because she felt unable to cope with her husband's odd and worrisome behavior. She confided with her oldest daughter (with whom she was very close), telling her the nature of her husband's illness and what the doctor had recommended. The oldest daughter agreed and felt that placing her father in a nursing home was the wisest alternative. However, when the matter was discussed with the two younger daughters, they were adamantly against nursing home placement. They felt their mother should hire a live-in nurse to care for their father. The family had reached an impasse and the strain of having to make a decision about Mr. B. that would be in everyone's best interest had caused Mrs. B. to become withdrawn and depressed. In addition, remnants of old anger, old hurts, and guilt over these feelings began to surface among the adult children and their aged parents.

Mrs. B. finally confided in a close friend about her dilemma. The friend suggested that the family seek the help of a family therapist. Since the family was experiencing a number of interpersonal stresses, Mrs. B. took her friend's advice and sought therapy for the family.

Many workers prefer to begin their work with a family group interview, a collective interview in which all of the members of the family are seen. If this is impractical, the family is asked to participate in one or more family meetings either at home or in the worker's office (Stamm, 1972). The initial family group meeting is the first step in an ongoing process of mutual exploration and discovery carried on throughout family therapy. The initial family group session is an important aspect of the worker's assessment process, which also includes direct observation carried on within a relationship with members of the family unit, as well as other exploratory activities for the purpose of enhancing knowledge about, and sensitivity to, family transactions and alignments among members (Stamm, 1972). In addition, the family group interview can increase the worker's understanding of each family member, since each person will tend to define himself in terms of his individual personality as well as in terms of his relationships with other family members.

A number of factors may preclude family group interviews during the initial exploration. For instance, the older person may be seriously physically ill, or so mentally disturbed as to be totally disoriented; he may be disinclined to come to the sessions at first; or he may be geographically inaccessible. These and other factors may make group sessions impractical.

Stamm (1972) points out the following:

> Whatever the pattern of beginning, it will have significance for the family system as well as for individual members. Its meaning will emerge slowly but the worker, by meeting the whole family in the beginning, communicates his own orientation and creates an opportunity to tune in directly and more quickly with family members and their transactions, the family's underlying motives, and its means of maintaining itself. (p. 211)

PSYCHOSEXUAL NEEDS OF THE ELDERLY

One area around which older men and women experience changes is in the pattern of their sexual responses. The most likely problem for men is enlargement of the prostate gland. Enlargement of this gland is very common, beginning in middle age, and may interfere with the free flow of urine. The gland may become cancerous. The traditional method of treatment has been removal of all or part of the prostate by surgery. For most men who experience it, this procedure is very threatening because the incisions are made near the genital area. Unless these are explained to them, few men really understand the functioning of the prostate gland or the consequences of the surgery.

Doctors have a responsibility to discuss the sexual consequences of medical procedures with patients, especially since many patients are too embarrassed to ask. Some men have been told by their doctors that they would become impotent after this operation. However, after prostate surgery many men are still able to obtain erections, to have orgasms, and to ejaculate. Wives should also be aware of the surgical procedures and the likely consequences, and should be sympathetic and understanding about any prostate problems.

Although a number of investigators have surveyed the sexual behavior of older persons, Masters and Johnson (1968) were the first to observe the anatomy and physiology of their sexual response under laboratory conditions. When the orgasmic cycles of the menopausal and post-menopausal women were studied, Masters and Johnson found that, for the most part, the intensity of physiologic reaction and the rapidity and duration of anatomic response to sexual stimulation were reduced with advancing years through all phases of the sexual act. That is, the sex flush was more limited and restricted in the older women, there was less lubrication, there was delay in reaction of the clitoris to direct stimulation, reduction in duration in orgasm time, and so forth. Nevertheless, they also found significant sexual capacity and effective sexual performance in these older women. These researchers concluded that:

> There seems to be no physiologic reason why the frequency of sexual expression found satisfactory for the younger woman should not be carried over into the post-menopausal years. The frequency of sexual intercourse or manipulative activity during the post-menopausal years is of little import, as long as the individuals concerned are healthy, active, well-adjusted members of society. (Masters & Johnson, 1968, pp. 238–247).

As in the female, Masters and Johnson found that in men after fifty the intensity and duration of physical responsiveness during the orgasmic cycle are lessened; particularly after sixty, erection takes much longer, ejaculation lacks the same force and duration, the sex flush is markedly reduced, and so forth. Masters and Johnson (1968) stress that the human male's responsiveness does wane as he ages. However, they conclude that

> The most important factor in the maintenance of effective sexuality for the aging male is consistency of active sexual expression. . . . If elevated levels of sexual activity are maintained from earlier years and neither acute nor chronic physical incapacity intervenes, aging males usually are able to continue some form of active sexual expression into the 70- and even 80-year age groups. (pp. 260–270)

The factors that prevent most older men and women from maintaining a normal sex life are financial, personal, family and societal attitudes, together with health problems and lack of a sex partner.

Parent-Adult Child Relationships

Once children leave home and establish a life of their own, parents begin to relate to their children as adults. The child is not only a child to his parents—he may be a parent himself. Parents and children have more in common as they grow older. Daughters may seek out their mothers for advice about child-rearing, tips on cooking and entertaining, and assistance with babysitting. Sons may receive helpful handyman tips from their fathers. The two generations may share similar hobbies, recreational activities, and a love of sports.

In many cases, the emotional ties between parents and their adult children seem to deepen as parents and children grow older. Social ties between elderly parents and their children may also grow stronger over time. Children tend to visit or call their parents frequently and spend leisure and recreation time with them as often as possible. In addition, the adult child joins parents in upholding family traditions (Sussman & Burchinal, 1962).

In other instances, ties between parents and children are anything but strong. Such situations often date back to the early years when there was constant strife between parents and children. Most of these earlier conflicts have never been adequately resolved and have widened the gap between children and their parents. The two parties have never been able to sit down together to talk things over. Instead, they have fortified the barriers against one another.

A social worker may be very helpful to both aging parents and their adult children. The worker needs to understand both sides of the situation and the feelings involved; she may then be able to help the parties get a better grasp of why an impasse has been reached. It is essential for the worker to accustom herself to listening to what both parties *mean,* as well as to what they *say.* The older woman who asserts that she doesn't want to see her son again, and the son who, in turn, says, ''That's fine with me,'' may be concealing their deep hurt at how each has disappointed the other. These are concealed feelings and the worker must listen carefully for them. In addition, guilt feelings on both parts may also be present, and the worker must be able to help alleviate these feelings.

The Meaning of Religion

Sometimes people deal with the difficult facets of their daily experiences through religion. The ability to come to God in prayer and turn unsolvable difficulties over to Him is a source of relief for young and old alike. Such an act demonstrates faith in the power of God to change the unchangeable, and at the same time, acknowledges man's limited abilities to right what is wrong. Once the person has turned the problem over to God, there is a sense of relief, a feeling of confidence that God will bring good out of the situation, and a positive feeling about the future. The person in a sense "transcends" the unpleasant realities and waits for God's answer to the present difficulty.

SUMMARY

It is within the family context that the individual first experiences himself as a social being. The two most fundamental tasks of the family are to provide care and socialization for the young and a network of interpersonal support and personal identity for adults.

Despite its ever-changing forms and functions, the family remains the crucial reference point for most older persons. There is evidence that most older people have considerable involvement with their families.

There is a variety of family forms and relationships, ranging from the traditional nuclear family to the untraditional homosexual couple with a child. However, the most common family form is the nuclear family. Older people are frequently members of extended families.

Retirement and widowhood are two major milestones that aging families frequently encounter. Retirement is a major role change that may or may not represent a crisis for the older person.

In those cases when the older person is experiencing difficulty adjusting to retirement, the social worker needs to understand and then focus on the main area(s) of difficulty that are interfering with the individual's adjustment. In addition, a number of aspects of family functioning should be examined. Emphasis is placed on working with the family as a unit because the worker is then better able to understand the underlying dynamics among the family members.

Sexual behavior during the later years is important to both older men and women. In the past, the failure of society to recognize the sexual needs of older people was serious, but not crucial. Today, when over twenty-five million people have reached the age of sixty-five, society can hardly afford to retain the myth of sexlessness in these years.

Emotional and social ties between parents and their adult children often seem to grow stronger over time. Children visit or call their parents frequently and engage in recreational activities with them as often as possible. In some instances, however, constant strife exists between parents and children. Many of the conflicts date back to the early years and have never been completely resolved.

Sometimes older people deal with difficult experiences in their lives through religion. Once the problem has been turned over to God in prayer, the older person feels a sense of relief and a feeling of confidence that God will bring forth positive results.

Family counseling is a useful method for helping older people and their families deal with problematic situations. During the total family interview the family members begin to recognize their interdependence.

chapter 10

PRACTICE
WITH GROUPS

As people grow older their circle of friends, relatives, and close associates becomes increasingly narrow. Their social contacts decrease as friends die or move away to other areas, as children leave home, and as health problems interfere with their normal style of living. Many older people feel the need to develop new and meaningful relationships with others.

Some older persons seek group contacts on their own. For example, some become actively involved in the social life of the church; some have their lives enriched through programs and contacts at multipurpose senior centers; some become active in political groups; and some seek to enhance their social contacts by taking adult courses at nearby schools. Other older people, beset by emotional and physical problems, have difficulty making contacts of this kind on their own, and may require help through individual or group counseling.

Traditionally, group work with the elderly has consisted of activity, recreation, and entertainment. Staff at institutions and community centers have tended to utilize groups as the principal means of filling leisure hours. However, group intervention is a mode of treatment that appears to be extremely useful in working with a number of older adults simultaneously.

THE PURPOSES OF GROUPS

Groups may be formed for a wide variety of purposes: to discuss current events, to carry on arts and crafts activities, to discuss fears and anxieties around a health problem, or to plan for departure from the hospital and return home. Miller and Solomon (1979) point out that, from the social worker's point of view, the purposes of groups may be

> to help elderly people to develop new and caring relationships, to maintain and enhance feelings of self-worth through continuity of social roles and the development of new ones, and to exert control over their lives through confronting and engaging some of the problems of living in the institutions or in the community. (pp. 87–88).

Natural Groups and Formed Groups

A number of definitions of what a group is have been advanced. One of the most useful definitions is this: ''a collection of people who need each other to work together on a common task, in an agency that is hospitable to the execution of that task" (Schwartz, 1971, p. 1258).

Some groups to which older people belong are natural groups; others are formed. Natural groups are those organized by the members themselves. Formed groups are those organized by outside agents to meet one or more needs of the members through professional help (Harbert & Ginsberg, 1979). For example, therapy or counseling groups for the elderly may be formed by social workers, nurses, or psychologists in a variety of settings such as Veterans Administration hospitals, nursing homes, and community mental health centers. A community senior center crafts group that is selected by the instructor is also a formed group (Harbert & Ginsberg, 1979).

Whether groups are natural or formed, they play an important part in the lines of older people. For example, life-task or problem solving groups are designed to do the following:

> help people who share similar concerns work together to overcome feelings of being alone and hopeless. Included here are groups that deal with life crises and their associated developmental tasks. For example, groups for recent retirees, for couples where one or both are recent retirees, for recent widows and widowers, for people who have recently become disabled, for people living in foster care or adult home settings, and for people who are contemplating a move from independent to institutional living. (Miller & Solomon, 1979, p. 89)

Another type of group to which older people belong is the social action group.

> Social action groups provide opportunities for people to continue to exert control over their lives by affecting political and social issues of concern to old people (as well as issues of general concern), e.g., a change in the mandatory retirement age, problems of housing, transportation, public amenities, traffic lights, increased police protection, increase in Medicare and Medicaid benefits, etc. (Miller & Solomon, 1979, p. 91)

It is especially important for social workers to understand the meaning that belonging to a group has for the older person, and how the group impacts on its members. Harbert and Ginsberg (1979) point out that "group relationships may be the most significant part of life for some older people'' (p. 124). A corollary to this is that most people derive a great deal of emotional support from those groups with which they interact. Most older people belong to more than one group. Some groups are organized social or service groups; others are less formal and more loosely structured. Groups of both kinds serve a very useful purpose for the older person.

In order to understand the significance the group has for the older person, it is necessary to identify the group's purpose(s) or goal(s). If it is a friendship or social group, then the purpose may simply be friendly and effective use of leisure time (Harbert & Ginsberg, 1979). If it is a self-government group, the purpose may be to help people maintain some control over what happens to them in the senior center or in the residential institution. If it is a formal or informal educational group, the purpose may be to help people develop or maintain mastery and competence in areas of common interest.

SOCIAL GROUP WORK WITH THE ELDERLY

Group methods of treatment have been shown to be extremely useful for certain older people with certain types of needs. There are several reasons why group procedures are beneficial. Some of the major ones are these: first, participating in groups promotes a sense of belonging; second, the group serves to enhance communication and interpersonal skills among the members. In addition, groups are facilitative —that is, group members encourage one another, serve as role models and provide direct and immediate feedback to each other (Goldberg & Deutsch, 1977).

Groups vary in many respects, such as in size. They may be small gatherings with as few as three or four people; they may comprise as many as fifteen members, as in some remotivation groups. Too many members may make management of the group unwieldy, and may result in early termination of some of the members. The size of the group will inevitably depend on the level and type of the group and whether there are co-leaders (Burnside, 1978).

Group work with the elderly has become an increasingly popular form of treatment since World War II. As more people began to seek professional help and as fewer trained people were available to help them, group work became a viable method of serving people. Current group procedures range from relatively traditional group psychotherapy patterned after individual treatment approaches to creativity/growth groups. The latter may or may not have a leader and may incorporate a wide range of specific techniques, for example, finger-painting or photography (Goldberg & Deutsch, 1977).

In general, group work with the aged involves a directive approach (Corey & Corey, 1977); leaders must take an active role in giving information, answering questions, and sharing themselves with the group members (Burnside, 1978). Further, the group members may be actively involved in solving their own problems.

Group members often have had no prior familiarity with each other. They may, however, be experiencing similar problems. For instance, some of the members may be experiencing difficulty adjusting to retirement, some are dealing with problems of loneliness, while others are struggling to overcome the use of drugs and/or alcohol. In addition, some come with the physical problems that accompany the normal process of aging. These must be recognized and dealt with. Such problems include declining vision, hearing loss, and limited mobility. Chronic health problems are also common. The group leader must be aware of these limitations and know how to deal with them. For instance, for those group members with a hearing loss, it is essential that the group leader speak slowly and as clearly as possible. Sitting close to the affected members is also helpful. The group leader should strive to keep the groups and circles small and manageable.

Another important point is that the group leader should be supportive of the members both when the group is in session and when it is not. She must demonstrate her continued interest in and concern for the older group member. For instance, the group leader should attend to physical complaints and personally visit or telephone group members. Sometimes older people may use their illness as an excuse for not attending the group. Such work can be demanding and require a great deal of patience, energy, and time.

The worker may also have to allow for a certain amount of dependency on the part of older group members. This is because a distinctive feature of work with older people is their tendency to view themselves—both individually and when in a group—as powerless to control their lives and effect changes in their environment. However, the worker can begin to encourage independent behavior among group members by identifying tasks that can be performed within the group. For instance, when the worker is defining the division of labor within groups of elderly people,

> the statement over who does what can be eliminated, or at least attenuated, by the worker's sharing with members of the group her perception of what tasks they can, in fact, perform. The worker can also offer to accompany and help group members with task performance or invite them to join her as she performs the tasks. (Miller & Solomon, 1979, p. 98)

Common Types of Groups and Group Methods with the Elderly

An exhaustive listing and description of the various kinds of groups and of group methods used with the aged is beyond the purview of this book. However, some of the more common groups and methods will be briefly described.

Reality Orientation Groups.   Reality orientation groups are useful for those older persons experiencing a moderate to severe degree of memory loss, confusion, and disorientation. Reality orientation is, therefore, a phase of rehabilitation for the institutionalized geriatric patient. In terms of procedure, the older person is placed in a group which is intended to wean him or her out of isolation and move him back into the community as a functioning contributor. Group meetings are scheduled regularly. The members are continually stimulated by repeated presentation of fundamental information, such as the day of the week, date, year, weather, next holiday, next meal (Barnes, 1974). To be effective, the reality-orientation process should be continued throughout the waking hours. A basic assumption is that keeping older people active mentally is as crucial as keeping them alive physically (Keller & Hughston, 1981).

An important aspect of reality orientation groups is reality testing, and it is essential that correct information be continuously given to the confused disoriented elderly person (Burnside, 1978). The patient should be told where he is going, what the occasion is, and what is expected of him. For example: "It's time to go to the classroom for lessons, Mr. Smith." "Today we want you to read the board." "Mrs. Johnson, you go to eat your lunch at twelve o'clock every day." "It is time to take a nap, Mr. Jones. This is your bed. See, it has your name on it—John Jones." The group leader should continue to reward the patient for his successes in finding his way around by praising him or giving him other appropriate rewards. Other essential points for the group leader to remember include the following:

1 Speak slowly and distinctly because many times older patients are hard of hearing.
2 Speak in a friendly manner, but do not talk to the patient as though he were a child.
3 Look directly at the patient when addressing him.
4 Maintain a calm, friendly approach.
5 Give the patient adequate time to respond.

Reminiscing Groups. Reminiscing groups have been in existence since 1970. These groups are based on the concept of the "life review" postulated by Robert N. Butler in 1961. This concept assumes that reminiscence in the aged is part of a normal life review process brought about by realization of approaching dissolution and death. The life review process "is characterized by the progressive return to consciousness of past experiences and particularly the resurgence of unresolved conflicts which can be looked at again and reintegrated" (Butler & Lewis, 1977, p. 49).

The purpose of the groups is to explore the memories of at least six to eight elderly persons (Burnside, 1978). Meetings are held once or twice a week. The sessions last about an hour and may be held in institutional or noninstitutional settings. Memories run the gamut from happy to sad, serious to somber, and include all states of life (Burnside, 1978).

In remembering his past life, the older person is engaged in ordering his life, accepting what has been, sometimes reworking aspects of the past to make them more acceptable to him (Butler, 1964). Older people who are mentally intact often recount the same event again and again as they reminisce. No matter how many times the older person repeats himself, the group leader must not "tune out," but rather in these situations offer the acceptance and appreciation that is being sought (Miller & Solomon, 1979).

Remotivation Therapy Groups. Remotivation groups are popular for reaching those long-term, chronic patients residing in large mental hospitals, who are reluctant to move toward improvement or discharge. The remotivation technique consists of the following five steps:

1   The climate of acceptance—establishing a warm, friendly relationship in the group.

2   A bridge to reality—reading poetry, keeping up with current events, etc.

3   Sharing the world—development of the topic through planned questions, use of props, etc.

4   An appreciation of the work of the world—stimulating the patients to think about work in relation to themselves.

5   The climate of appreciation—expressing enjoyment at getting together, etc.

The goals of remotivation therapy are (1) to assist the resident in resocialization and organization of thought; (2) to stimulate communication among individuals in a group; and (3) to provide opportunities for residents to share ideas, opinions and life experiences with those who will recognize and reward their participation (Health Careers Education, Training and Consultation Service, 1978).

Remotivation groups are generally composed of six to ten residents, with two people who are alert and talkative and at least two who are regressed. Patients, both men and women, are placed in a circle, with the group leader or remotivator in the center, moving about freely. As he moves about the group, the group leader greets each person by name, shakes his hand, and welcomes him. He also tries to say something nice that he has noticed about the older person.

The group leader may then interject some interest-gathering questions into the group to stimulate response among the members—for example, "When does the snow fall?" "When the sky is gray, what kind of weather do we expect?" "What do people do on rainy days?" "How do people enjoy sunny, warm days?" "If you went for a walk in the country on a nice day, what would you be most likely to see?" Any response obtained is accepted by the group leader, who may repeat what was said, or comment "That's right..." "Good..." "Yes..." "Fine..." "Great..." This procedure is always followed by the reading by the group leader of a short poem with a regular, even rhythm and rhyme. Following the reading of the poem, discussion is stimulated through the leader's questions: "What...?" "When...?" "Where...?" "How...?" "Why...?"

There are those who believe this approach has merit because it has resocialized and reinvolved many elderly patients in the ideas of the world outside the institution (Health Careers Education, Training and Consultation Service, 1978).

Topic-Specific Groups. There are a number of other groups that are recommended for use with the elderly. Such groups include art therapy groups, health-related groups, music groups, poetry groups, and so forth. They are designed ultimately to improve the quality of daily living for older people and to assist them to live in the community for as long as possible. Thus, the forming of a group should depend upon the purposes of that group. Since a group formed by the social worker will be based on some specific objective, the members selected will have similar problems or difficulties.

Every social worker will not have the knowledge, skills, or inclination to work with groups of older people. The worker's ability to lead groups will be based in large part on his knowledge of group dynamics, group theory, psychodynamics and a background in social work and gerontology. However, the student/worker must have the skills and motivation required to begin a group.

The chronic shortages of helping professionals such as psychiatrists, psychologists, and social workers underscore the need for a variety of human services workers including volunteers and paraprofessionals to provide services to the elderly. However, the need for professionals with group leadership skills will continue.

BASIC CONCEPTS FOR GROUP WORK WITH THE ELDERLY

Background Information for Potential Members

Before the older person joins a group, he or she has the right to information as to what the group is all about. He or she should know something about the purposes of the group and the time, place, and length of group sessions, how long the group is expected to last, who the other members are, and who the group leader will be (Burnside,

1976). Even when a potential group member is disoriented and confused, every attempt should be made to communicate this information to him.

Selection of Group Members

This is in many ways a process of sizing up who will be the members of the group, a weighing of factors about what persons will benefit most from the group experience. Before a contract is negotiated, both the older adult and the social worker will want to obtain more information about how the group can be of benefit.

The leader will want to select members who are manageable in a group. For instance, if one member is extremely outspoken, belligerent, and upsetting to the other group members, this would be counterproductive to group work. If all of the members of the group are frail and in poor physical health, this would overtax the capacities of a single group leader. In such a case, it would be beneficial to have a co-leader.

There are some who believe that random selection of group members is the preferred approach (Harbert & Ginsberg, 1979). As long as people want to spend their time together and enjoy each other's company, then this is perhaps the wisest way to proceed in selecting group members. However, the value of pre-membership interviews cannot be underestimated in making group membership selections.

The Early Stages of the Group

The early stages of the group are characterized by the members' cautiousness and their disinclination to reveal much about themselves. The group leader will be faced with a variety of personalities. Some members will rarely talk during the early stages, one or two others may monopolize the group. Eventually the members will take on certain roles and tasks. Some members will be mistrustful of other members until they become more familiar with them.

The members should be informed at the beginning about the group objectives. The worker should also state briefly the concerns that the members share and make some attempt to connect people with one another through their shared concerns.

A certain amount of anxiety may be apparent among the

members, especially during the early stages of the group. Some members will appear to be uneasy, nervous, worried, and a bit apprehensive. This is a natural occurrence especially if the group members are not familiar with each other. However, the degree of anxiety should diminish as they become more familiar and more comfortable with each other, become more familiar with the group process and the benefits to be derived, and begin to reach out to each other.

Throughout the life of the group, the worker must be aware of any medical and physical problems of older group members. A group member with diabetes, arthritis, or emphysema may have difficulty attending the group sessions on his own on a regular basis. In that case, transportation may have to be arranged.

The Middle Stage of the Group

Group cohesion does not come easily. There will be a lot of testing as group members struggle with the issues of acceptance and nonacceptance, support, and willingness to interact with and communicate with one another. The worker may find this an especially difficult time, as he attempts to hold the group together.

A number of individual personality factors emerge at this time. A few older members may monopolize the group; there may be silent member(s), hostile member(s), and members who operate at the group's periphery. These last sit at a distance from the others, appear to be paying little attention, and generally seem to have little interest in the group. Yet their attendance level is high.

These personality factors will come together in the context of the group and may result in a certain amount of conflict. Group conflict in and of itself is a normal aspect of group growth (Harbert & Ginsberg, 1979). If the conflict (that is, struggle, strife) becomes extreme, it may disrupt the meeting altogether and cause the group to fall apart. This phenomenon has not only been observed in groups for therapy, but also for education, for tasks, for problem-solving, and so on. As the group members settle in and become better acquainted with each other a period of testing seems to occur. The group members may become disenchanted with each other, the group, the group's tasks, and whatever independence they may have given up by becoming a member of the group. Hartford (1971) vividly points out that

> the discomfort emerging from the participants' reaction to belonging may show itself in hostilities, resistances, anger, striking out, or withdrawal. It may show itself in confusion. There may be denial of having heard or participated in any preliminary development of group purposes and tasks. (p. 81)

In order for the group to go on with the business at hand, it may first have to deal with these conflicts around interpersonal issues.

Group conflict must be skillfully handled. The leadership role requires that the group worker must allow for open discussion on all sides of the issue. Each person must be given an opportunity to speak. Thus the group may be a useful tool for releasing the range of feelings and concerns that exist among the members.

Once the group is more firmly established, subgrouping among the group members is almost inevitable. This may be of extreme importance to the older person whose circle of friendships has narrowed. Sometimes friendships formed in groups are carried over into the older person's life outside of the group.

As the group stabilizes, the worker helps the members communicate more effectively with one another, develop group norms, and mobilize to use their energies in carrying out the group's activities. Differences may still arise from time to time but they are resolved within the context of democratic decision-making (Harbert & Ginsberg, 1979). The atmosphere of the group is without tension or strife; members feel free to risk themselves more; they communicate more easily. The group members also look forward to coming to the meetings. Relationships among the members become more meaningful during this phase. In fact, some members may show up an hour or more before the group actually meets.

A ten-week experimental task-directed group led by a certified painting instructor met on a weekly basis in a local Jewish community service center. The leader was paid for her services. The group consisted of twelve community-based marginal elderly persons ranging in age from sixty-five to eight-seven years. They had limited educational backgrounds, were living on fixed incomes, and were relatively culturally and socially disadvantaged. Most were isolated and relatively shy. The major goal of the group was to provide the members with a personally enriching experience through painting. Specific objectives were: (1) to increase communication and interaction with peers, family, and friends;

(2) to increase opportunities for personal self-fulfillment; (3) to increase feelings of self-worth; (4) to establish personal bonds among group members; and (5) to develop basic skills in painting.

During the early sessions, the members appeared shy and reluctant to talk. None had ever painted before. The group leader took the initiative by giving the members a general introduction to painting and allowing them to examine, visually and by touching, the materials to be used during the sessions. The materials included paper, brushes, paints, plastic spoons, paper plates, plastic containers, canvas board, spatulas for mixing, etc. They examined still life paintings of fruit such as apples, pears, and oranges. The students were shown how to make easels out of cardboard boxes. They became familiar with paints. An early exercise was to bring in a picture or a subject to paint.

During the first four sessions, most of those members of the group who were actively participating stayed to themselves and concentrated on their own painting. Peer interaction was low even into the fifth session, though interaction with the group's instructor was high. The leader used this session to give individual instruction to the group members on such topics as light, color, depth, special qualities, and shadows. She also provided positive feedback, and encouraged the non-participants to become more actively involved.

This activity was carried over into the sixth session. By this time, more members began to paint, the level of interaction among peers increased, and the class began to come alive. Several members of the group started arriving at least an hour before the class was scheduled to begin.

A new dimension was added at the seventh session. The members began to critique each other's paintings and eventually their own. The leader always initiated the process, offering positive feedback about the various aspects of the paintings. At first, some of the group members were shy about accepting criticism and reluctant to give it. Once they became more comfortable about the purpose of the criticism, however, their attitude changed. Group members became more cohesive and actively involved with both their own and each other's paintings. Interaction and communication among members was high.

Some new people wanted to join the group. However, their presence was resented by the original group members, who felt that their progress would be impeded.

During the remaining sessions, the bonds between members were strengthened. Some of the group members were coming to class in carpools; a few were being driven to class by the group leader. Coming to the sessions in carpools afforded the members an opportunity to interact on a more intimate and personal level.

The worker is very active during the middle phase. She sets the pace and tone for the group. She models behavior and encourages the members to interact with each other in a forthright, nondefensive, and nonjudgmental manner (Burnside, 1978). Older people who are not familiar with this way of behaving may be somewhat reluctant to approach another member in this manner. But as they see the worker interacting without adverse effects, they feel more comfortable in trying it out themselves. Notice, for example, the elderly members' initial reluctance to criticize each other's paintings. However, as the leader assumed the role of model for the members, they began to follow her lead. By emulating the leader, these members were also increasing their own self-esteem.

As a group continues to meet, the older members who have remained throughout the early and middle stages will continue to attend on a regular basis—unless they experience a personal problem in their own lives. For older community-based group members, the group may be among the significant and meaningful outlets within the context of their lives. For those older group members who reside in institutions, the group at this stage may become overriding, all-consuming and dominant.

The Termination Phase of the Group

Ideally, each group member should know from the beginning the plan for the termination of the group. For instance, in a therapy group, the members should be told at the outset the number of sessions or the length of time that the group will exist. In a task-directed group, the members should know that the group will terminate when it has completed its tasks. Since all relationships eventually must come to an end, so the life of the group cannot go on forever, although some groups go on for years, adding new members as other members drop out. However, most groups established for some purpose eventually come to an end.

Termination with groups must be planned appropriately so that the members may move on from this experience to something else. Although the worker and the group members should all be actively involved in the termination process, the group worker's skills are especially important in helping the members work through this experience. Hartford (1971) stresses that the termination phase includes enumerating and evaluating the group's accomplishments and failures, planning for recognition of individual members and leaders, and a period of working through the difficulties that some members may feel in breaking the ties. (p. 87)

Most members anticipate the ending of the group, although some may need to be reminded that the ending was scheduled from the beginning. Some may avoid termination by not coming to meetings. Others may come late and minimize their involvement and interaction with the other members. Some may want to continue the group beyond the current experience. In that case, the members should explore their reasons for continuing and talk about what they expect to accomplish with another group experience.

All group members should be involved in the termination process, since termination is a normal life experience. The group experience has a special meaning for each individual member, and giving up that experience may be hard for some. Nevertheless, if the members are helped to deal with this experience appropriately and in a healthy way, then this may prepare them for other terminations that will confront them in life. Termination may thus help them on to other experiences (Hartford, 1971).

GROUP WORK WITH THE ELDERLY: DEMANDING AND REWARDING

Group work with the elderly can be extremely demanding, especially if the members making up the group are regressed. Regressed elderly group members tend to be overly dependent, listless, apathetic, and have relatively low energy levels. It may be helpful to the worker to balance the membership in such a way that some members are less regressed than others.

Group workers will need as much support as possible from other staff members. For instance, the supervisor should be available to the new group worker, particularly during the beginning of the group experience. The supervisor's presence and feedback should help the new worker deal with anxiety, depression, and lack of self-esteem that members may experience during the early phase of the group.

Group work with the elderly can also be extremely rewarding.

This is especially the case in task-directed groups when relatively isolated and shy elderly people have come together to learn a new task such as finger painting, ceramics, puppet-making, or photography. Such a group, as it exists in the life of a multipurpose senior center, a housing project, or a community center, can bring heightened interest and unanticipated benefits. Curiosity is aroused among staff and other older people outside the group, other older people want to join, family members are especially satisfied, and members themselves develop increased feelings of confidence and self-worth.

For instance, the group in painting aroused great interest in the community center. Some older people with serious physical handicaps wanted to join the group. A stroke victim who only painted numbers decided he wanted something more. Seniors with eye problems and some who had trouble standing wanted to become members of the group. The varied painting exercises, the flexibility of the group, the sensitivity of the leader to the needs of the older members, the positive regard she demonstrated toward both the students and their efforts, and the feelings of concern and goodwill that existed among the group members—all contributed toward the achievement of the group's objectives.

SUMMARY

Social group work is a useful method for intervening with older adults. Groups are formed for many purposes and play an important part in the lives of older people. To understand the meaning the group has for the older person, it is necessary to identify the group's purpose(s) or goal(s). Formed groups may be organized for the expressed purpose of dealing with such problems as adjustment to retirement, widowhood, or substance abuse.

Social work with the elderly in groups can be demanding and require a great deal of patience, energy, and time. A number of questions may have to be answered and leaders must take an active role in information-giving.

The four types of groups identified in this chapter are reality orientation, reminiscing, remotivation therapy and topic-specific groups. Reality orientation groups are useful for those older persons experiencing a moderate to severe degree of memory loss, confusion, and disorientation. Reminiscing groups are guided by the "life review" concept developed by Robert N. Butler in 1961. This concept assumes that reminiscence in older people is part of a normal life review process. Remotivation therapy stresses resocialization and reinvolvement in patients who are reluctant to move toward improvement or discharge. Topic-specific groups are designed to improve the quality of daily life for older people, and to assist them in living in the community for as long as possible.

A number of ideas are suggested for working with older persons in groups. Prior to joining a group, the older persons should be given some background information about the group. Thought should be given to the selection of group members. The early stages of the group are characterized by the members' cautiousness. There is also a certain amount of anxiety and sizing each other up.

Before the group coalesces, there will be a lot of testing as the members struggle with such issues as acceptance, support, and willingness to interact with one another. During the middle phase of the group, various personality styles may surface and create a certain amount of group conflict. At this stage, the group takes on considerable significance for the members.

Most groups established for some purpose must come to an end. Although termination is discussed during the early phases of the group, many members forget and have to be reminded of this during the termination phase. Most members anticipate the end. Even though the group may terminate, some members continue to keep in touch with each other on an on-going basis.

chapter 11

COMMUNITY SERVICES

Community services consist of a fabric of institutional services that have been developed to meet the needs of individuals and families. The services of this system vary from one community to another, but they usually include the following: public transportation, religion, recreation, public health and safety, sanitation, housing, employment and legal systems (Goldberg & Deutsch, 1977). These services meet many individual needs. However, problematic situations may arise among and between people that are not addressed by these major community services. For example, noninstitutionalized, elderly, frail clients who may need help from several agencies may be unable to negotiate the services they need or to protect themselves from overzealous caretakers. Such older clients may be in need of protective services. Other older people who have difficulty getting around because of physical disabilities or language barriers may require escort services. An information and referral service can be of invaluable assistance to those older people who are experiencing difficulty in finding resources to help resolve such difficulties as leaky faucets, problems in receiving their social security checks, or the dilemma of finding assistance for an older parent diagnosed as having organic brain syndrome.

·   Protective, escort, and information and referral services were developed in response to specialized needs and are concerned with promoting and improving the social functioning and self-actualization of individuals and families. They are part of what is frequently referred to as the human services system. These services exist in a number of different communities throughout the country. In some communities human service systems function reasonably well; in others, human services offer very little to the citizens (Goldberg & Deutsch, 1977). Ideally, for human service systems to function effectively, there must be a comprehensive range of services available to the citizens. Instead, in many communities, such service systems are characterized by fragmentation, duplication, and obvious gaps in service delivery.

COMMUNITY-BASED HUMAN SERVICES
AND SOCIAL WORK: AN HISTORICAL OVERVIEW

Social work has wrestled for years with the issue of whether community organizations should stress the delivery of services to individuals in need, or should emphasize the modification of social conditions which predispose some people to dysfunction or disadvantage. Social work from its inception had two aspects: social treatment and social reform. These were spelled out to mean the care and rehabilitation of troubled individuals and the elimination of social conditions which bring on hardship (Cox et al., 1970). These approaches were recognized as complementary to each other and had a single objective —the well-being of the individual.

The early years of the development of social work were characterized by social action movements. For instance, settlement houses fought for more and better schools, better working conditions, and safer and healthier recreational and living environments. The Progressive Era (1900-1915) produced a large number of dedicated, social reformers imbued with the ideal of service—service to the ill-housed and ill-fed and to the community. Their vision of a classless, democratic society was belied by the stratifications of race and class (Lubove, 1963). Many early social reformers such as Florence Kelley, Jane Addams, Edward T. Devine, Joseph Goldmark, and Mary Richmond demonstrated through their humanitarian efforts that social action was a viable method for solving key social problems of the time. Thus, in its early years, social work made a two-pronged attack on human disability and injustice through casework and social action.

Shortly after World War I, social casework was greatly influenced by the new psychoanalytic theory. According to Friedlander and Apte (1980), the new insights into human behavior and personality developed by Sigmund Freud spread quickly into the social work arena. "Psychoanalytic concepts, which offered psychodynamic examinations of client behavior, became of primary interest to workers" (p. 116). Social workers embraced the psychoanalytic model of practice to the extent that it overshadowed social reform activities. Social casework became the model of practice in social work. This trend continued for years as there was a dearth of systematic literature or explicit theory from the busy action-oriented community practitioners (Cox et al., 1970).

Interest in social reform activities was given new impetus in the years following World War II. This was due primarily to the empirical knowledge originating in the social sciences. The social sciences provided a knowledge base for the planning and social

change area comparable to the base provided earlier for the treatment area by psychoanalysis (Cox et al., 1970).

During the 1960's, society exerted a great deal of pressure on various professions, among them social work, to address themselves to social injustice and dysfunction. Individualized services were not sufficient to deal with such problems as discrimination, poverty, urban blight, racial conflict, certain types of delinquency, unemployment, and educational disability. A number of programs designed to improve the social conditions among the poor and disadvantaged came into existence. Such programs included Office of Economic Opportunity, Model Cities, School Improvement Projects, and Volunteers in Service to America (VISTA).

In many instances, these antipoverty programs were extremely beneficial to the clientele they assisted; in other instances, questions were raised about their effectiveness. Many community-based services developed in a relatively haphazard manner. No doubt public and fiscal policies contributed to this situation (Goldberg & Deutsch, 1977). Government agencies became increasingly involved in mandating and funding a variety of programs. Such programs continued to mushroom in both the public and private sectors and there was little or no interrelation between them. Many communities developed their own backup system of human services. These latter service systems also were poorly developed because in some areas there were gaps, and in others duplication or a great deal of fragmentation.

There were also questions about service delivery. Some service delivery systems failed to provide services to those targeted for the services. Such targeted groups included the poor, minority groups, those living in rural communities, and the elderly. Many service agencies were designed to serve people with specific problems (the mentally retarded, the physically handicapped, the blind, and so forth) rather than various categories of people (the elderly, the unemployed, the poor, and so forth). An individual with multiple problems might have to travel to agencies scattered all over the community before all his needs could be met.

In addition, the cost of community services skyrocketed and questions were raised about their effectiveness. To what extent were they benefiting the clients served? According to Goldberg & Deutsch (1977) when information about the effectiveness of the various ser-

vices was collected, it was discovered that a discouragingly high proportion of people were not being helped.

Most agencies, particularly public agencies funded by taxpayers' monies, responded to the push for accountability. Attempts were made, and are being made, to cut out waste, upgrade staff, develop innovative service techniques, and redesign the entire service network.

INTERVENTION AT THE COMMUNITY LEVEL

Community organization has been variously defined by educators and practitioners, and yet has seemed to defy or elude definition. Currently, there is no universally held or used definition of the community organization method in social work (Moore, 1970). Nevertheless, the concept, community organization, covers a number of related activities at the community level aimed at bringing about desired improvement in the social well-being of individuals, groups, neighborhoods (Brager & Specht, 1973). Under whatever name, intervention at the community level is oriented toward influencing community institutions and solving community welfare problems (Cox et al., 1970).

Community organization owes allegiance to the great social reformers of the early 1900s and their crusades to improve social institutions and social conditions. Community organization has passed through a number of stages of development; a major emphasis today is on program development that generally involves planning, community influences on planning, the role of the planner, and so forth. Planning for social needs has been expanding and proliferating fairly rapidly in recent years.

However, planning is not the whole of community organization. Community organization has always involved direct work with people in the community for neighborhood development or social action purposes. The historical precedent for this aspect of community organization in social work is the settlement house movement, beginning with the Neighborhood Guild in New York in 1886, and the Hull-House in Chicago in 1889. The settlement approach was a total identification by the settlement workers with the disadvantaged neighborhood and its people, and an attempt to elevate socially whole

groups of people through improved housing, sanitation, education, recreation, medical care, in an effort to create a sense of community (Moore, 1970).

There has been renewed interest in community organization practice at the neighborhood level in a number of cities around the country. At least a part of community organization practice continues to be focused on direct organizational work with low-income populations—for example, the frail or at risk elderly who are not affiliated with the major institutional systems and are not using available services in the community.

What distinguishes community organization from the other methods of practice? Some practitioners are of the opinion that the field and content determine the nature of the community organization process. The field is conceptualized as being made up of coordinating (planning) and "promotional" (fund-raising, educational) agencies. The processes are those of social change through democratic procedures which seek to unite rather than to divide groups, and to plan "with" rather than "for" people (Moore, 1967).

For Ross (1967), neither setting nor content determines the nature of the community organization process. Community organization to Ross is a distinctive pattern of work which has wide application in both community development and community relations. Ross stresses that the process and the end product must always be the enhancement of "community integration." By integration Ross means the community's "capacity to function as a unit in solving its own problems."

Ross (1967) defined community organization as:

> . . . a process by which a community identifies its needs or objectives, orders (or ranks) these needs or objectives, develops the confidence and will to work at these needs or objectives, finds the resources (internal and/or external) to deal with these needs or objectives, takes action in respect to them, and in so doing extends and develops cooperative and collaborative attitudes and practices in the community. (Chapter I)

Two assumptions held by Ross are that "communities of people can develop the capacity to deal with their problems," and that "people should participate in major changes in the communities" (p. 13). According to Ross (1967), communities will change their ways only if forced or highly motivated to change.

In the 1959 Curriculum-Study of Social Work, Boehm stated that

> community organization is conceived to be a direct service method whose aim is to provide services to community agencies for the enhancement of community life and the functioning of community groups, and thereby indirectly contribute to the enhancement of the social functioning of individuals. (1959, p. 136)

This conceptualization embodies the core values, goals, knowledge, and methods common to both casework and group work. Thus, the worker should have an understanding of social work knowledge and skill in methods to enhance his problem-solving activities in the community. According to this definition, in order for change to occur there must first be recognition that a social problem exists. Also, the community must focus on some attainable group goal through activities that are designed to move the people of the affected community toward that goal (Moore, 1967).

In the last several years, strong emphasis has been placed on "lay" or citizen leadership in the affected neighborhoods or communities. It has been stressed that residents of the community should be actively involved in any decisions that concern them. Much of the focus since the Civil Rights Movement and the War on Poverty in the 1960s has been on change at the neighborhood level. People who live in close proximity to each other often have certain special needs or interests in common. The worker's role in this instance would be to organize people to be consumers of social welfare goods and services in the community.

Many older people live in areas where resources are scarce and knowledge of how to reach them is nonexistent. Even where services exist, they may go unused. Leadership capabilities among the elderly are also scarce, and when leaders do emerge, they are uncertain how to organize their activities and mobilize community residents for action. Consider the following case example:

> Mr. and Mrs. Jones lived in a low-income urban community. The housing projects in which they lived were

subsidized by federal funds. All of the residents of the community were elderly and living on fixed incomes. Social work counseling services were provided the residents through the housing authority. Concrete services such as help in processing housing complaints or in consumer problems were also provided. These services were located in the main office of the housing project, but few project residents used them. A tenant association was organized by a few key residents (including Mr. Jones and his wife) and the community organizer (CO) whose office was in the central building.

Meetings were held once every two weeks in a meeting room in the main building. Issues of concern to the elderly residents were discussed—most of which related to housing problems and housing policy. The CO and key leaders of the group thought that the most effective way to improve and utilize existing services was to get the elderly residents together to register joint complaints. Notices were sent out in advance of each meeting to remind tenants of the next meeting as well as to provide information about what was discussed during the previous meeting. These meetings were thought to be helpful to the few who came faithfully, but concern was expressed about the low attendance.

Mr. Jones (who had been elected president of the tenant association), his wife, a few other key people and the CO held a strategy session for facilitating resident participation. A decision was made to interview each elderly person in his or her own home to find out what, if any, were the barriers to participation. Once the interviewing was underway it became clear that a number of problems existed. Many elderly people did not know what to expect from these meetings and thought that if they complained too much they would be evicted; some were frail and afraid to risk falling on the street; others did not come because of transportation problems and felt the main office was much too far to walk. The major problem, however, was fear of crime. Several families had moved into low-rent apartment buildings on the other side of the street. Most of these families included teenagers. Some of the elderly residents had already been victims of purse-snatching and other forms of intimidation. News of these incidents spread rapidly and even though the tenants were safe within their own homes, they feared going out.

Armed with this input, key leaders and the CO once again convened to develop the kind of linkage services that would assist elderly people in using the services available. A door to door transportation system was developed: older people were picked up at their door and returned to their door whenever they needed to go shopping, to meetings, to the bank, and to the doctor. A citizen watch was also developed. Teams of older people took turns in watching the homes on their block. A direct line to the local police was in operation at all times. Lighting on the streets was improved. Lights were also kept on all night in each building.

As a result of these improvements, elderly residents felt safer in leaving their homes to utilize and participate more in community programs and services.

Objectives of Community Organization

Several related objectives of community organization have been identified. The objectives may be described as the coordination of existing services, extension of or change in existing services, the planning of future services, and the development and implementation of new services (Friedlander & Apte, 1980). Each of these goals is intended to enhance the quality and coverage of service delivery to the client and target group. Another essential aim of community organization activities is the enhancement of human relationships and opportunities through engagement in the process of shared responsibility to bring about change (Friedlander & Apte, 1980).

One means of bringing about change or working for improvements is to organize the people who require institutional services—that is, the consumers. With this approach, residents of communities learn by experience that they can be effective in changing certain unacceptable conditions.

Another approach, the organizational, focuses on the performance of institutions in meeting human needs. A basic aim of the social worker in this area is to improve that performance. Moore (1970) sees the organizational approach as "a method of effecting social change in all or any part of a community through the modification of the behavior of its institutions and its ways of using resources in social welfare matters" (p. 239). Thus, the social worker may strive to change the institutions directly, that is, to concentrate on the providers of social welfare (Klenk & Ryan, 1970).

Friedlander and Apte (1980) state that:

> The social worker in the field of community organization must become well acquainted with the social needs in the community and with the most vital desires of its population for improvement of services and

changes in conditions. The task then is to mobilize those forces that enable the public and private social service organizations and indigenous groups to coordinate their activities toward common goals. (p. 150)

Community Practice

The social sciences have made major contributions to the practice of community organization. One vital contribution has been in understanding the settings in which community organizers work. These are frequently referred to as the settings or arenas of community practice. Such settings include interpersonal relations, small groups, formal organizations, neighborhoods, communities, and societies (Cox et al., 1970). It is the community that will be singled out here for special attention. A sense of community is important if the reader is to understand the contexts within which community organizers work.

Communities have been variously defined. One frequently cited definition is that of Roland L. Warren (1963) who defines a community as

> ...that combination of social units and systems which perform the major social functions having locality relevance. This is another way of saying that by "community" we mean the organization of social activities to afford people daily local access to those broad areas of activity which are necessary in day to day living. (p. 9)

Warren identified five major functions of the community: (1) production-distribution-consumption; (2) socialization; (3) social control; (4) social participation; and (5) major support. Each of these functions is carried out by collections of groups and formal organizations, partly dependent on one another but in no way centrally controlled. A community is not planned nor is it centrally directed, as are parts of a formal organization.

Another way of defining a community is to view it as the territorial organization of people, goods, services, and commitments. It is an important subsystem of the society, and one in which many "locality relevant" functions are carried on (Cox et al., 1970). The social worker's influence may be directed within the community for the purpose of changing local attitudes, administrative practices, and so on. Cox and colleagues (1970) suggest that

> The worker may do this directly by working with the individuals in
> groups and organizations, and indirectly by influencing the
> characteristics of the groups and organizations themselves such as size,
> representativeness, operating procedures, etc. as well as intervening in
> the relations between individuals, groups and organizations, i.e.,
> bringing them into closer communication or cooperation, increasing their
> autonomy, facilitating confrontation and contention, etc. (pp. 59–60)

The social worker may also direct his efforts toward the larger society and attempt to affect national opinion and legislation.

Three models of community organization practice are briefly described below, together with examples that relate specifically to the elderly and the community. Each model suggests that the worker performs various roles and strategies for planning and bringing about change. Rothman (1968) refers to these community organization methods as locality development, social planning, and social action.

Locality Development.   Locality development presumes that community change can be pursued optimally through broadly based participation in goal determination and action by a wide spectrum of people at the local community level. Community development is perhaps the archetype for locality development. As stated in a major United Nations publication:

> Community development can be tentatively defined as a process designed
> to create conditions of economic and social progress for the whole
> community with its active participation and the fullest possible reliance
> on the community's initiative. (United Nations, 1955, p. 6)

Essential themes emphasized in locality development include democratic procedures, voluntary cooperation, self-help, development of indigenous leadership, and educational objectives (Dunham, 1963). Thus, a broad cross-section of people is involved in determining and solving problems. Salient practitioner roles include enabler, catalyst, coordinator, teacher of problem-solving skills and ethical values.

Some examples of locality development in the field of aging that use this approach include community efforts to provide supportive services to allow older individuals to remain in the community; the home delivery of medical services; day care centers for the elderly;

meals-on-wheels; and outreach programs designed to seek out older people in the community who need help.

Many communities throughout the country provide supportive services to the elderly. Supportive services are designed to compensate for the reduced functions of the aged and help them to remain independent. If such services were not provided, many elderly might have to enter institutions unnecessarily. Blonsky (1973) has described how one community started a supportive service program and the effect it had on the older residents of that community. The program was based on the principle of using the strengths and resources of older persons to help older persons. A store-front office staffed by older people was set up. Older residents of the community were informed of its existence. Among the available services were a bus service, a tenant-landlord complaint bureau, a neighborhood improvement association, a cooperative food service, and an information referral desk that directed all types of problems to an appropriate source. The program was effective in maintaining in the community many aged people who would otherwise have been forced to enter institutions.

There are several other supportive services that the community can offer its older citizens, drawing on the strengths and resources of older people to help older people. It is the social worker in the role of enabler who can facilitate this process by encouraging organization, helping people express their needs, nourishing good interpersonal relationships, and emphasizing common objectives (Biddle & Biddle, 1965). For instance, through friendly visiting programs, older persons can be assisted in relieving a sense of loneliness and boredom. Telephone reassurance programs are similar to friendly visiting programs, in that loneliness can be lessened and reassurance given. Telephone reassurance and friendly visiting are supportive services ideal for volunteers, particularly older volunteers. Homemaker services provide a competent person to come into the home and to perform essential housekeeping tasks for older persons who cannot perform basic tasks for themselves. The duties include cleaning the home, planning meals, shopping for food, preparing meals, doing the laundry, and so forth. Outreach programs are designed to locate older people who do not know of a program's existence, or are too proud to ask for help, and inform them about the services that may be available to them (Crandall, 1980). The purpose of outreach is to help with a specific problem by informing older peo-

ple about the services that are available in the community (Harbert & Ginsberg, 1979). Supportive community services may also include transportation services, employment counseling, shopping assistance, escort services, and various types of protective services. Each of these services is designed to help older people cope more effectively with the complex matrix of problems confronting them (Harbert & Ginsberg, 1979).

The Social Planning Approach.   The social planning approach stresses a technical process of solving substantive social problems such as those involving housing, mental and physical health, or recreation. Social planning organizations, themselves, are often mandated specifically to deal with concrete social problems, and their official names signify this—mental health departments, city planning and urban renewal authorities, alcoholism rehabilitation centers, and so forth (Rothman, 1968). Rational deliberation and controlled change have a central place in the social planning model. The degree of community involvement may vary from a great deal to little, depending on what organizational variables are present. This approach presumes that planned change in a complex industrial environment requires experts to guide change processes through the exercise of technical skills, including the ability to manipulate large bureaucratic organizations. The basic concern here is delivering goods and services to people who need them. Building community capacity and fostering radical or fundamental social change do not play an essential part (Rothman, 1968).

Salient practitioner roles include fact-gatherer and analyst, program implementer, and facilitator. In terms of change strategy, emphasis is always placed on gathering pertinent facts about the problem, and then deciding on a rational and feasible course of action. Thus, the practitioner plays a central role in gathering and analyzing facts and determining appropriate services, programs, and actions.

Sometimes essential programs and services that are needed by older people do not actually exist. This may mean that to serve an older clientele effectively a program or service must be created or developed. Program development always involves planning. Harbert and Ginsberg (1979) define planning as the ''systematic process of decision-making through which one makes rational choices among

alternative problem solutions'' (p. 196). Thus the worker moves through a series of steps leading to logical choices about the most effective ways of meeting the needs of the older adult. People engaged in program development attempt to find the most desirable solution to an existing service need. An example given by Harbert and Ginsberg (1979) demonstrates this point:

> The director of a meals program, in looking through the agency files, may discover that a number of older people who would like to receive hot meals aren't able to, because they cannot get to the meals program. After discussing this matter, the director learns that other meals program directors have identified a similar problem. The director of the meals program may then make contact with service agencies in the community to determine if they provide transportation to older people. If they do not offer transportation service either, the program director will probably conclude that transportation is a problem not only for prospective participants of the meals program but for all the elderly of the community, and something should be done about it.
>
> The "something to be done" may involve any of a number of solutions. For example, in the situation stated above, the need perceived by the meals program director is for transportation services. However, does this mean that older people need access to public transportation or financial aid in order to use transportation? If older people do not have access to public transportation, then the service needed is a transportation system. If, on the other hand, they do not have money to pay for public transportation, then the service needed may be an income subsidy to be used for public transportation. The planning process enables the planner to make the correct choices among the various alternatives available. (pp. 197–198)

Morris and Binstock (1966) identify six major steps in the planning process which, if engaged in, should lead to an ultimate goal. The six steps are: (1) problem identification; (2) problem analysis; (3) involvement of interested people; (4) development of a plan of action; (5) program implementation; and (6) program evaluation. It is these steps that Morris and Binstock believe are the logical ones to follow in the planning process. If carried out conscientiously, they should lead to rational decisions about program development (Harbert & Ginsberg, 1979).

This approach is practiced in a number of federal, state, and local agencies, in social planning divisions of urban renewal authorities, in some community welfare councils, and in various facets of community mental health planning.

The Social Action Approach.   The social action approach presupposes a disadvantaged segment of the population that needs to be organized, perhaps in alliance with others, for the purpose of making adequate demands on the larger community for increased resources or treatment more in accordance with social justice or democracy (Rothman, 1968). Its practitioners aim at making basic changes in major institutions or in community practices. They seek redistribution of power, resources, or decision-making in the community, or changes in the basic policies of formal organizations. Characteristic change tactics and techniques used include confrontation, direct action, and negotiation. Salient practitioner roles are activist-advocate, agitator, broker, negotiator, and partisan. Political action groups and, in many instances, political pressure groups composed of "fed up" older adults, provide an example of the use of the social action approach.

The following illustrations demonstrate how older adults are exerting their influence on the political process.

1   In Ohio, members of senior citizens groups converged on the state capitol to support a bill requiring sprinkler systems to be installed in nursing homes, which they referred to as death traps. They wrote and visited their state legislators, and as the bill came up for a final vote, they did more. They filed into the visitors galleries and knelt for a pray-in. With their senior constituents watching and praying above them, the legislators voted the bill into law.

2   In Boston, Massachusetts, older people went even further. They stormed the office of a state legislator who had refused to let several bills out of his committee that would have benefited older people. The older adults barricaded the state legislator in his office, knowing that he would have to leave to take medication at a certain time. Sitting in front of his office door, they refused to let him leave until he promised to let the bills they wanted out of his committee. Only after he did so was he permitted to leave his office.

3   In Pontiac, Michigan, older adults tired of unfulfilled promises

to install traffic lights at busy intersections, staged sit-ins that snarled traffic for miles. Embarrassed by the demonstrating senior citizens and swamped by complaints from angry motorists, the city leaders quickly installed the much-needed traffic lights (Jones, 1977).

These incidents illustrate the growing political consciousness among older people. Across the country, older people are forming political action groups, seeking to improve their lives. Three such groups, the National Association of Retired Federal Employees, the National Council of Senior Citizens, and the American Association of Retired Persons/National Retired Teachers Association, have headquarters in Washington, D.C. These groups have a national staff, a nationwide membership, and a network of local affiliates across the country. In addition, they have a legislative affairs staff to maintain contact with Congress, testify at Congressional hearings on behalf of senior citizens, and publish newsletters to keep members informed on developments in Washington.

The political potential of the elderly is not fully known. What is known, however, is that most politicians are sensitive to the political demands of their older constituents. It goes without saying that the mobilization of masses of people to challenge the power structure can result in dramatic changes (Friedlander & Apte, 1980).

Social action is a strategy that has been used in recent years by political action groups composed of people sixty-five years of age and over. Seemingly powerless groups of older people are joining forces in an effort to get what they need. They have already won significant victories in many places. Older adults have been particularly successful in winning lower fares on public transportation and in gaining property tax relief. They have found that the tactics of conflict, confrontation, and lobbying have met with reasonable success.

Margaret (Maggie) Kuhn, an elderly Philadelphian who founded the organization, the Gray Panthers, has emerged as an outspoken leader for the elderly. It is her desire to liberate older adults from "endless rounds of shuffleboard, the paternalism of old age homes, and their 'fuddy-duddy' image" (Jones, 1977, p. 233). She is willing to lead (and has led) numerous demonstrations to win new life-styles, freedom, and justice for older adults.

Social workers who work with the elderly must be aware of the struggle to improve the rights of older people, and the tactics older adults are taking to try to put an end to ageism and gerontophobia. Working with older people in the community requires knowledge of the elderly as members of the community, of the community as a social system, and of the social system of the larger society. In addition, the community worker must master a multiplicity of roles in the realm of intervention skills—advocate, broker, enabler, activist, consultant, educator, and so on, (Friedlander and Apte, 1980). Each role requires certain tasks and responsibilities, and differing applications of knowledge. As the worker gains experience in each role, she or he develops a more conscious use of self and is able to choose the most appropriate role for the particular situation.

INFORMAL NETWORKS

When problems in interpersonal relations or living develop, people frequently make use of informal resources to meet their needs. Abrahams (1976) contends that informal resources support a wide range of interpersonal activities and exchanges by aiding individuals and families to cope adaptively with stress and problems of transition. Included among informal resources are self-help groups, social networks, and persons such as teachers, police, clergy, and postal service personnel who represent a variety of community services.

Self-help groups, which have emerged relatively recently as a valuable method of providing supportive services on an informal basis, are a significant part of the range of support services available to individuals who have special needs not being met by natural or formal support systems. Generally small voluntary associations and self-help groups supplement the support system in a way that is particularly helpful to the elderly, who often experience increasing losses in their natural support systems and have very specialized needs and problems.

The advantages of self-help groups for the elderly are twofold: first, the older person receives the support of a peer group which is sensitive to his or her problems and is motivated by a sincere desire to help others; and second, self-help groups can reduce the need for support services from formal service providers, which can be expensive and insensitive—and may often be unavailable.

SUMMARY

Community services consist of a network of institutional services that has been developed to meet a range of individual and family needs. The services of this system vary from one community to another.

An early form of community organization was characterized by social action. For instance, settlement leaders fought for more and better schools, better working conditions, and safer and healthier recreational and living environments. Beginning in the years after World War I, however, emphasis on social reform activities was largely superseded by stress on treatment, stemming from the psychoanalytic model.

The 1960s brought to the fore a number of issues of social injustice, discrimination, racial conflict and social dysfunction. Individualized services proved insufficient to deal with these problems. A number of programs designed to improve social conditions among the poor and disadvantaged came into existence, among them OEO, Model Cities, and VISTA. Programs such as these benefited a number of people. However, the programs began to proliferate and were developed in a haphazard manner. Questions began to be raised about cost, effectiveness, and accountability. In many instances, those older people for whom the services were originally developed were not receiving them. Changes were needed in the service delivery system to cut out waste, upgrade staff, and redesign the entire service network.

Much emphasis in community organization today is on organizational work with low-income populations such as the frail or the at risk elderly. These persons are perceived of as not being affiliated with the major institutional systems and are thus not using available services in the community.

A number of definitions of community organization have been advanced. Intervention at the community level is oriented toward influencing community institutions and solving community welfare problems. Working with older people in the community requires knowledge of the elderly as members of the community. It also requires knowledge of the community as a social system, as well as of the social system of the larger society.

When problems on living arise, people frequently seek out help from informal networks—self-help groups, police, clergy, and so on.

REFERENCES

ABRAHAMS, R. B. Mutual Helping: Styles of Care-Giving in a Mutual Aid Program—The Widowed Service Line. In G. Caplan & M. Killilea (Eds.), *Support Systems and Mutual Help: Multidisciplinary Explorations.* New York: Grune & Stratton, 1976.

ARISTOTLE. *Treatise on Rhetoric* (T. Buckley. trans.) London: Bell, 1883.

ARY, D., JACOBS, L. C., AND RAZAVIEH, A. *Introduction to Research in Education,* 2nd ed. New York: Holt, Rinehart & Winston, 1979.

ATCHLEY, R. C. *The Social Forces in Later Life* (2nd ed.). Belmont, California: Wadsworth, 1977.

AXINN, J., & LEVIN, H. *Social Welfare—A History of the American Response to Need.* New York: Dodd, Mead, 1975.

BARNES, J. A. Effects of Reality Orientation Classroom on Memory Loss, Confusion, and Disorientation in Geriatric Patients. *Gerontologist,* 1974, *14,* 139–142.

BARRY, A. J., DALY, J. W., PRUETT, E. D. R., STEINMETZ, J. R., PAGE, H. F., BIRKHEAD, N. C., & RODAHL, K. The Effects of Physical Conditioning on Older Individuals. *Journal of Gerontology,* 1966, *21,* 182–191.

BEATTIE, W. M. Aging and the Social Services. In R. H. Binstock & E. Shanas (Eds.), *Handbook of Aging and the Social Sciences.* New York: Van Nostrand Reinhold, 1976.

BEAUVOIR, S. DE. *The Coming of Age.* New York: Putnam, 1972.

BELL, A. G. *The Duration of Life and Conditions Associated with Longevity, A Study of the Hyde Genealogy.* Monograph. Washington, D.C.: Genealogical Record Office, 1918.

BELL, B. Maintenance Therapy in Vision and Hearing for Geriatrics Patients. In J. Rudd & R. J. Margolins (Eds.), *Maintenance Therapy for the Geriatrics Patient.* Springfield, Illinois: Thomas, 1968.

BELL, B., & ROSE, C. L. The Interdisciplinary Study of the Life Span. In M. G. Spencer & C. J. Dorr (Eds.), *Understanding Aging: A Multidisciplinary Approach.* New York: Appleton-Century-Crofts, 1975.

BENEDICT, R. A Profile of Indian Aged. In Institute of Gerontology, University of Michigan/Wayne State University, *Minority Aged in America.* Ann Arbor: University of Michigan Press, 1972.

BENGTSON, V. L., & HABER, D. Sociological Approaches to Aging. In D. S. Woodruff & J. E. Birren (Eds.), *Aging—Scientific Perspectives and Social Issues.* New York: Van Nostrand, 1975.

BENSMAN, J., & ROSENBERG, B. *An Introduction to Sociology.* New York: Praeger, 1976.

BENSON, R. A., & BRODIE, D. C. Suicide by Overdose of Medicines Among the Aged. *Journal of the American Geriatrics Society,* 1975, *23,* 304–308.

BIDDLE, W. W., & BIDDLE, L. J. *The Community Development Process: The Re-*

discovery of Local Initiative. New York: Holt, Rinehart & Winston, 1965.

BIERMAN, E. L., & HAZZARD, W. R. Old Age, Including Death and Dying. In D. W. Smith & E. L. Bierman (Eds.), *The Biologic Ages of Man.* Philadelphia: Saunders, 1973.

BIRREN, J. E. Age Changes in Speed of Behavior: Its Central Nature and Physiological Correlates. In A. T. Welford & J. E. Birren (Eds.), *Behavior, Aging and the Nervous System.* Springfield, Illinois: Thomas, 1965.

BIRREN, J. E. & CLAYTON, V. History of Gerontology. In D. S. Woodruff & J. E. Birren (Eds.), *Aging: Scientific Perspectives and Social Issues.* New York: D. Van Nostrand Company, 1975.

BLENKNER, M., BLOOM, M., WASSER, E., AND NIELSON, M. Protective Services for Old People: Findings from the Benjamin Rose Institute Study. *Social Casework,* 1971, *52,* 483–522.

BLONSKY, L. E. An Innovative Service for the Elderly. *Gerontologist,* 1973, *13,* 189–196.

BOEHM, W. W. *Objectives of the Social Work Curriculum of the Future. Vol. 1, Curriculum Study.* New York: Council on Social Work Education, 1959.

BONDAREFF, W. The Neural Basis of Aging. In J. E. Birren & K. W. Schaie (Eds.), *Handbook of the Psychology of Aging.* New York: Van Nostrand Reinhold, 1977.

BOTWINICK, J. *Cognitive Processes in Maturity and Old Age.* New York: Springer, 1967.

BOTWINICK, J. *Aging and Behavior.* New York: Springer, 1973.

BOTWINICK, J., Intelligence and Aging. In J. E. Birren & K. W. Schaie (Eds.), *Handbook of the Psychology of Aging.* New York: Van Nostrand Reinhold, 1977.

BOTWINICK, J. *We Are Aging.* New York: Springer, 1981.

BOTWINICK, J. & STORANDT, M. Cardiovascular Status, Depressive Affect, and Other Factors in Reaction Time. *Journal of Gerontology,* 1974, *29,* 543–548.

BOTWINICK, J. & THOMPSON, L. W. Age Difference in Reaction Time: An Artifact? *Gerontologist,* 1968, *8,* 25–28.

BRAGER, G. & SPECHT, H. *Community Organization.* New York: Columbia University Press, 1973.

BREMNER, R. H. *American Philanthropy.* Chicago: University of Chicago Press, 1960.

BRIAR, S. & MILLER, H. *Problems and Issues in Social Casework.* New York: Columbia University Press, 1971.

BRILL, N. *Working with People—The Helping Process.* Philadelphia: Lippincott, 1973.

BRODY, E. M. Aging and Family Personality: A Developmental View. *Family Process Magazine,* 1974, *13,* 23–37.

BRODY, E. M. Aging. In *Encyclopedia of Social Work* (17th ed.). Washington, D.C.: National Association of Social Workers, 1977.

BURNSIDE, I. M. Formation of a Group. In I. M. Burnside (Ed.), *Nursing and the Aged.* New York: McGraw-Hill, 1976.

BURNSIDE, I. M. *Working with the Elderly—Group Processes and Techniques.* North Scituate, Massachusetts: Duxbury Press, 1978.

BUTLER, R. N. The Life Review: An Interpretation of Reminiscence in the Aged. *Psychiatry,* 1963, *26,* 65–76.

BUTLER, R. N. The Life Review: An Interpretation of Reminiscence in the Aged. In R. Kastenbaum (Ed.), *New Thoughts on Old Age.* New York: Springer, 1964.

BUTLER, R. N. *Why Survive? Being Old in America.* New York: Harper & Row, 1975.

BUTLER, R. N. *Medicine and Aging: An Assessment of Opportunities and Neglect.* National Institute of Health, Education, and Welfare (NIH Publication Number 79–1699). Washington D.C.: U.S. Government Printing Office, 1979.

BUTLER, R. N. & LEWIS, M. I. *Aging and Mental Health* (2nd ed.). Saint Louis: Mosby, 1977.

BUTLER, R. N. & LEWIS, M. I. *Aging and Mental Health* (3rd ed.). St. Louis: Mosby, 1982.

CAMPBELL, A. The American Way of Mating: Marriage Si, Children Only Maybe. *Psychology Today,* 1975, pp. 37–42.

CARP, F. M. Housing and Minority-Group Elderly. *Gerontologist,* 1969, *9,* 20–24.

CARP, F. M., & KATAOKA, E. Health Care Problems of the Elderly of San Francisco's Chinatown. *Gerontologist,* 1976, *16,* 30–38.

Casebook on Family Diagnosis and Treatment. New York: Family Service Association of America, 1965.

CHALMERS, T. C., & STERN, A. R. The Staggering Cost of Prolonging Life. *Business Week,* Feb. 23, 1981, p. 19.

COHEN, E. S. An Overview of Long-Term Care Facilities. In E. M. Brody (Ed.), *A Social Work Guide for Long-Term Care Facilities.* Rockville, Maryland: National Institute of Mental Health, 1974.

COLL, B. D. *Perspectives in Public Welfare—A History.* U.S. Department of Health, Education, and Welfare. Washington, D.C.: U.S. Government Printing Office, 1969.

COMBS, A. W., AVILA, D. L., & PURKEY, W. W. *Helping Relationships—Basic Concepts for the Helping Professions.* Boston: Allyn & Bacon, 1971.

CONGER, J. J. A World They Never Knew: The Family and Social Change. *Daedalus,* 1971, *100,* 1105–1138.

COREY, J., & COREY, M. Groups with the Elderly. In *Groups: Process and Practice.* Monterey, California: Brooks/Cole, 1977.

CORSO, J. F., Auditory Perception and Communication. In J. E. Birren & K. W. Schaie (Eds.), *Handbook of the Psychology of Aging.* New York: Van Nostrand Reinhold, 1977.

COX, F. M., ERLICH, J. L., ROTHMAN, J., & TROPMAN, J. E. *Strategies of Community Organization* (3rd ed.). Itasca, Illinois: Peacock, 1979.

CRAIK, F. I. M. Two Components in Free Recall. *Journal of Verbal Learning and Verbal Behavior,* 1968, *7,* 996–1004.

CRAIK, F. I. M. Age Differences in Human Memory. In J. E. Birren & K. W. Schaie (Eds.), *Handbook of the Psychology of Aging.* New York: Van Nostrand Reinhold, 1977.

CRANDALL, R. C. *Gerontology—A Behavioral Science Approach.* Reading, Massachusetts: Addison-Wesley, 1980.

CROUCH, B. M. Age and Institutional Support: Perceptions of Older Mexican-Americans. *Journal of Gerontology,* 1972, *27,* 524–529.

Current Population Reports, Special Studies. Demographic Aspects of Aging and the Older Population in the United States. Series P-23, No. 59. Washington, D.C.: U.S. Government Printing Office, 1976.

CUTLER, N. E., & HAROOTYAN, R. A. Demography of the Aged. In D. S. Woodruff & J. E. Birren (Eds.), *Aging.* New York: Van Nostrand, 1975.

DAVIS-WONG, D. *Poverty Among Black Elderly Rising.* Washington, D.C.: The National Caucus and Center on Black Aged, 1981.

DENNEY, N. W., & WRIGHT, J. C. Cognitive Changes during the Adult Years: Implications for Developmental Theory and Research. In H. W. Reese & L. P. Lipsitt (Eds.), *Advances in Child Development and Behavior.* (Vol 11). New York: Academic Press, 1976.

DENNIS, W. Age and Achievement: A Critique. *Journal of Gerontology,* 1956, *11,* 331–333.

DENNIS, W. Creative Productivity between Ages of 20 to 80 Years. *Journal of Gerontology,* 1966, *21,* 1–8.

DENTLER, R. A. *Major Social Problems* (2nd ed.). Chicago: Rand McNally, 1967.

deVRIES, H. A. Physiological Effects of an Exercise Training Regimen Upon Men Aged 52–88. *Journal of Gerontology,* 1970, *24,* 325–336.

deVRIES, H. A. *Vigor Regained.* Englewood Cliffs, New Jersey: Prentice-Hall, 1974.

DEWALD, P. A. *Psychotherapy—A Dynamic Approach.* New York: Basic Books, 1964.

DIAMOND, S. Social Security. In R. A. Dentler (Ed.), *Major Social Problems* (2nd ed.). Chicago: Rand McNally, 1967.

DIBNER, A. S. The Psychology of Normal Aging. In M. G. Spencer & C. J. Dorr (Eds.), *Understanding Aging: A Multidisciplinary Approach.* New York: Appleton-Century-Crofts, 1975.

DUFFY, B. J., JR. Medical Care of the Elderly. In M. G. Spencer & C. J. Dorr (Eds.), *Understanding Aging: A Multidisciplinary Approach.* New York: Appleton-Century-Crofts, 1975.

DULLES, F. R. *The United States Since 1865.* Ann Arbor: University of Michigan Press, 1959.

DUNHAM, A. Some Principles of Community Development. *International Review of Community Development,* 1963, *11,* 141–151.

EARLEY, L. W., & VON MERING, O. Growing Old the Out-Patient Way. *American Journal of Psychiatry,* 1969, *125,* 963–967.

EHRLICH, E., FLEXNER, S. B., CARRUTH, G., & HAWKINS, J. M. *Oxford American Dictionary.* New York: Oxford University Press, 1980.

EISDORFER, C. Health Planning for the Aged. *Gerontologist,* 1976, *16,* 12–16.

EISDORFER, C., & WILKIE, F. Stress, Disease, Aging and Behavior. In J. E. Birren & K. W. Schaie (Eds.), *Handbook of the Psychology of Aging.* New York: Van Nostrand Reinhold, 1977.

ELKIND, D. Erik Erikson's Eight Ages of Man. In L. R. Allman & D. T. Jaffe (Eds.), *Readings in Adult Psychology: Contemporary Perspectives.* New York: Harper & Row, 1977.

ENGEL, G. L., & ROMANO, J. Delirium, A Syndrome of Cerebral Insufficiency. *Journal of Chronic Diseases,* 1959, *9,* 260–277.

ENGEN, T. Taste and Smell. In J. E. Birren & K. W. Schaie (Eds.), *Handbook of the Psychology of Aging.* New York: Van Nostrand Reinhold, 1977.

ERIKSON, E. H. *Childhood and Society* (2nd ed.). New York: Norton, 1963.

ERNST, M. & SHORE, H. *Sensitizing People to the Processes of Aging: The In-Service Educator's Guide* (2nd ed.). Denton, Texas: North State Texas University, 1976.

Facts About Older Americans. U.S. Department of Health, Education and Welfare. OHDS 79-20006. Washington, D.C.: Administration on Aging, 1978.

FELDMAN, A. G., & FELDMAN, F. L. Community Strategies and the Aged. In A. N. Schwartz & I. N. Mensh (Eds.), *Professional Obligations and Approaches to the Aged.* Springfield, Illinois: Thomas, 1974.

FELDMAN, F. L., & SCHERZ, F. H. *Family Social Welfare.* New York: Atherton Press, 1967.

FISH, F. J. Senile Paranoid States. *Gerontologia Clinica,* 1959, *1,* 127–131.

FISCHER, A., PARISKOVA, J., & ROTH, Z. The Effect of Systematic Physical Activity on Maximal Performance and Functional Capacity in Senescent Men. *Internationale Zeitschrift Fuer Angewandte Physiologie Einschliesslich Arbeitsphysiologie,* 1965, *21,* 269–304.

FISCHER, D. H. *Growing Old in America.* New York: Oxford University Press, 1977.

FISCHER, J. *Effective Casework Practice.* New York: McGraw-Hill, 1978.

FOLLETT, S. Protective Services for Adults. In *Encyclopedia of Social Work,* Vol. II (17th ed.). Washington, D.C.: National Association of Social Workers, 1977.

FOZARD, J. L., & THOMAS, J. C. *Why Aging Engineering Psychologists Should Get Interested in Aging.* Paper presented at American Psychological Association, Montreal, Canada, August, 1973.

FREEMAN, J. T. *Clinical Features of the Older Patient.* Springfield, Illinois: Thomas, 1965.

FRIEDLANDER, W. A., & APTE, R. Z. *Introduction to Social Welfare* (5th ed.). Englewood Cliffs, New Jersey: Prentice-Hall, 1980.

GARRETT, A. *Interviewing—Its Principles and Methods* (25th ed.). New York: Family Service Association of America, 1966.

GELFAND, D. E., & OLSEN, J. K. *The Aging Network—Programs and Services.* New York: Springer, 1980.

GERONTOLOGY AND GERIATRICS, *Encyclopaedia Britannica.* London: Encyclopaedia Britannica, 1969.

GILBERT, N., MILLER, H., & SPECHT, H. *An Introduction to Social Work Practice.* Englewood Cliffs, New Jersey: Prentice-Hall, 1980.

GITTERMAN, A., & SCHAEFFER, A. The White Professional and the Black Client. *Social Casework,* 1972, *53,* 280–291.

GLASSCOTE, R., BREGEL, A., BUTTERFIELD, A., JR., CLARK, E., COX, B., ELPERS, J. R., GUDERMAN, J., GOREL, L., LEWIS, R., MILES, D., RAYBIN, J., REISLER, C., & VITO, E., JR. *Old Folks at Homes.* Washington, D.C.: Joint Information Service of the American Psychiatric Association and the National Association of Mental Health, 1976.

GOLDBERG, S. R., & DEUTSCH, F. *Life-Span Individual and Family Development.* Monterey, California: Brooks/Cole, 1977.

GOLDENBERG, I., & GOLDENBERG, H. *Family Therapy: An Overview.* Monterey, California: Brooks/Cole, 1980.

GRUMAN, G. J. *A History of Ideas About the Prolongation of Life: The Evolution of Prolongevity Hypothesis to 1800.* Philadelphia: American Philosophical Society, 1966.

Guide to the Census 1980. U.S. Department of Commerce. Washington, D.C.: U.S. Government Printing Office, 1979.

GUTTMAN, N. D., & CUELLAR, J. B. Barriers to Equitable Service. *Generations,* Spring, 1982, 31–32.

HALL, G. *Senescence, the Last Half of Life.* New York: Appleton, 1922.

HAMILTON, G. *Theory and Practice of Social Casework* (4th ed.). New York: Columbia University Press, 1954.

HANDEL, G. *Social Welfare in Western Society.* New York: Random House, 1982.

HARBERT, A. S., & GINSBERG, L. H. *Human Services for Older Adults: Concepts and Skills.* Belmont, California: Wadsworth, 1979.

HARRIS, C. *Fact Book on Aging: A Profile of America's Older Population.* Washington, D.C.: National Council on the Aging, 1978.

HARRIS, L. AND ASSOCIATES. *The Myth and Reality of Aging in America.* Washington, D.C.: National Council on the Aging, 1975.

HARTFORD, M. E., *Groups in Social Work.* New York: Columbia University Press, 1971.

HAVIGHURST, R. J. Personality and Patterns of Aging, *Gerontologist,* 1968, *8,* 20–23.

Health Careers Education, Training and Consultation Service. The Burke Rehabilitation Center, White Plains, New York, 1978.

HENDRICKS, J., & HENDRICKS, C. D. *Aging in Mass Society.* Cambridge, Massachusetts: Winthrop, 1977.

HENDRICKS, J., & HENDRICKS, C. D. *Aging in Mass Society* (2nd ed.). Cambridge, Mass: Winthrop, 1981.

HERTZLER, J. O. *A Sociology of Language.* New York: Random House, 1965.

HESS, B. B., & MARKSON, E. W. *Aging and Old Age.* New York: Macmillan, 1980.

HILL, R. B. *A Profile of Black Aged.* In J. J. Johnson (Ed.), *Proceedings of Research Conference on Minority Group Aged in the South.* Durham: Duke University Press, 1971.

HILL, R. B. *The Strengths of Black Families.* New York: Emerson Hall, 1972.

HOLLIS, F. *Casework—A Psychosocial Therapy* (2nd ed.). New York: Random House, 1972.

HOLLIS, F. Social Casework: The Psychosocial Approach. In *Encyclopedia of Social Work,* Vol. II (17th ed.). Washington, D.C.: National Association of Social Workers, 1977.

HUYCK, M. H. *Growing Older.* Englewood Cliffs, New Jersey: Prentice-Hall, 1974.

JARVIK, L. F., & COHEN, D. A Biobehavioral Approach to Intellectual Changes with Aging. In C. Eisdorfer & M. P. Lawton (Eds.), *The Psychology of Adult Development and Aging.* Washington, D.C.: American Psychological Association, 1974.

JOHNSON, H. R., BRITTON, J. H., LANG, C. A., SELTZER, M. M., STANFORD, E. P., YANCIK, R., MAKLAN, C. W., & MIDDLESWARTH,

A. B. Foundations for Gerontological Education. *Gerontologist,* 1980, *20,* 1–61.

JONES, R. *The Other Generation.* Englewood Cliffs, New Jersey: Prentice-Hall, 1977.

KADUSHIN, A. *The Social Work Interview.* New York: Columbia University Press, 1972.

KAHANA, E., & KAHANA, B. Theoretical and Research Perspectives on Grandparenthood. *Aging and Human Development,* 1971, *2,* 261–268.

KALISH, R. A. *Late Adulthood: Perspectives on Human Development.* Monterey, California: Brooks/Cole, 1975.

KALLMANN, F. J., & JARVIK, L. F. Individual Differences in Constitution and Genetic Background. In J. E. Birren (Ed.), *Handbook of Aging and the Individual.* Chicago: University of Chicago Press, 1959.

KART, C. S. *The Realities of Aging.* Boston: Allyn & Bacon, 1981.

KELLER, J. F., & HUGHSTON, G. A. *Counseling the Elderly.* New York: Harper & Row, 1981.

KELTNER, J. W. *Elements of Interpersonal Communication.* Belmont, California: Wadsworth, 1973.

KENNEDY, C. E. *Human Development: The Adult Years and Aging.* New York: Macmillan, 1978.

KENSHALO, D. R. Age Changes in Touch, Vibration, Temperature, Kinesthesis and Pain Sensitivity. In J. E. Birren & K. W. Schaie (Eds.), *Handbook of the Psychology of Aging.* New York: Van Nostrand Reinhold, 1977.

KIMMEL, D. C. *Adulthood and Aging.* New York: Wiley, 1974.

KLENK, R. W., & RYAN, R. M. *The Practice of Social Work.* Belmont, California: Wadsworth, 1970.

KOLLER, M. R. *Social Gerontology.* New York: Random House, 1968.

KOSBERG, J. I. Nursing Homes. In *Encyclopedia of Social Work* Vol II (17th ed.). Washington, D.C.: National Association of Social Workers, 1977.

KOSBERG, J. I., & GORMAN, J. F., Perceptions Toward the Rehabilitation Potential of Institutionalized Aged. *Gerontologist,* 1975, *15,* 398–403.

LEHMAN, H. C. *Age and Achievement.* Princeton: Princeton University Press, 1953.

LEHMAN, H. C. Reply to Dennis' Critique of Age and Achievement. *Journal of Gerontology,* 1956, *11,* 333–337.

LEHMAN, H. C. The Influence of Longevity upon Curves Showing Man's Creative Production Rate at Successive Age Levels. *Journal of Gerontology,* 1958, *13,* 187–191.

LEHMAN, H. C. Chronological Age Versus Present-Day Contributions to Medical Progress. *Gerontologist,* 1963, *3,* 71–75.

LEHMAN, H. C. The Psychologist's Most Creative Years. *American Psychologist,* 1966, *21,* 363–369.

LEMON, B. W., BENGTSON, V. L., & PETERSON, J. A. An Exploration of the Activity of Aging: Activity Types and Satisfaction Among Inmovers to a Retirement Community. *Journal of Gerontology,* 1972, *27,* 511–523.

LEUCHTENBURG, W. E. *The Perils of Prosperity 1914-32.* Chicago: University of Chicago Press, 1958.

LEVINE, R. A. *Culture, Behavior, and Personality.* Chicago: Aldine, 1973.

LEVITON, L. C. Implications of an Aging Population for the Health Care System in Southwestern Pennsylvania. Health Policy Institute, Graduate School of Public Health, University of Pittsburgh. Pittsburgh: HPI Policy Series No. 2, May 1981.

LOETHER, H. J. *Problems of Aging* (2nd ed.). Encino, California: Dickenson, 1975.

LOPATA, H. Z. *Widowhood in an American City.* Cambridge, Massachusetts: Schenkman, 1973.

LOWENTHAL, M. F. *Psychosocial Variations across the Adult Life Course: Frontiers for Research and Policy.* Robert W. Kleemeir Memorial Lecture, Gerontological Society, Portland, Oregon, October, 1974.

LOWENTHAL, M. F., BRISSETTE, G. G., BUEHLER, J. A., PIERCE, R. C., ROBINSON, B. C., & INER, M. L. *Aging and Mental Disorder in San Francisco.* San Francisco: Jossey-Bass, 1967.

LOWENTHAL, M. F., & HAVEN, C. Interaction and Adaptation: Intimacy as a Critical Variable. In B. L. Neugarten (Ed.), *Middle Age and Aging: A Reader in Social Psychology.* Chicago: University of Chicago Press, 1968.

LOWY, L. *Social Work with the Aging.* New York: Harper & Row, 1979.

LUBOVE, R. *The Progressives and the Slums.* Pittsburgh: University of Pittsburgh Press, 1963.

LYMAN, S. M. *Chinese Americans.* New York: Random House, 1974.

MADDOX, G. L. Activity and Morale: A Longitudinal Study of Selected Elderly Subjects. *Social Forces,* 1963, *42,* 195–204.

MADDOX, G. L., & WILEY, J. Scope, Concepts and Methods in the Study of Aging. In R. H. Binstock & E. Shanas (Eds.), *Handbook of Aging and the Social Sciences.* New York: Van Nostrand Reinhold, 1976.

MANSVELT, J. *Pick's Disease, A Syndrome of Lobar Cerebral Atrophy.* Enchede, The Netherlands: Van Der Loeff, 1954.

MARMOR, T. *The Politics of Medicare.* Chicago: Aldine, 1973.

MASTERS, W. H., & JOHNSON, V. E. *Human Sexual Response.* Boston: Little, Brown, 1966.

MASTERS, W. H., & JOHNSON, V. E. Human Sexual Response: The Aging Female and the Aging Male. In B. L. Neugarten (Ed.), *Middle Age and Aging.* Chicago: University of Chicago Press, 1968.

MASTERS, W. H., & JOHNSON, V. E. *Human Sexual Inadequacy.* Boston: Little, Brown, 1970.

MATHIASEN, G. The Aging. In *Encyclopedia of Social Work* (15th ed.). New York: National Association of Social Workers, 1965.

MERSKEY, H. *Psychiatric Illness* (3rd ed.). London: Baillier, Tindall, Cassell, 1980.

MILLER, I., & SOLOMON, R. The Development of Group Services for the Elderly. In C. B. Germain (Ed.), *Social Work Practice: People and Environments.* New York: Columbia University Press, 1979.

MILLER, S. J. The Social Dilemma of the Aging Leisure Participant. In A. M. Rose & W. A. Peterson (Eds.), *Older People and Their Social World.* Philadelphia: Davis, 1965.

MISCHEL, W. Continuity and Change in Personality. *American Psychologist,* 1969, *24,* 1012–1018.

MOORE, N. R. The Practice of Community Organization. In R. W. Klenk & R. M. Ryan (Eds.), *The Practice of Social Work.* Belmont, California: Wadsworth, 1970.

MORRIS, R. Aging and the Field of Social Work. In M. Riley, J. W. Riley & M. E. Johnson (Eds.), *Aging and Society. Vol. 2: Aging and the Professions.* New York: Russell Sage Foundation, 1969.

MORRIS, R., & BINSTOCK, R. H. *Feasible Planning for Social Change.* New York: Columbia University Press, 1966.

MURPHY, M. J. Financing Social Welfare: Voluntary Organizations. In *Encyclopedia of Social Work* (17th ed.). Washington, D.C.: National Association of Social Workers, 1977.

National Association of Social Workers. Code of Ethics. In *NASW Personnel Standards and Adjudication Procedures.* New York: National Association of Social Workers, 1963.

NEUGARTEN, B. L., BERKOWITZ, H., & ASSOCIATES (EDS.). *Personality in Middle and Late Life.* New York: Atherton Press, 1964.

NEUGARTEN, B. L., MOORE, J. W., & LOWE, J. C. Age Norms, Age Constraints, and Adult Socialization. *American Journal of Sociology,* 1965, *70,* 710–717.

NEUGARTEN, B. L., & WEINSTEIN, K. K. The Changing American Grandparent. *Journal of Marriage and the Family,* 1964, *26,* 199–204.

NEUGARTEN, B. L., WOOD, V., KRAINES, R. J., & LOOMIS, B. Women's Attitudes toward the Menopause. In B. L. Neugarten (Ed.), *Middle Age and Aging.* Chicago: University of Chicago Press, 1968.

NORTHEN, H. *Social Work with Groups.* New York: Columbia University Press, 1969.

OKUN, B. F. *Effective Helping: Interviewing and Counseling Techniques.* North Scituate, Massachusetts: Duxbury Press, 1976.

Older American Reports, December, 1981, *5,* (no. 49), 1–8. Arlington, Virginia: Capitol Publications.

PFEIFFER, E. Successful Aging. In L. E. Brown & E. O. Ellis (Eds.),

Quality of Life: The Later Years. Acton, Massachusetts: Publishing Science Group, 1975.

PFEIFFER, E. Psychopathology and Social Pathology. In J. E. Birren & K. W. Schaie (Eds.), *Handbook of the Psychology of Aging.* New York: Van Nostrand Reinhold, 1976.

PIORE, N. Health as a Social Problem. In *Encyclopedia of Social Work* (17th ed.) Vol. I. Washington, D.C.: National Association of Social Workers, 1977.

POST, F. *Persistent Persecutory States of the Elderly.* London: Pergamon, 1966.

PRESSEY, S. L., & PRESSEY, A. D. Major Neglected Need Opportunity: Old Age Counseling. *Journal of Counseling Psychology,* 1972, *19,* 362–366.

PUMPHREY, R. E. Social Welfare in the United States. In *Encyclopedia of Social Work* (15th ed.). New York: National Association of Social Workers, 1965.

PUMPHREY, R. E., & PUMPHREY, M. W. (Eds.). *The Heritage of American Social Work.* New York: Columbia University Press, 1961.

RABBITT, P. Changes in Problem Solving Ability in Old Age. In J. E. Birren & K. W. Schaie (Eds.), *Handbook of the Psychology of Aging.* New York: Van Nostrand Reinhold, 1977.

RAMOS, R. Participation Observation. In R. M. Grinnell, Jr. (Ed.), *Social Work Research and Evaluation.* Itasca, Illinois: F. E. Peacock, 1981.

RANSFORD, E. H. On Isolation, Powerlessness, and Violence. In M. P. Golden (Ed.), *The Research Experience.* Itasca, Illinois: Peacock, 1976.

RAYMOND, B. J. Free Recall Among the Aged. *Psychological Reports,* 1971, *29,* 1179–1182.

REDICK, R. W., KRAMER, M., & TAUBE, C. A. Epidemiology of Mental Illness and Utilization of Psychiatric Facilities among Older Persons. In E. W. Busse & E. Pfeiffer (Eds.), *Mental Illness in Later Life.* Washington, D.C.: American Psychiatric Association, 1973.

REIK, T. *Listening with the Third Ear* (5th ed.). New York: Pyramid Publications, 1971.

Resource Guide for Mental Health and Support Services for the Elderly. National Institute of Mental Health. Washington, D.C.: U.S. Government Printing Office, 1981.

RETHERFORD, R. D. *The Changing Sex Differential in Mortality.* Westport, Connecticut: Greenwood Press, 1975.

RETTERSTOL, N. *Paranoid and Paranoiac Psychoses.* Oslo: Universitetsforlaget, 1966.

RILEY, M. W., & FONER, A. *Aging and Society: Volume I, An Inventory of Research Findings.* New York: Russell Sage, 1968.

ROGERS, D. *The Adult Years—An Introduction to Aging.* Englewood Cliffs, New Jersey: Prentice-Hall, 1979.

Rose, A. M. The Subculture of the Aging: A Framework for Research in Social Gerontology. In A. M. Rose & W. Peterson (Eds.), *Older People and Their Social Worlds*. Philadelphia: Davis, 1965.

Rosenfeld, A. H. *New Views on Older Lives*. U.S. Department of Health, Education, and Welfare. Washington, D.C.: U.S. Government Printing Office, 1978.

Rosow, I. *Social Integration of the Aged*. New York: Free Press, 1967.

Rosow, I. *Socialization to Old Age*. Berkeley, California: University of California Press, 1974.

Ross, M. G. *Community Organization: Theory and Principles* (2nd ed.). New York: Harper, 1967.

Rothman, J. Three Models of Community Organization Practice. In National Conference on Social Welfare, *Social Work Practice*. New York: Columbia University Press, 1968.

Schlossberg, N. K., Troll, L. E., & Leibowitz, Z. *Perspectives on Counseling Adults: Issues and Skills*. Monterey, California: Brooks/Cole, 1978.

Schulman, E. D. *Intervention in Human Services*. St. Louis: Mosby, 1974.

Schwartz, A. N. A Transactional View of the Aging Process. In A. N. Schwartz & I. N. Mensh (Eds.), *Professional Obligations and Approaches to the Aged*. Springfield, Illinois: Thomas, 1974.

Schwartz, A. N., & Peterson, J. A. *Introduction to Gerontology*. New York: Holt, Rinehart & Winston, 1979.

Schwartz, W. Social Group Work: Interactionist Approaches. In *Encyclopedia of Social Work* (16th ed.). New York: National Association of Social Workers, 1971.

Shock, N. Physiological Aspects of Aging in Man. *Annual Review of Physiology*, 1961, *23*, 97–122.

Siegel, J. S., Herrenbruck, M. D., Akers, D. S., & Passel, J. S. Introduction. *Demographic Aspects of Aging and the Older Population in the United States*. Series P-23, No. 59. Washington, D.C.: U.S. Government Printing Office, 1976.

Sinex, F. M. The Biochemistry of Aging. In M. G. Spencer & C. J. Dorr (Eds.), Understanding Aging: A Multidisciplinary Approach. New York: Appleton-Century-Crofts, 1975.

Smith, D. W., & Bierman, E. L. *The Biologic Ages of Man*. Philadelphia: Saunders, 1973.

Smith, T. L., & Zopf, P. E., Jr. *Demography—Principles and Methods*. New York: Alfred, 1976.

Social Security Programs in the United States. U.S. Department of Health, Education, and Welfare. Washington, D.C.: U.S. Government Printing Office, 1973.

SOLDO, B. America's Elderly in the 1980's. *Population Bulletin,* 1980, *35,* (4), 3–47.

STAMM, I. L. Family Therapy. In F. Hollis (Ed.), *Casework—A Psychosocial Therapy.* New York: Random House, 1972.

STEIN, B. *On Relief.* New York: Basic Books, 1971.

STREAN, H. S. *The Social Worker as Psychotherapist.* Metuchen, New Jersey: Scarecrow Press, 1974.

STREAN, H. S. *Personality Theory and Social Work Practice.* Metuchen, New Jersey: Scarecrow Press, 1975.

STREAN, H. S. *Clinical Social Work—Theory and Practice.* New York: Free Press, 1978.

STREIB, G. F. Are the Aged a Minority Group? In A. W. Gouldner & W. A. Peterson (Eds.), *Applied Sociology.* New York: Free Press, 1965.

STREIB, G. F., & SCHNEIDER, C. J. *Retirement in American Society, Impact and Process.* Ithaca: Cornell University Press.

SUSSMAN, M. S., & BURCHINAL, L. Kin Family Network: Unheralded Structure in Current Conceptualizations of Family Functioning. *Marriage and Family Living,* 1962, *24,* 231–240.

TALLMER, M., & KUTNER, B. Disengagement and the Stresses of Aging. *Journal of Gerontology,* 1969, *24,* 70–75.

TIBBITTS, C. The Future of Research in Social Gerontology. In P. F. Hansen (Ed.), *Age with a Future.* Copenhagen: Munksgaard, 1964.

TITMUSS, R. M. *Commitment to Welfare.* New York: Pantheon, 1968.

TRIPODI, T., FELLIN, P., & MEYER, H. J. *The Assessment of Social Research.* Itasca, Illinois: F. E. Peacock, 1969.

TROLL, L. E. *Early and Middle Adulthood.* Monterey, California: Brooks/Cole, 1975.

TURNER, F. *Psychosocial Therapy.* New York: Free Press, 1978.

UNITED NATIONS. *Social Progress through Community Development.* New York: United Nations, 1955.

UNITED STATES BUREAU OF THE CENSUS. *Census of Population: 1970 Volume 1, Characteristics of the Population, Part I, United States Summary, Section 1.* Washington, D.C.: U.S. Government Printing Office, 1973.

UNITED STATES BUREAU OF THE CENSUS. *Statistical Abstracts of the United States* (97th ed.). Washington, D.C.: U.S. Government Printing Office, 1976.

UNITED STATES BUREAU OF THE CENSUS. *Statistical Abstracts of the United States* (99th ed.). Washington, D.C.: U.S. Government Printing Office, 1978.

UPHAM, F. *A Dynamic Approach to Illness—A Social Work Guide.* New York: Family Service Association of America, 1949.

WALSH, D. A., Age Differences in Learning and Memory. In D. S. Woodruff & J. E. Birren (Eds.), *Aging: Scientific Perspectives and Social Issues.* New York: D. Van Nostrand, 1975.

WALSH, D. A., & JENKINS, J. J. Effects of Orienting Tasks on Free Recall in Incidental Learning: Difficulty, Effort, and Process Explanations. *Journal of Verbal Learning and Verbal Behavior,* 1975, *12,* 481–488.

WARD, L. F. *Dynamic Sociology* (reprint of 1883 ed.). New York: Johnson Reprint, 1968.

WARD, R. A. *The Aging Experience.* New York: Lippincott, 1979.

WARREN, R. L. *The Community in America.* Chicago: Rand McNally, 1963.

WEAVER, E. T. Public Assistance and Supplemental Security Income. In *Encyclopedia of Social Work.* New York: National Association of Social Workers, 1977.

WEBSTER'S NEW WORLD DICTIONARY. New York: World Publishing, 1970.

WEG, R. B. Changing Physiology of Aging: Normal and Pathological. In D. S. Woodruff & J. E. Birren (Eds.), *Aging—Scientific Perspectives and Social Issues.* New York: Van Nostrand, 1975.

WELFORD, A. T. Motor Performance. In J. E. Birren & K. W. Schaie (Eds.). *Handbook of the Psychology of Aging.* New York: Van Nostrand Reinhold, 1977.

WHIPPLE, D. V. *Dynamics of Development: Euthenic Pediatrics.* New York: McGraw-Hill, 1966.

WHITTOUVRIE, S. K., & WEINSTOCK, C. S. Adult Development. New York: Holt, Rinehart & Winston, 1979.

WHITE HOUSE CONFERENCE ON AGING. *Toward a National Policy on Aging* Vol. 1. Washington, D.C.: White House Conference on Aging, 1971.

WILSON, D. L. The Programmed Theory of Aging. In M. Rockstein (Ed.), *Theoretical Aspects of Aging.* New York: Academic Press, 1974.

WIRTH, L. The Problem of Minority Groups. In R. Linton (Ed.), *The Science of Man in the World Crisis.* New York: Columbia University Press, 1945.

WOOD, V., & ROBERTSON, J. F. Friendship and Interaction: Differential Effect on the Morale of the Elderly. *Journal of Marriage and the Family,* 1978, *40,* 367–375.

WOODRUFF, D. S. Relationships between EEG Alpha Frequency, Reaction, Time, and Age: A Biofeedback Study. *Psychophysiology,* 1975,

WOODRUFF, D. S., & BIRREN, J. E. *Aging—Scientific Perspectives and Social Issues.* New York: Van Nostrand, 1975.

ZARO, J. S., BARACH, R., NEDELMAN, D. J., & DREIBLATT, I. S. *A Guide for Beginning Psychotherapists.* Cambridge: Cambridge University Press, 1977.

ZASTROW, C. *Introduction to Social Welfare Institutions* (revised ed.). Homewood, Illinois: Dorsey Press, 1982.

author index

subject index